ANT-MAN

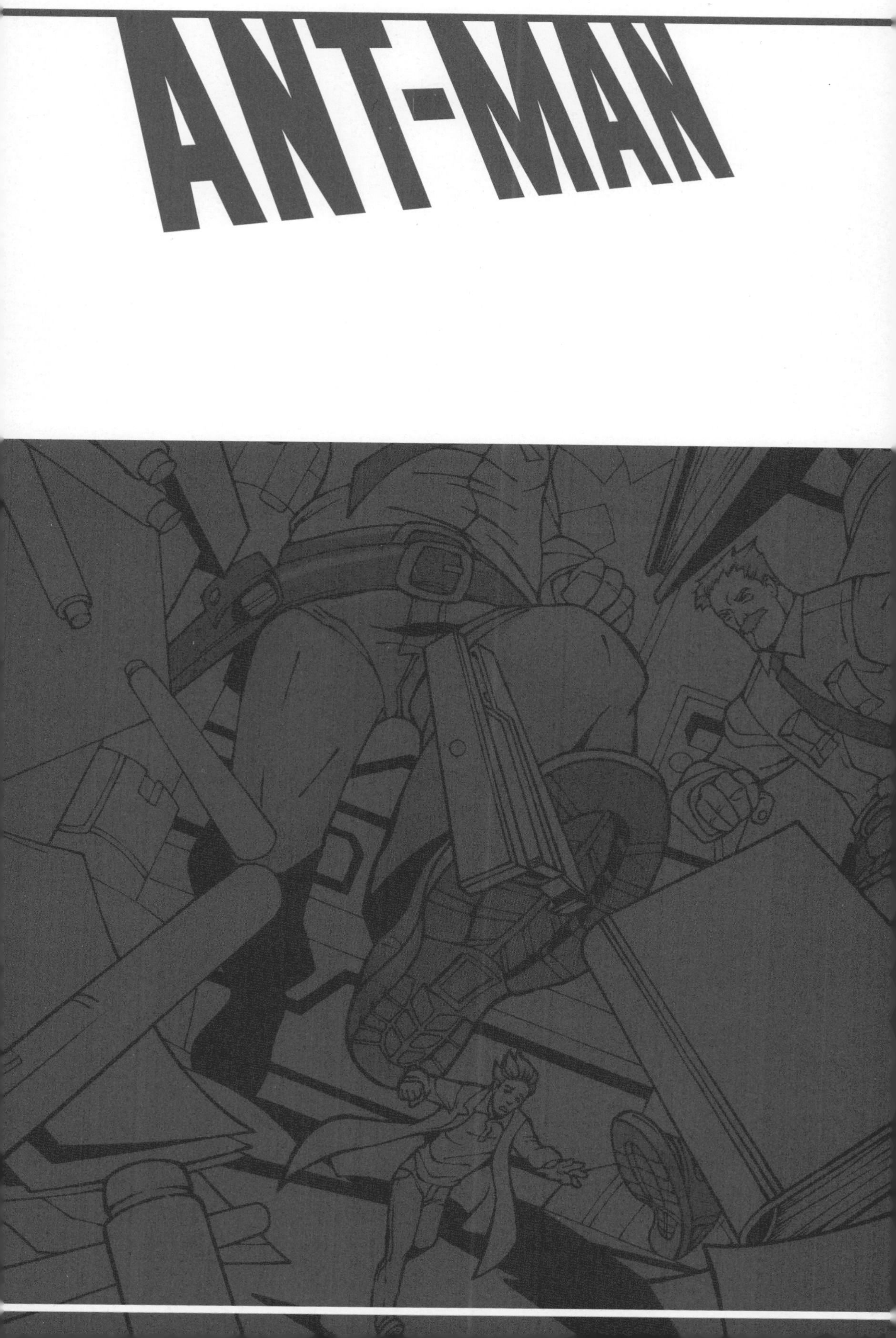

COLLECTION EDITOR: **JENNIFER GRÜNWALD**
ASSISTANT EDITORS: **ALEX STARBUCK & NELSON RIBEIRO**
EDITOR, SPECIAL PROJECTS: **MARK D. BEAZLEY**
SENIOR EDITOR, SPECIAL PROJECTS: **JEFF YOUNGQUIST**
SENIOR VICE PRESIDENT OF SALES: **DAVID GABRIEL**
SVP OF BRAND PLANNING & COMMUNICATIONS: **MICHAEL PASCIULLO**
COVER & BOOK DESIGN: **JEFF POWELL**

EDITOR IN CHIEF: **AXEL ALONSO**
CHIEF CREATIVE OFFICER: **JOE QUESADA**
PUBLISHER: **DAN BUCKLEY**
EXECUTIVE PRODUCER: **ALAN FINE**

ANT-MAN: SEASON ONE. Contains material originally published in magazine form as AVENGERS ACADEMY #1. First printing 2012. ISBN# 978-0-7851-6386-2. Published by MARVEL WORLDWIDE, INC., a subsidiar MARVEL ENTERTAINMENT, LLC. OFFICE OF PUBLICATION: 135 West 50th Street, New York, NY 10020. $24.99 per copy in the U.S. and $27.99 in Car (GST #R127032852); Canadian Agreement #40668537. **Printe the U.S.A.** ALAN FINE, EVP - Office of the President, Marvel Worldwide, Inc. and EVP & CMO Marvel Characters B.V.; DAN BUCKLEY, Publisher & President - Print, Animation & Digital Divisions; JOE QUESADA, Chief Crea Officer; TOM BREVOORT, SVP of Publishing; DAVID BOGART, SVP of Operations & Procurement, Publishing; RUWAN JAYATILLEKE, SVP & Associate Publisher, Publishing; C.B. CEBULSKI, SVP of Creator & Content Developm DAVID GABRIEL, SVP of Publishing Sales & Circulation; MICHAEL PASCIULLO, SVP of Brand Planning & Communications; JIM O'KEEFE, VP of Operations & Logistics; DAN CARR, Executive Director of Publishing Technol SUSAN CRESPI, Editorial Operations Manager; ALEX MORALES, Publishing Operations Manager; STAN LEE, Chairman Emeritus. For information regarding advertising in Marvel Comics or on Marvel.com, please contact Disla, Director of Marvel Partnerships, at ndisla@marvel.com. For Marvel subscription inquiries, please call 800-217-9158. **Manufactured between 5/21/2012 and 6/25/2012 by R.R. DONNELLEY, INC., SALEM, VA,**

10 9 8 7 6 5 4 3 2 1

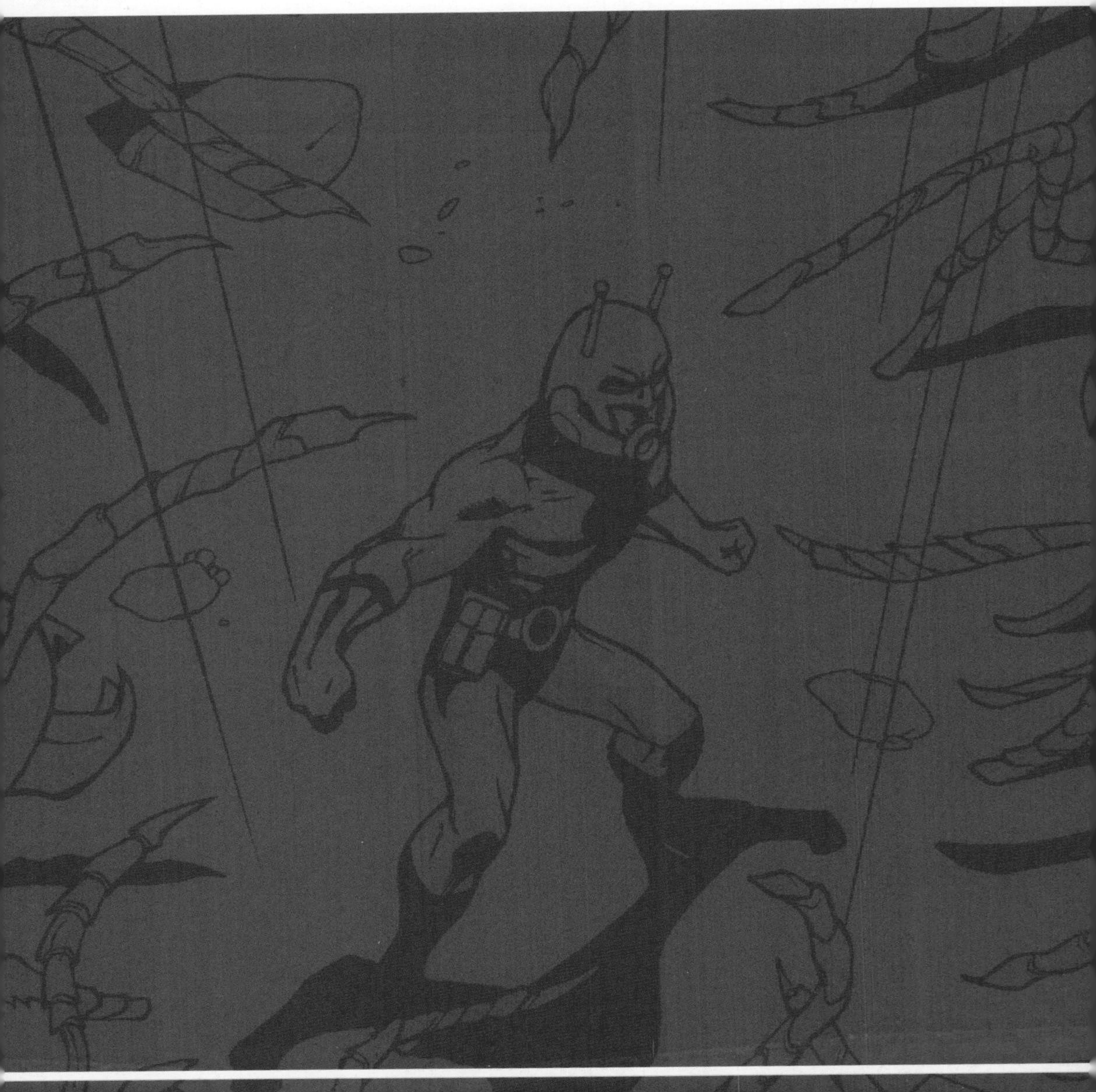

ANT-MAN

WRITER
TOM DEFALCO
ARTIST
HORACIO DOMINGUES
ART ASSISTANTS
RUBEN GONZALEZ & ANDRES PONCE
COLOR ARTIST
CHRIS SOTOMAYOR
LETTERERS
VC'S CHRIS ELIOPOULOS
& JOE SABINO

COVER ARTIST
JULIAN TOTINO TEDESCO

EDITOR
TOM BRENNAN
EXECUTIVE EDITOR
TOM BREVOORT

SEASON ONE

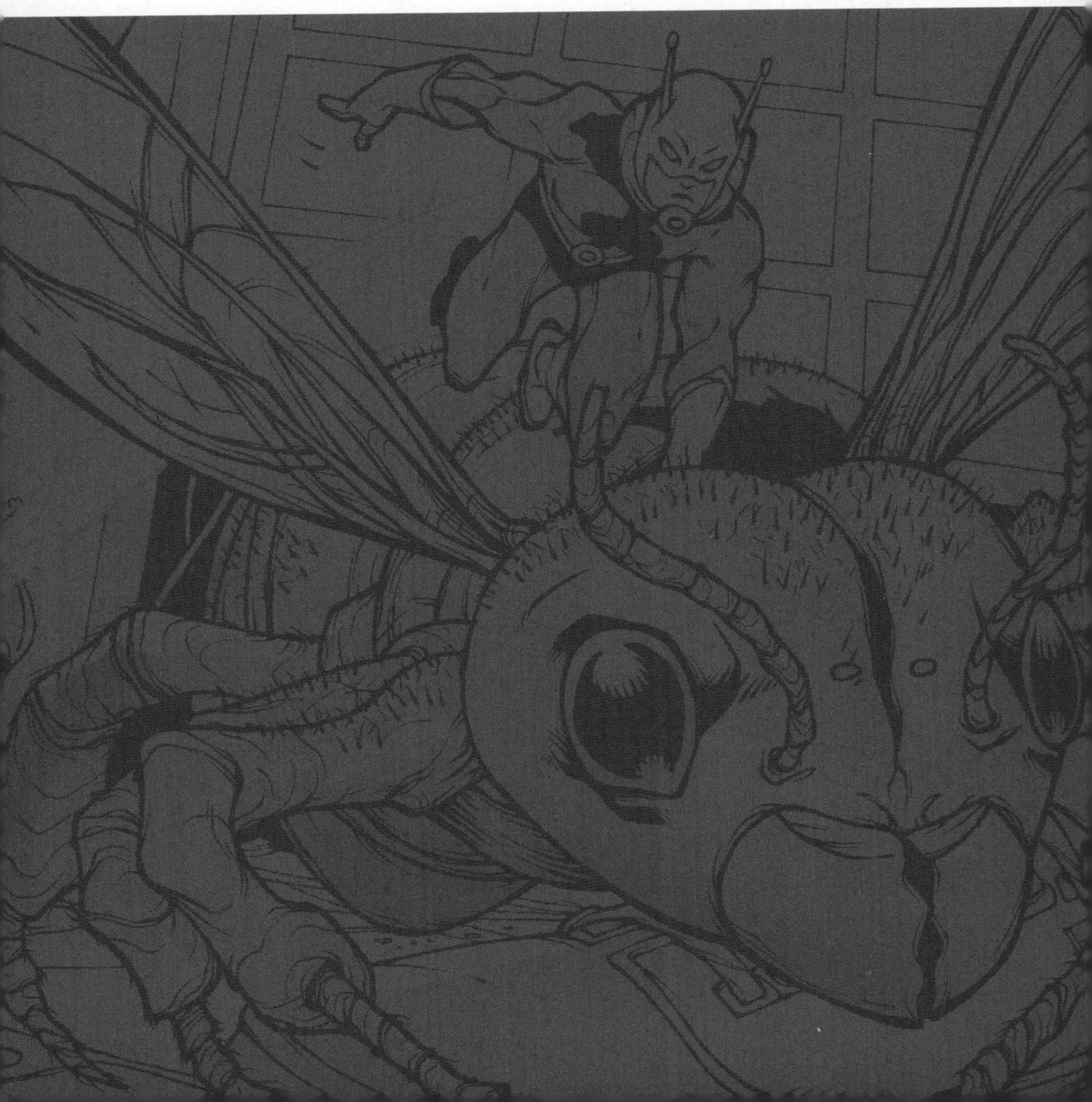

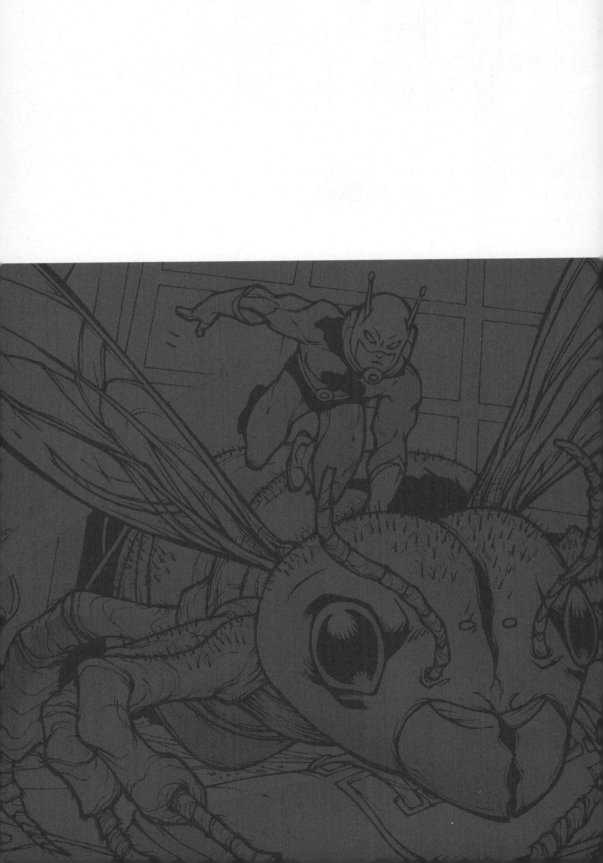

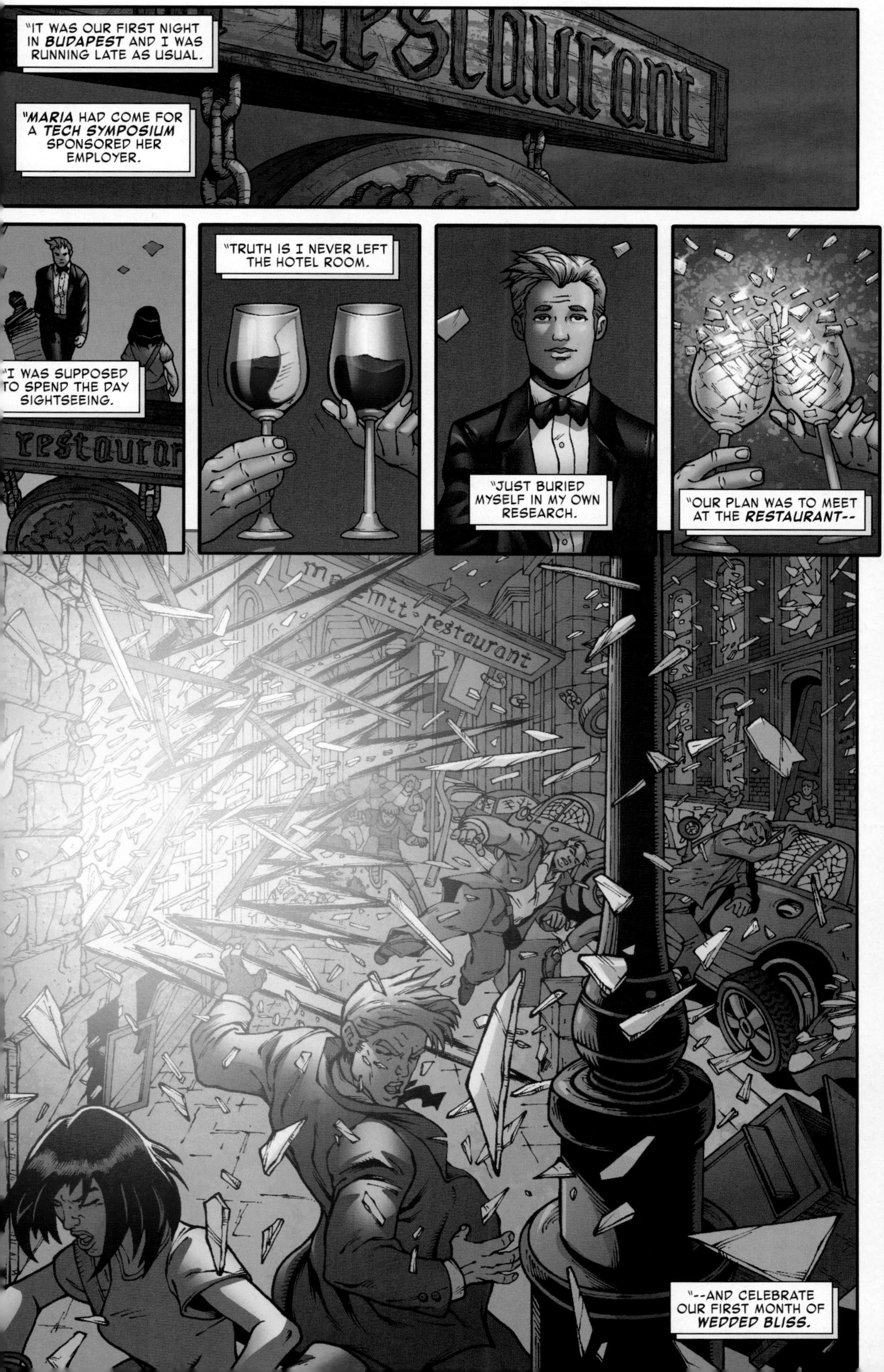
"IT WAS OUR FIRST NIGHT IN BUDAPEST AND I WAS RUNNING LATE AS USUAL.
restaurant
"MARIA HAD COME FOR A TECH SYMPOSIUM SPONSORED HER EMPLOYER.
"I WAS SUPPOSED TO SPEND THE DAY SIGHTSEEING.
restaurant
"TRUTH IS I NEVER LEFT THE HOTEL ROOM.
"JUST BURIED MYSELF IN MY OWN RESEARCH.
"OUR PLAN WAS TO MEET AT THE RESTAURANT--
restaurant
"--AND CELEBRATE OUR FIRST MONTH OF WEDDED BLISS.

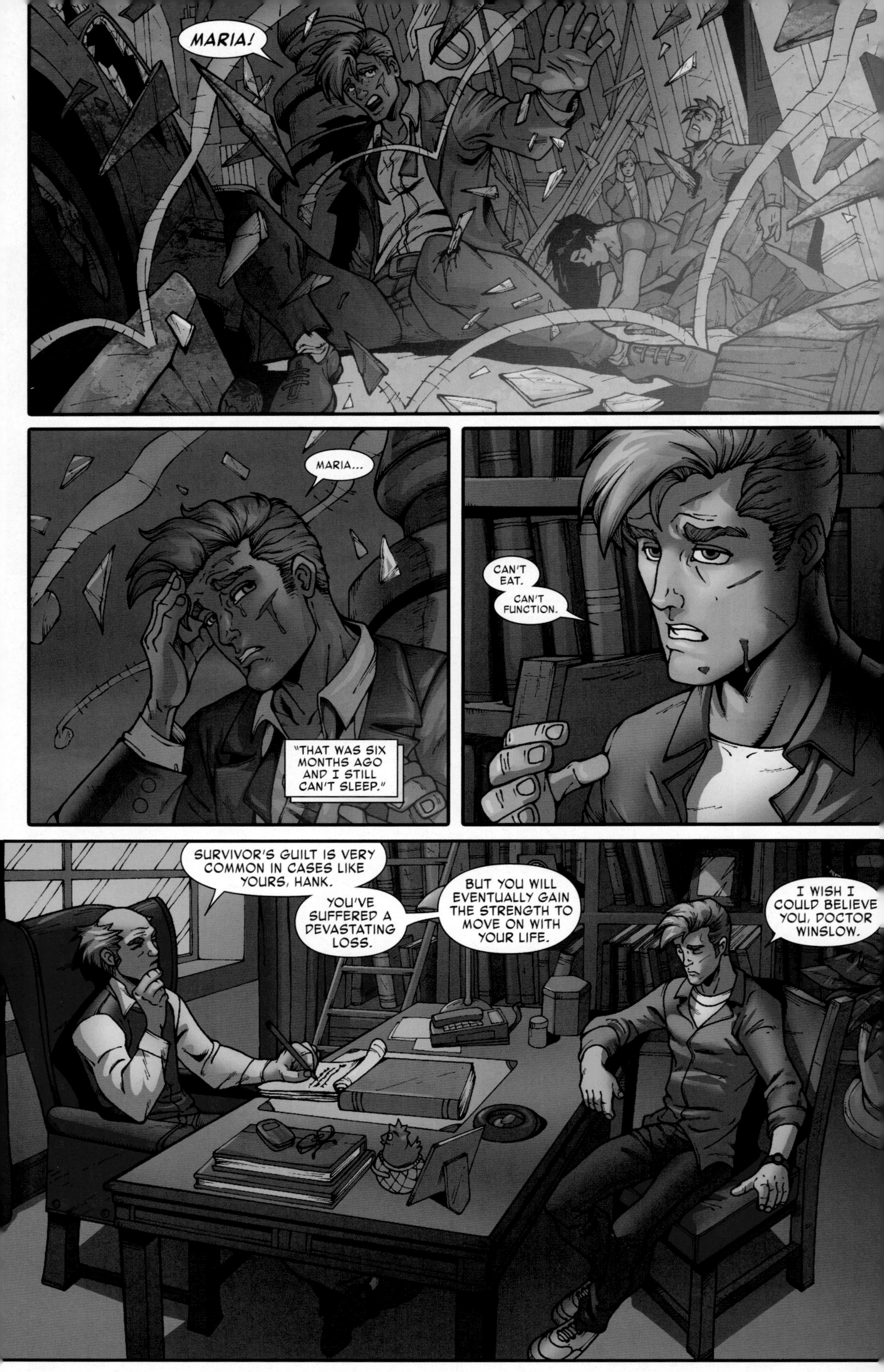
MARIA!
MARIA...
"THAT WAS SIX MONTHS AGO AND I STILL CAN'T SLEEP."
CAN'T EAT.
CAN'T FUNCTION.
SURVIVOR'S GUILT IS VERY COMMON IN CASES LIKE YOURS, HANK.
YOU'VE SUFFERED A DEVASTATING LOSS.
BUT YOU WILL EVENTUALLY GAIN THE STRENGTH TO MOVE ON WITH YOUR LIFE.
I WISH I COULD BELIEVE YOU, DOCTOR WINSLOW.

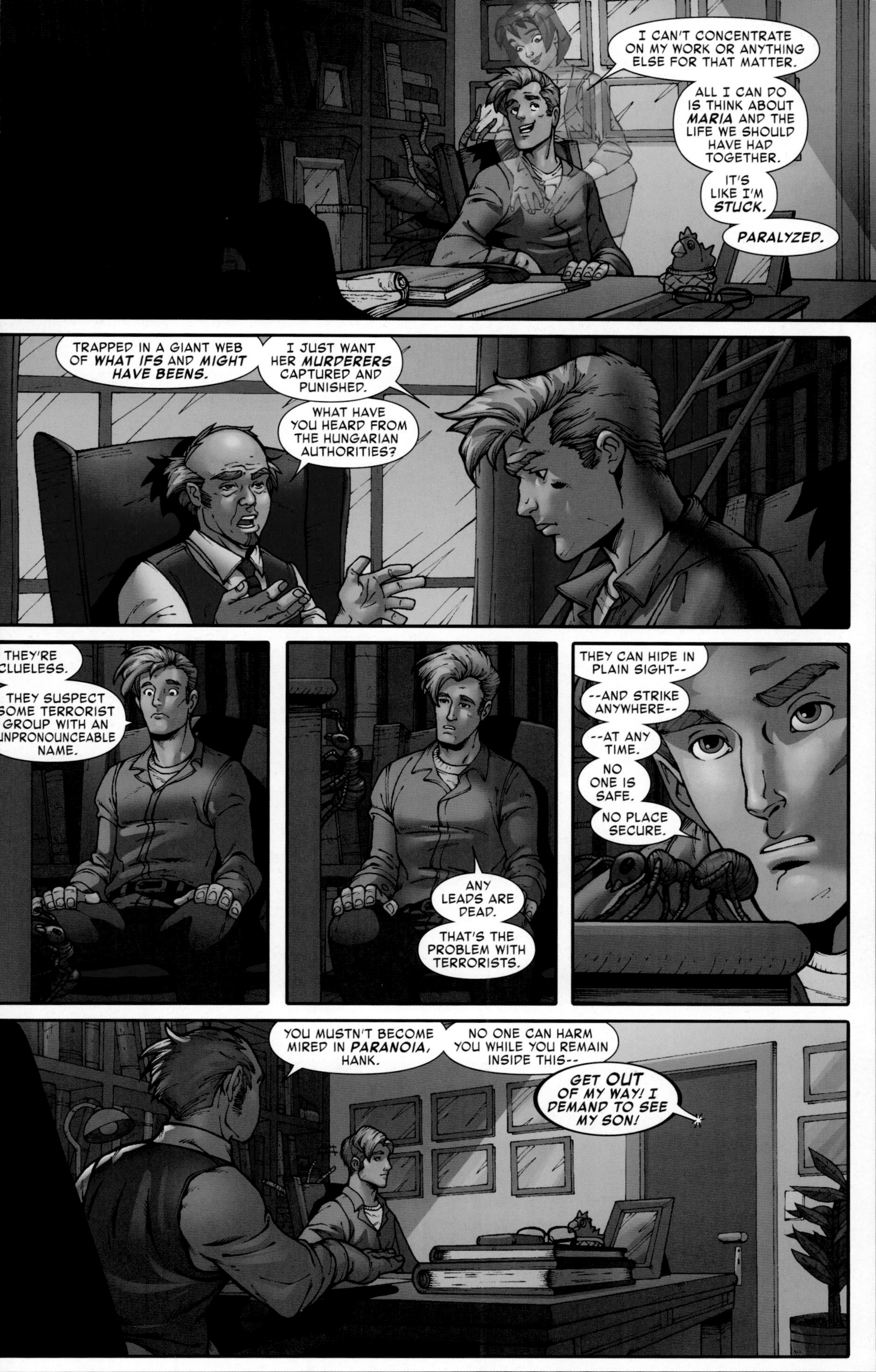

I CAN'T CONCENTRATE ON MY WORK OR ANYTHING ELSE FOR THAT MATTER.
ALL I CAN DO IS THINK ABOUT MARIA AND THE LIFE WE SHOULD HAVE HAD TOGETHER.
IT'S LIKE I'M STUCK.
PARALYZED.
TRAPPED IN A GIANT WEB OF WHAT IFS AND MIGHT HAVE BEENS.
I JUST WANT HER MURDERERS CAPTURED AND PUNISHED.
WHAT HAVE YOU HEARD FROM THE HUNGARIAN AUTHORITIES?
THEY'RE CLUELESS.
THEY SUSPECT SOME TERRORIST GROUP WITH AN UNPRONOUNCEABLE NAME.
ANY LEADS ARE DEAD.
THAT'S THE PROBLEM WITH TERRORISTS.
THEY CAN HIDE IN PLAIN SIGHT--
--AND STRIKE ANYWHERE--
--AT ANY TIME.
NO ONE IS SAFE.
NO PLACE SECURE.
YOU MUSTN'T BECOME MIRED IN PARANOIA, HANK.
NO ONE CAN HARM YOU WHILE YOU REMAIN INSIDE THIS--
GET OUT OF MY WAY! I DEMAND TO SEE MY SON!

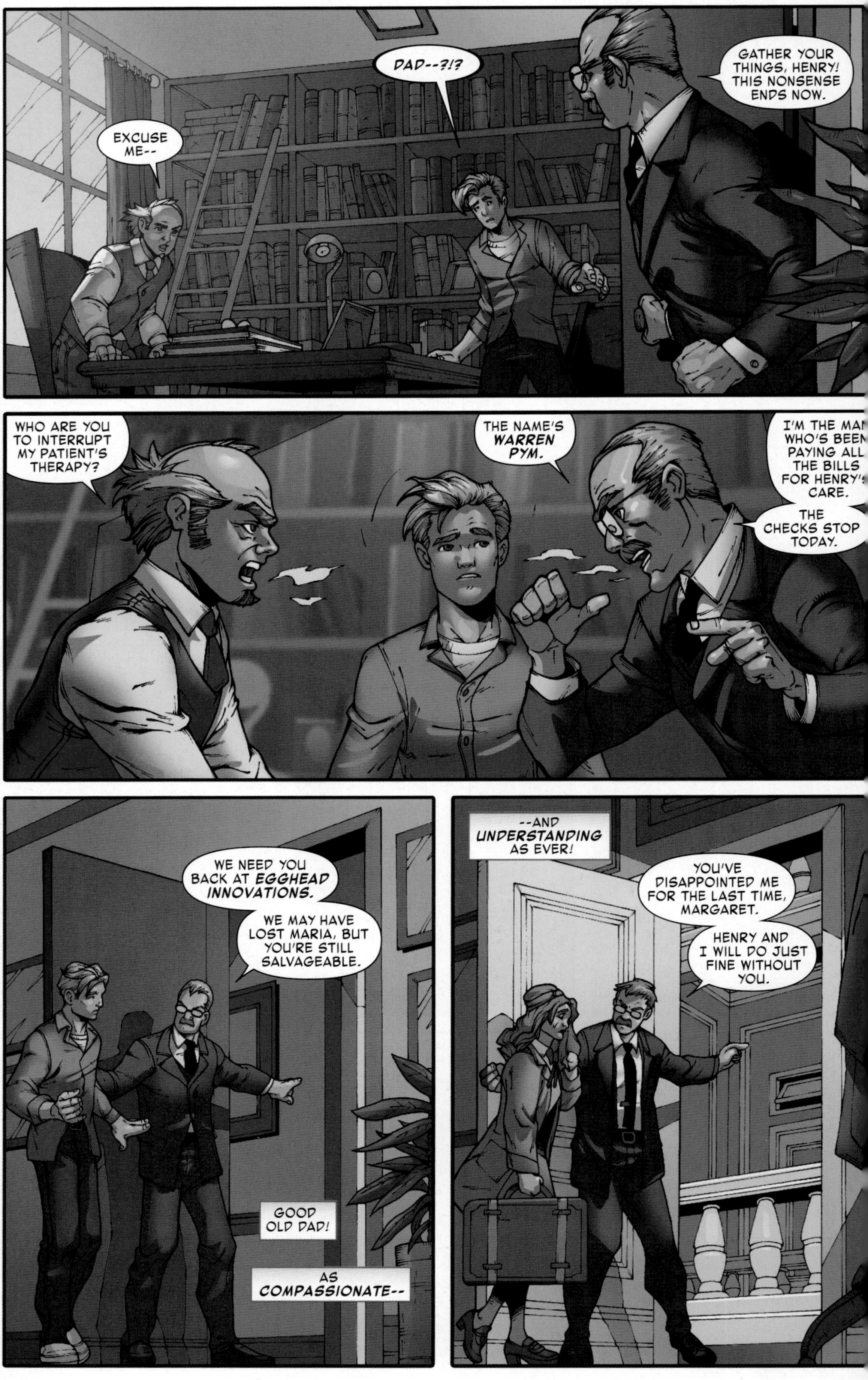
GATHER YOUR THINGS, HENRY! THIS NONSENSE ENDS NOW.
DAD--?!?
EXCUSE ME--
WHO ARE YOU TO INTERRUPT MY PATIENT'S THERAPY?
THE NAME'S WARREN PYM.
I'M THE MAN WHO'S BEEN PAYING ALL THE BILLS FOR HENRY'S CARE.
THE CHECKS STOP TODAY.
WE NEED YOU BACK AT EGGHEAD INNOVATIONS.
WE MAY HAVE LOST MARIA, BUT YOU'RE STILL SALVAGEABLE.
GOOD OLD DAD!
AS COMPASSIONATE--
--AND UNDERSTANDING AS EVER!
YOU'VE DISAPPOINTED ME FOR THE LAST TIME, MARGARET.
HENRY AND I WILL DO JUST FINE WITHOUT YOU.

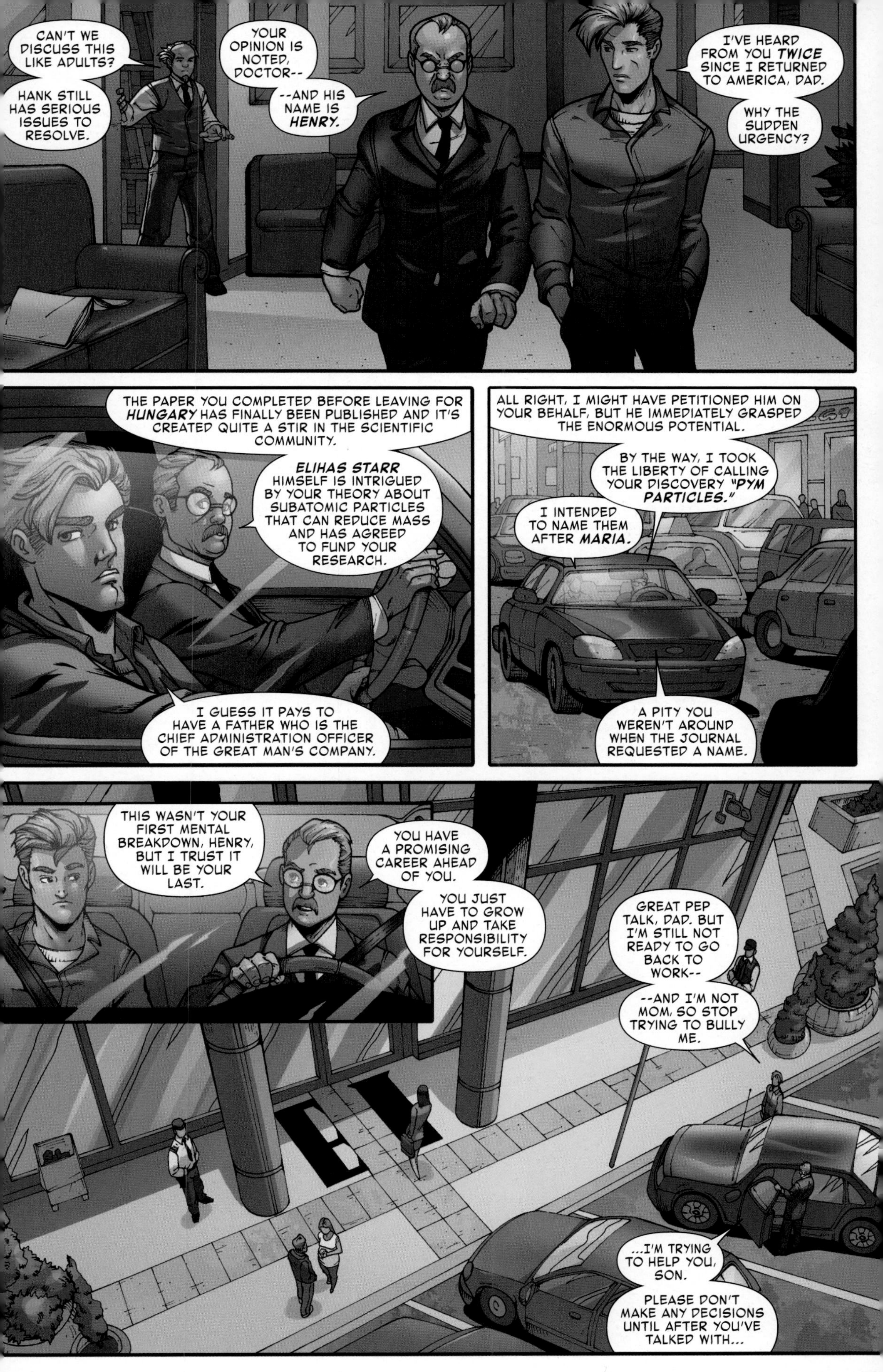
CAN'T WE DISCUSS THIS LIKE ADULTS?
HANK STILL HAS SERIOUS ISSUES TO RESOLVE.
YOUR OPINION IS NOTED, DOCTOR--
--AND HIS NAME IS HENRY.
I'VE HEARD FROM YOU TWICE SINCE I RETURNED TO AMERICA, DAD.
WHY THE SUDDEN URGENCY?
THE PAPER YOU COMPLETED BEFORE LEAVING FOR HUNGARY HAS FINALLY BEEN PUBLISHED AND IT'S CREATED QUITE A STIR IN THE SCIENTIFIC COMMUNITY.
ELIHAS STARR HIMSELF IS INTRIGUED BY YOUR THEORY ABOUT SUBATOMIC PARTICLES THAT CAN REDUCE MASS AND HAS AGREED TO FUND YOUR RESEARCH.
I GUESS IT PAYS TO HAVE A FATHER WHO IS THE CHIEF ADMINISTRATION OFFICER OF THE GREAT MAN'S COMPANY.
ALL RIGHT, I MIGHT HAVE PETITIONED HIM ON YOUR BEHALF, BUT HE IMMEDIATELY GRASPED THE ENORMOUS POTENTIAL.
BY THE WAY, I TOOK THE LIBERTY OF CALLING YOUR DISCOVERY "PYM PARTICLES."
I INTENDED TO NAME THEM AFTER MARIA.
A PITY YOU WEREN'T AROUND WHEN THE JOURNAL REQUESTED A NAME.
THIS WASN'T YOUR FIRST MENTAL BREAKDOWN, HENRY, BUT I TRUST IT WILL BE YOUR LAST.
YOU HAVE A PROMISING CAREER AHEAD OF YOU.
YOU JUST HAVE TO GROW UP AND TAKE RESPONSIBILITY FOR YOURSELF.
GREAT PEP TALK, DAD. BUT I'M STILL NOT READY TO GO BACK TO WORK--
--AND I'M NOT MOM, SO STOP TRYING TO BULLY ME.
...I'M TRYING TO HELP YOU, SON.
PLEASE DON'T MAKE ANY DECISIONS UNTIL AFTER YOU'VE TALKED WITH...

MR. STARR-- ELIHAS! WE WERE ON OUR WAY TO YOUR OFFICE.

I HAD THE DESK INFORM ME AS SOON AS YOU ARRIVED, WARREN.

I APOLOGIZE FOR ALL THE INTRUSIVE SECURITY, HENRY.

OUR GOVERNMENT CONTRACTS REQUIRE IT.

I WAS SO SORRY TO HEAR ABOUT MARIA.

SHE WAS A VALUED AND CHERISHED MEMBER OF OUR LITTLE FAMILY.

...THANK YOU, MR. STARR, I THANK YOU FOR ALL YOUR ASSISTANCE WITH THE EMBASSY IN TRANSPORTING MARIA'S REMAINS.

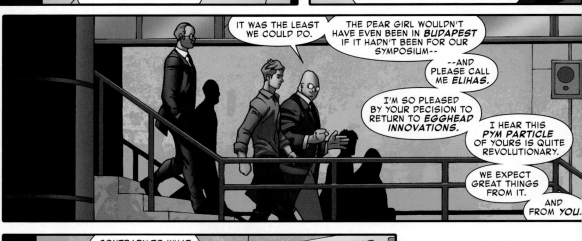

IT WAS THE LEAST WE COULD DO.

THE DEAR GIRL WOULDN'T HAVE EVEN BEEN IN BUDAPEST IF IT HADN'T BEEN FOR OUR SYMPOSIUM--

--AND PLEASE CALL ME ELIHAS.

I'M SO PLEASED BY YOUR DECISION TO RETURN TO EGGHEAD INNOVATIONS.

I HEAR THIS PYM PARTICLE OF YOURS IS QUITE REVOLUTIONARY.

WE EXPECT GREAT THINGS FROM IT.

AND FROM YOU.

CONTRARY TO WHAT MY FATHER MAY HAVE TOLD YOU, MR. STARR--

--I WOULDN'T EXPECT TOO MUCH.

WHAT ARE YOU SAYING, HENRY?

LEVEL 3

I HAVE NO IDEA WHEN OR EVEN IF MY RESEARCH WILL YIELD PRACTICAL RESULTS.

AND I WON'T BE RUSHED OR HELD TO AN ARTIFICIAL TIMETABLE.

I UNDERSTAND, HENRY.

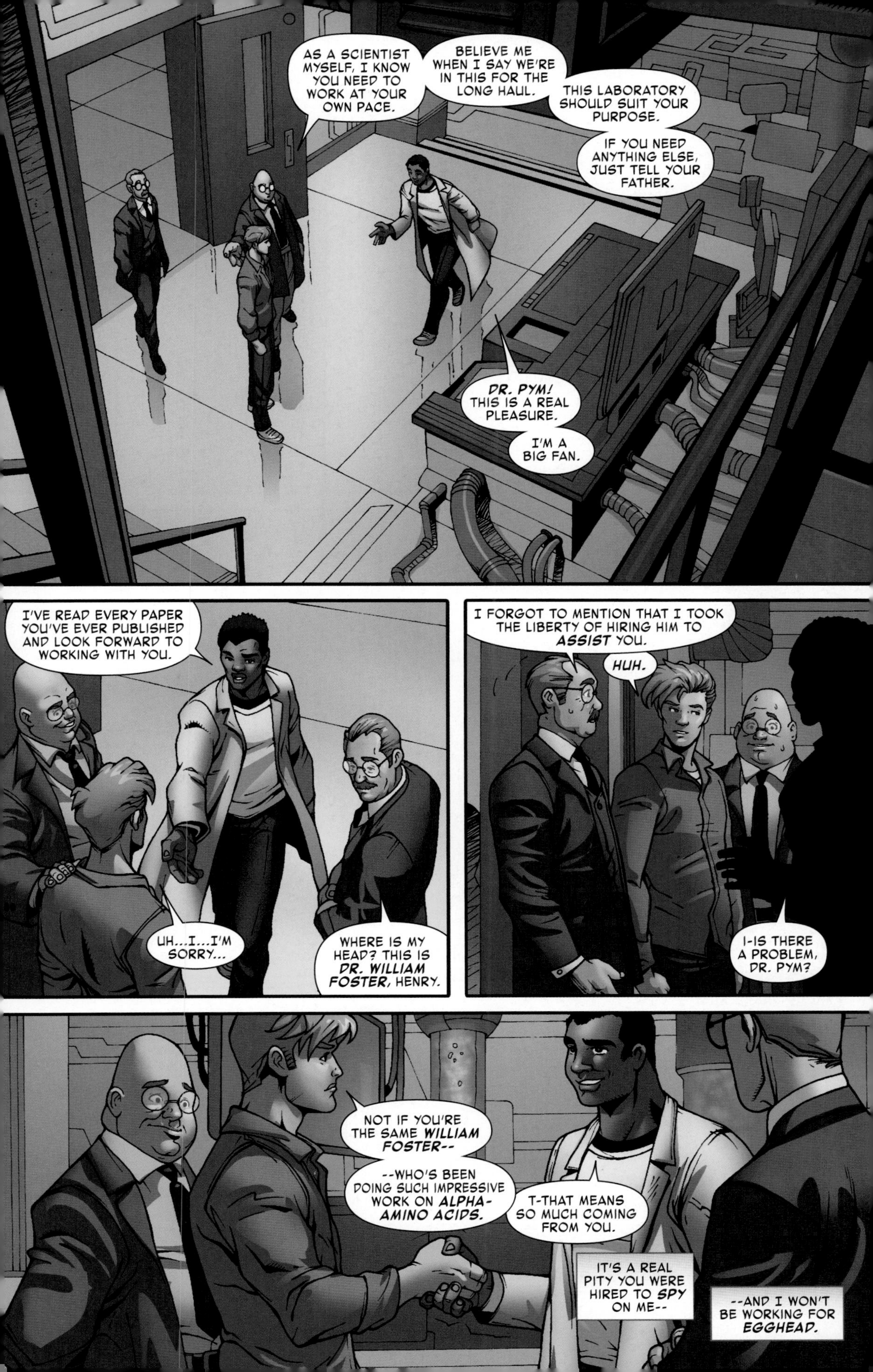
AS A SCIENTIST MYSELF, I KNOW YOU NEED TO WORK AT YOUR OWN PACE.
BELIEVE ME WHEN I SAY WE'RE IN THIS FOR THE LONG HAUL.
THIS LABORATORY SHOULD SUIT YOUR PURPOSE.
IF YOU NEED ANYTHING ELSE, JUST TELL YOUR FATHER.
DR. PYM! THIS IS A REAL PLEASURE.
I'M A BIG FAN.
I'VE READ EVERY PAPER YOU'VE EVER PUBLISHED AND LOOK FORWARD TO WORKING WITH YOU.
UH...I...I'M SORRY...
WHERE IS MY HEAD? THIS IS DR. WILLIAM FOSTER, HENRY.
I FORGOT TO MENTION THAT I TOOK THE LIBERTY OF HIRING HIM TO ASSIST YOU.
HUH.
I-IS THERE A PROBLEM, DR. PYM?
NOT IF YOU'RE THE SAME WILLIAM FOSTER--
--WHO'S BEEN DOING SUCH IMPRESSIVE WORK ON ALPHA-AMINO ACIDS.
T-THAT MEANS SO MUCH COMING FROM YOU.
IT'S A REAL PITY YOU WERE HIRED TO SPY ON ME--
--AND I WON'T BE WORKING FOR EGGHEAD.

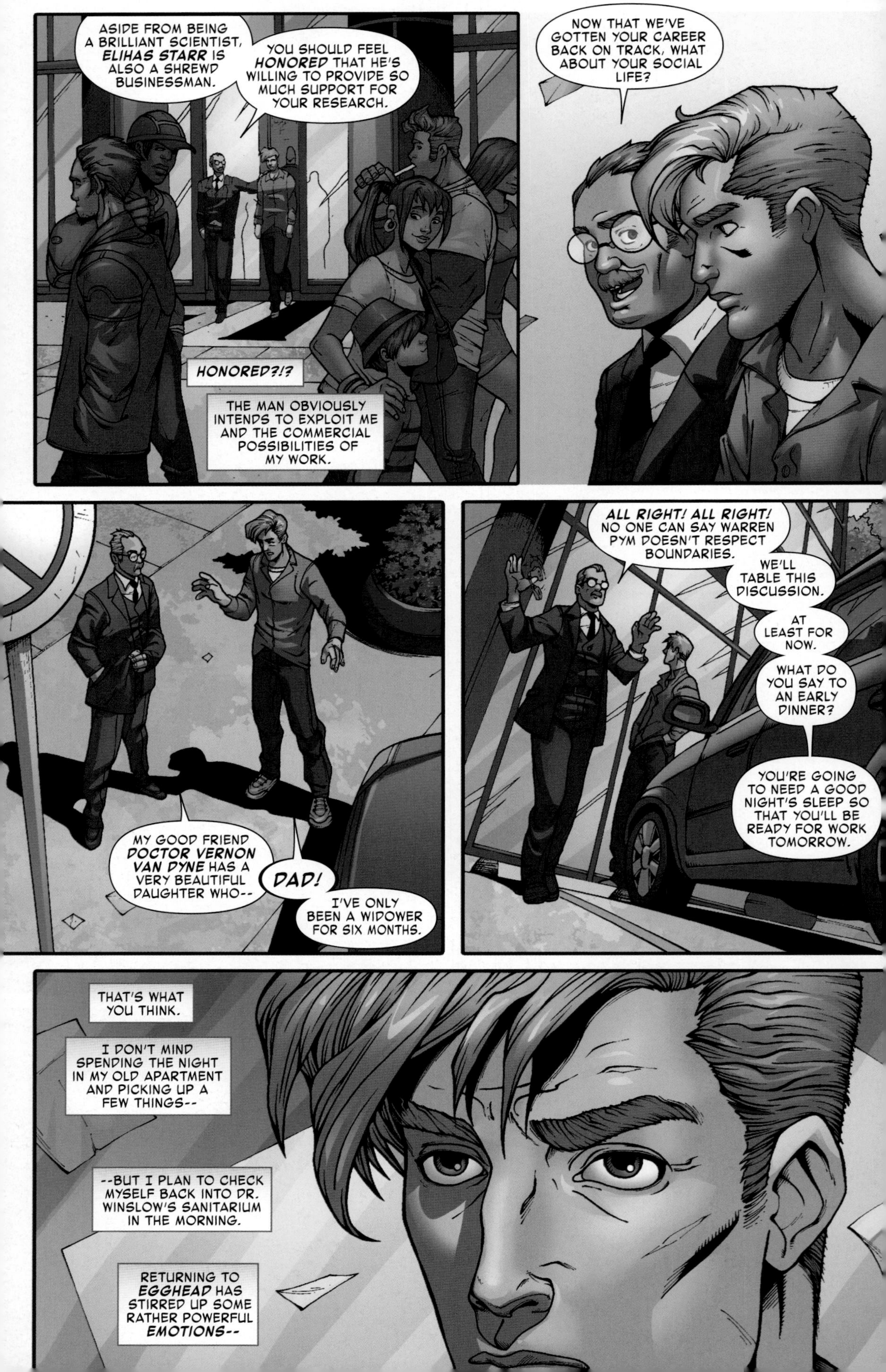
ASIDE FROM BEING A BRILLIANT SCIENTIST, ELIHAS STARR IS ALSO A SHREWD BUSINESSMAN.
YOU SHOULD FEEL HONORED THAT HE'S WILLING TO PROVIDE SO MUCH SUPPORT FOR YOUR RESEARCH.
HONORED?!?
THE MAN OBVIOUSLY INTENDS TO EXPLOIT ME AND THE COMMERCIAL POSSIBILITIES OF MY WORK.
NOW THAT WE'VE GOTTEN YOUR CAREER BACK ON TRACK, WHAT ABOUT YOUR SOCIAL LIFE?
MY GOOD FRIEND DOCTOR VERNON VAN DYNE HAS A VERY BEAUTIFUL DAUGHTER WHO--
DAD!
I'VE ONLY BEEN A WIDOWER FOR SIX MONTHS.
ALL RIGHT! ALL RIGHT! NO ONE CAN SAY WARREN PYM DOESN'T RESPECT BOUNDARIES.
WE'LL TABLE THIS DISCUSSION.
AT LEAST FOR NOW.
WHAT DO YOU SAY TO AN EARLY DINNER?
YOU'RE GOING TO NEED A GOOD NIGHT'S SLEEP SO THAT YOU'LL BE READY FOR WORK TOMORROW.
THAT'S WHAT YOU THINK.
I DON'T MIND SPENDING THE NIGHT IN MY OLD APARTMENT AND PICKING UP A FEW THINGS--
--BUT I PLAN TO CHECK MYSELF BACK INTO DR. WINSLOW'S SANITARIUM IN THE MORNING.
RETURNING TO EGGHEAD HAS STIRRED UP SOME RATHER POWERFUL EMOTIONS--

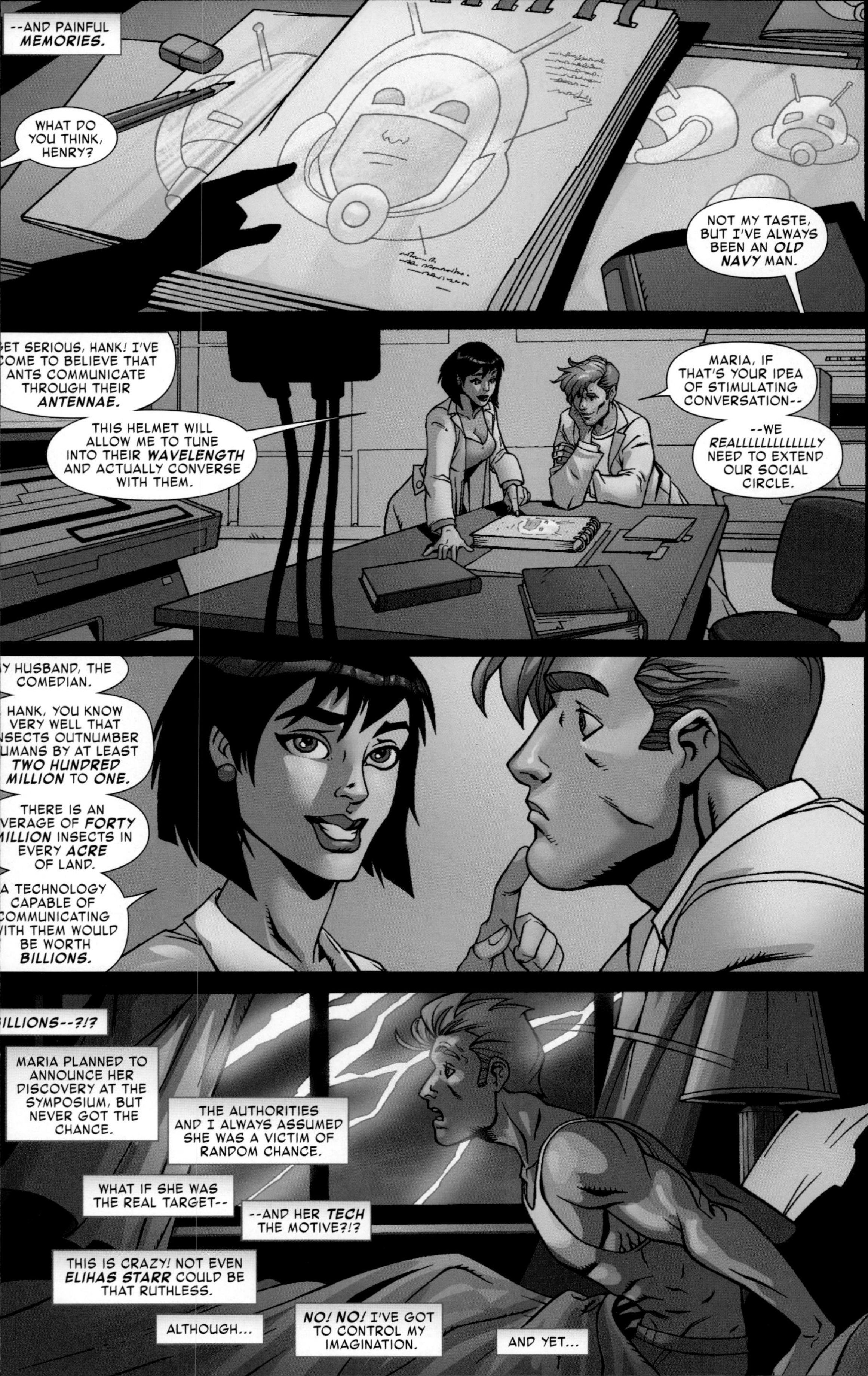
--AND PAINFUL MEMORIES.
WHAT DO YOU THINK, HENRY?
NOT MY TASTE, BUT I'VE ALWAYS BEEN AN OLD NAVY MAN.
ET SERIOUS, HANK! I'VE OME TO BELIEVE THAT ANTS COMMUNICATE THROUGH THEIR ANTENNAE.
THIS HELMET WILL ALLOW ME TO TUNE INTO THEIR WAVELENGTH AND ACTUALLY CONVERSE WITH THEM.
MARIA, IF THAT'S YOUR IDEA OF STIMULATING CONVERSATION--
--WE REALLLLLLLLLLLLLY NEED TO EXTEND OUR SOCIAL CIRCLE.
Y HUSBAND, THE COMEDIAN.
HANK, YOU KNOW VERY WELL THAT NSECTS OUTNUMBER UMANS BY AT LEAST TWO HUNDRED MILLION TO ONE.
THERE IS AN VERAGE OF FORTY MILLION INSECTS IN EVERY ACRE OF LAND.
A TECHNOLOGY CAPABLE OF COMMUNICATING WITH THEM WOULD BE WORTH BILLIONS.
ILLIONS--?!?
MARIA PLANNED TO ANNOUNCE HER DISCOVERY AT THE SYMPOSIUM, BUT NEVER GOT THE CHANCE.
THE AUTHORITIES AND I ALWAYS ASSUMED SHE WAS A VICTIM OF RANDOM CHANCE.
WHAT IF SHE WAS THE REAL TARGET--
--AND HER TECH THE MOTIVE?!?
THIS IS CRAZY! NOT EVEN ELIHAS STARR COULD BE THAT RUTHLESS.
ALTHOUGH...
NO! NO! I'VE GOT TO CONTROL MY IMAGINATION.
AND YET...

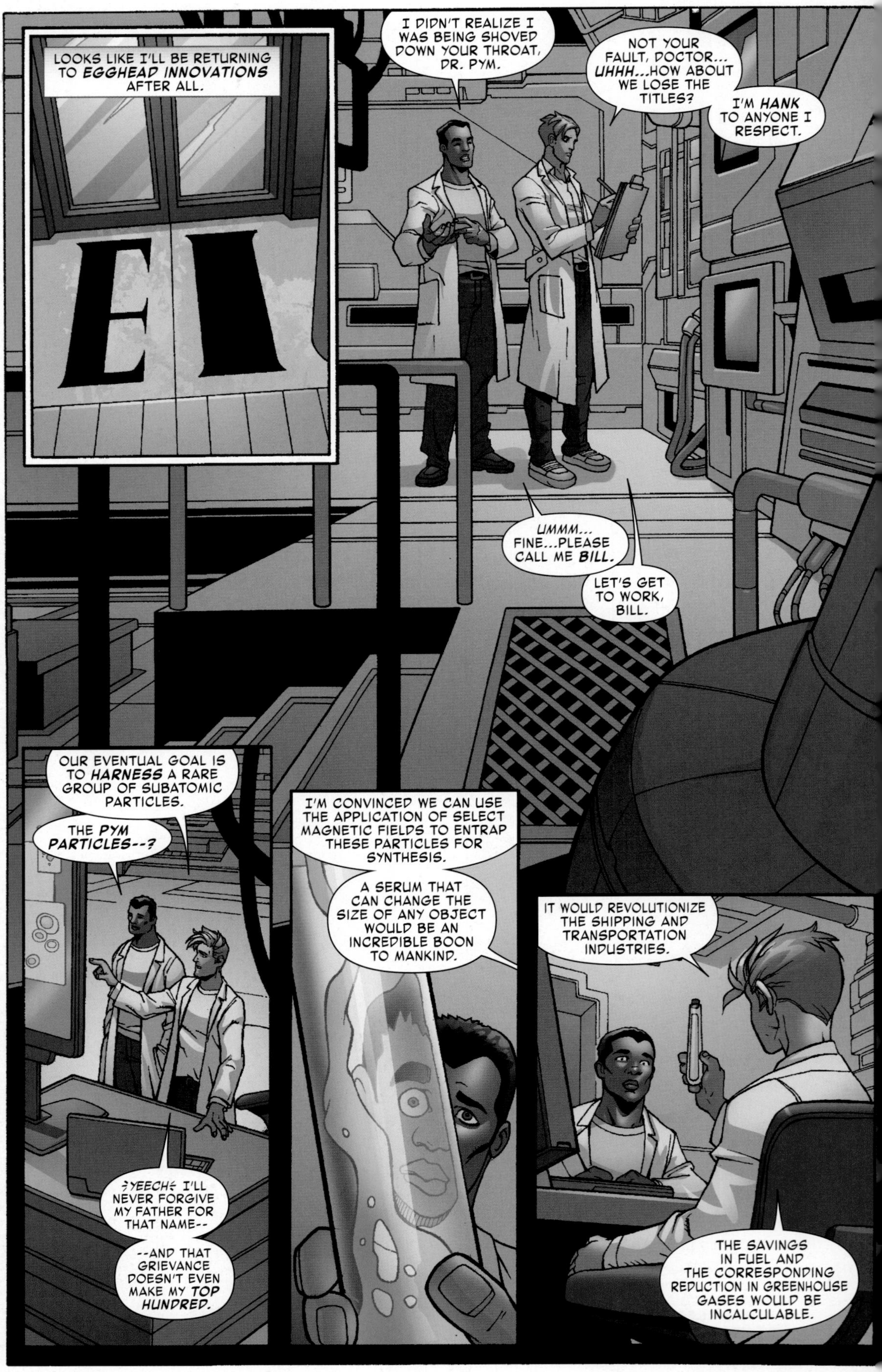

LOOKS LIKE I'LL BE RETURNING TO EGGHEAD INNOVATIONS AFTER ALL.
I DIDN'T REALIZE I WAS BEING SHOVED DOWN YOUR THROAT, DR. PYM.
NOT YOUR FAULT, DOCTOR... UHHH...HOW ABOUT WE LOSE THE TITLES?
I'M HANK TO ANYONE I RESPECT.
UMMM... FINE...PLEASE CALL ME BILL.
LET'S GET TO WORK, BILL.
OUR EVENTUAL GOAL IS TO HARNESS A RARE GROUP OF SUBATOMIC PARTICLES.
THE PYM PARTICLES--?
YEECH I'LL NEVER FORGIVE MY FATHER FOR THAT NAME--
--AND THAT GRIEVANCE DOESN'T EVEN MAKE MY TOP HUNDRED.
I'M CONVINCED WE CAN USE THE APPLICATION OF SELECT MAGNETIC FIELDS TO ENTRAP THESE PARTICLES FOR SYNTHESIS.
A SERUM THAT CAN CHANGE THE SIZE OF ANY OBJECT WOULD BE AN INCREDIBLE BOON TO MANKIND.
IT WOULD REVOLUTIONIZE THE SHIPPING AND TRANSPORTATION INDUSTRIES.
THE SAVINGS IN FUEL AND THE CORRESPONDING REDUCTION IN GREENHOUSE GASES WOULD BE INCALCULABLE.

FOSTER LIVES
UP TO HIS REP--

--CONTRIBUTING FAR
MORE THAN HIS SHARE
TO THE RESEARCH.

MORE'S THE PITY
I CAN'T TRUST HIM.

THE DAYS MORPH INTO
WEEKS AND THE SO-
CALLED PYM PARTICLES
STILL ELUDE US.

THE GUYS IN GENETICS
INVITED US TO JOIN THEM
FOR A BEER AFTER
WORK.

YOU GO AHEAD, BILL.
I JUST WANT TO PREP
THE LAB FOR TOMORROW
AND HAVE AN EARLY
NIGHT.

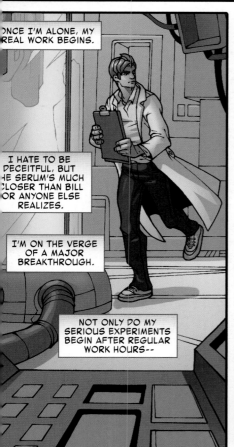

ONCE I'M ALONE, MY
REAL WORK BEGINS.

I HATE TO BE
DECEITFUL, BUT
THE SERUM'S MUCH
CLOSER THAN BILL
OR ANYONE ELSE
REALIZES.

I'M ON THE VERGE
OF A MAJOR
BREAKTHROUGH.

NOT ONLY DO MY
SERIOUS EXPERIMENTS
BEGIN AFTER REGULAR
WORK HOURS--

--I'VE ALSO HACKED
INTO ELIHAS STARR'S
PERSONAL COMPUTER--

--SEARCHING FOR
ANY CONNECTION
BETWEEN HIM AND
MARIA'S KILLERS.

OKAY, MAYBE I
AM ACTING A
LITTLE PARANOID--

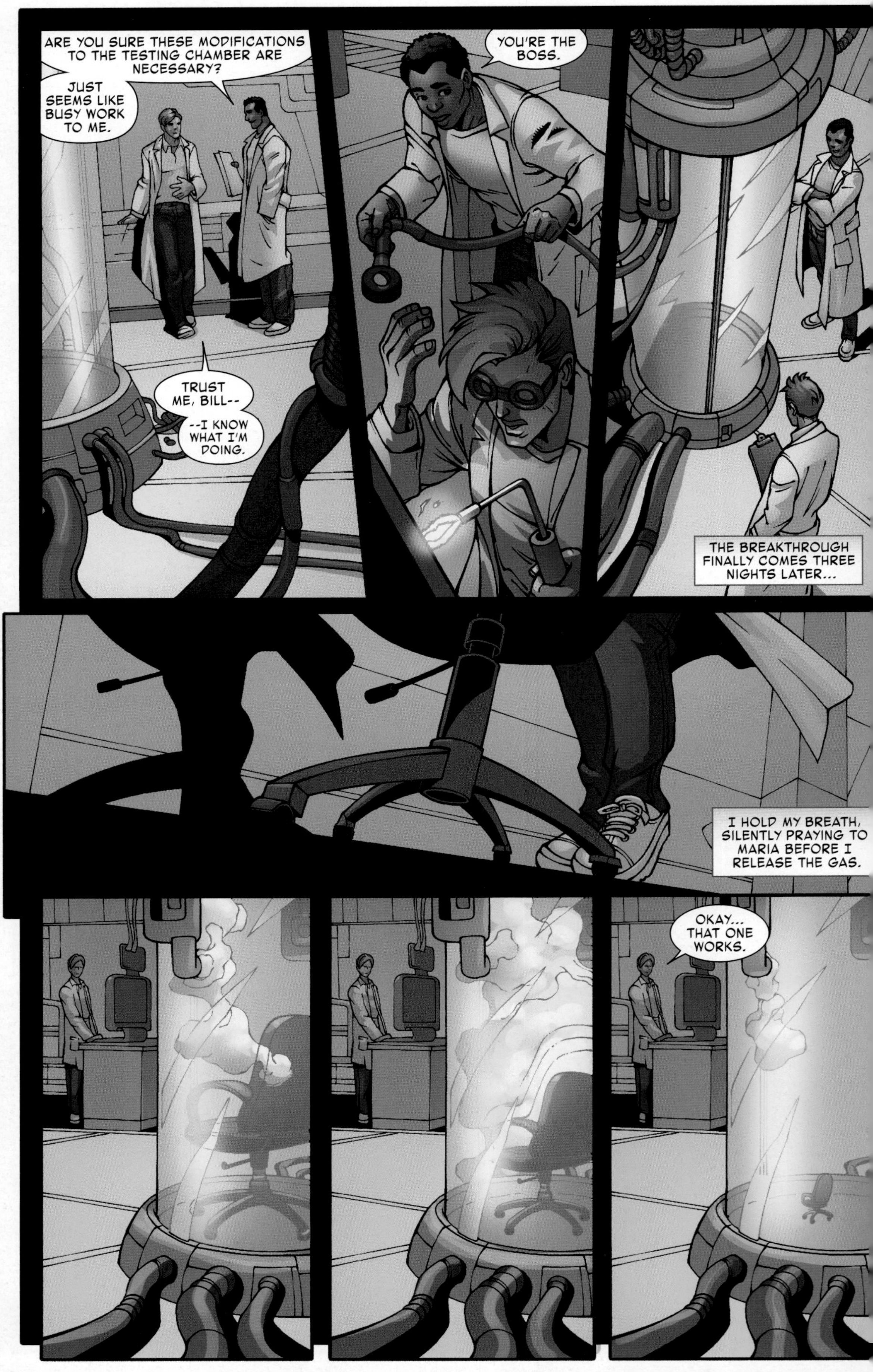
ARE YOU SURE THESE MODIFICATIONS TO THE TESTING CHAMBER ARE NECESSARY?
JUST SEEMS LIKE BUSY WORK TO ME.
TRUST ME, BILL--
--I KNOW WHAT I'M DOING.
YOU'RE THE BOSS.
THE BREAKTHROUGH FINALLY COMES THREE NIGHTS LATER...
I HOLD MY BREATH, SILENTLY PRAYING TO MARIA BEFORE I RELEASE THE GAS.
OKAY... THAT ONE WORKS.

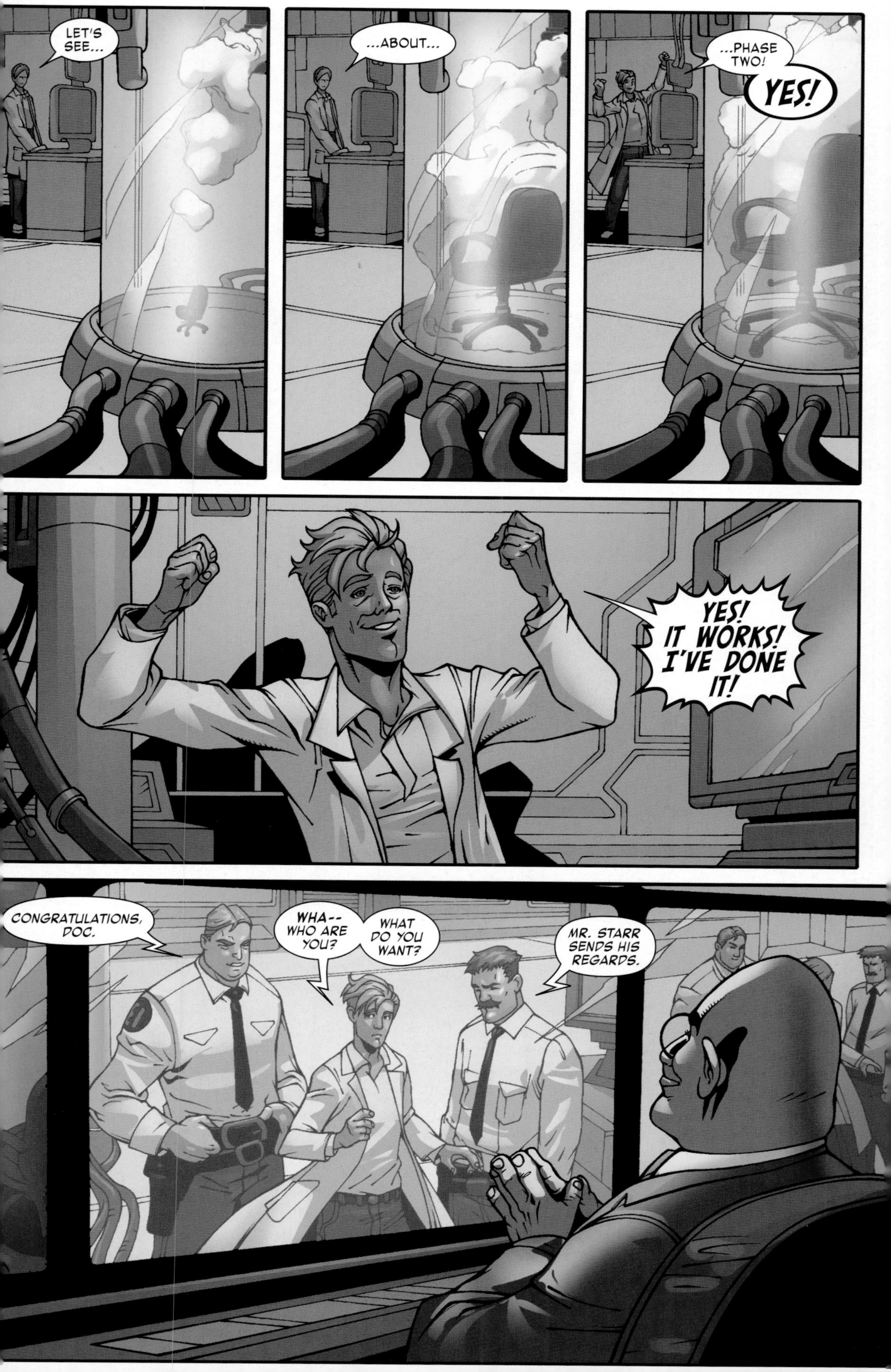
LET'S SEE...
...ABOUT...
...PHASE TWO!
YES!
YES! IT WORKS! I'VE DONE IT!
CONGRATULATIONS, DOC.
WHA-- WHO ARE YOU?
WHAT DO YOU WANT?
MR. STARR SENDS HIS REGARDS.

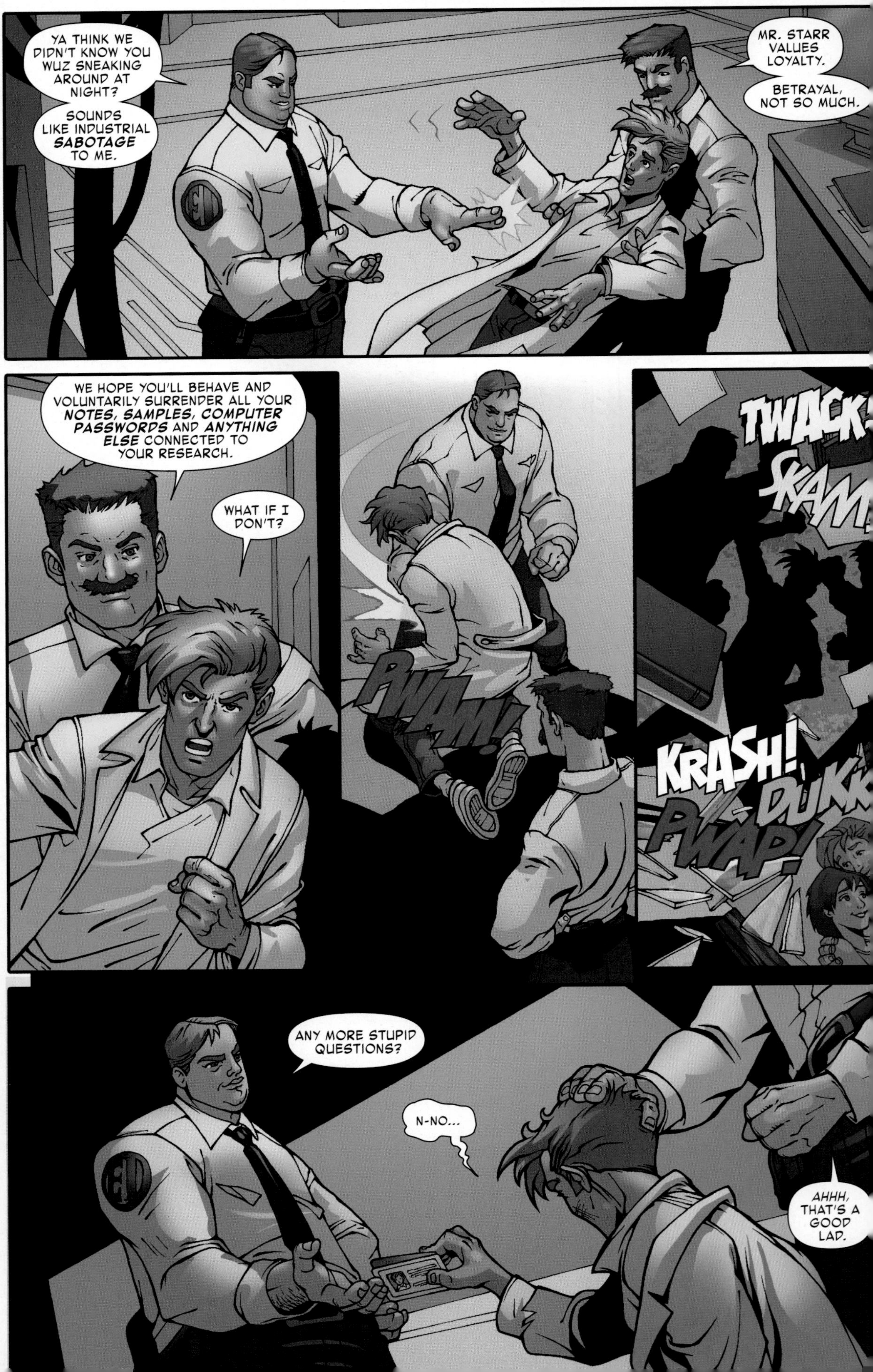
YA THINK WE DIDN'T KNOW YOU WUZ SNEAKING AROUND AT NIGHT?
SOUNDS LIKE INDUSTRIAL SABOTAGE TO ME.
MR. STARR VALUES LOYALTY.
BETRAYAL, NOT SO MUCH.
WE HOPE YOU'LL BEHAVE AND VOLUNTARILY SURRENDER ALL YOUR NOTES, SAMPLES, COMPUTER PASSWORDS AND ANYTHING ELSE CONNECTED TO YOUR RESEARCH.
WHAT IF I DON'T?
PWAM!
TWACK!
SKAM!
KRASH!
DUKK
PWAP!
ANY MORE STUPID QUESTIONS?
N-NO...
AHHH, THAT'S A GOOD LAD.

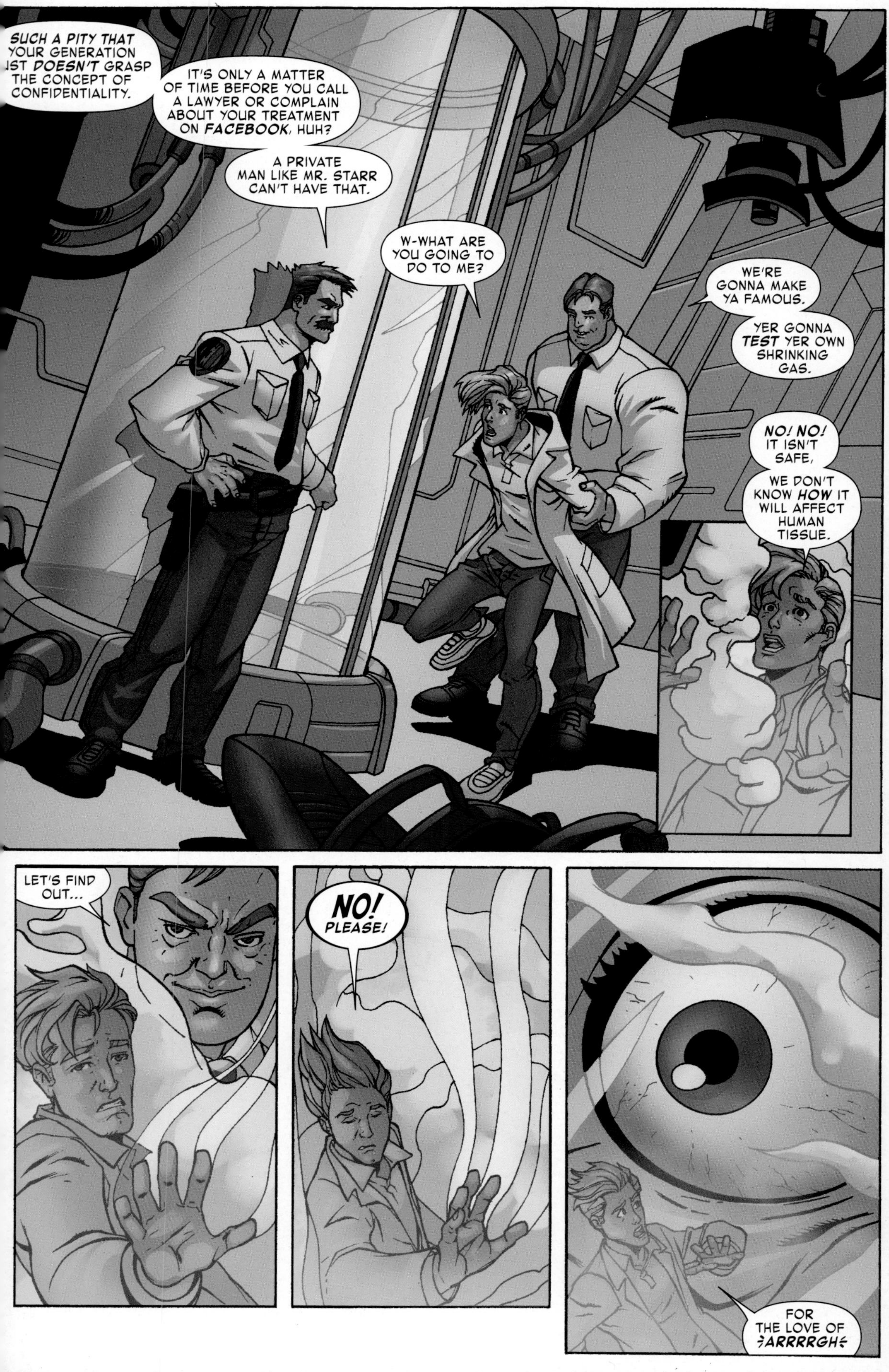
SUCH A PITY THAT YOUR GENERATION JUST DOESN'T GRASP THE CONCEPT OF CONFIDENTIALITY.
IT'S ONLY A MATTER OF TIME BEFORE YOU CALL A LAWYER OR COMPLAIN ABOUT YOUR TREATMENT ON FACEBOOK, HUH?
A PRIVATE MAN LIKE MR. STARR CAN'T HAVE THAT.
W-WHAT ARE YOU GOING TO DO TO ME?
WE'RE GONNA MAKE YA FAMOUS.
YER GONNA TEST YER OWN SHRINKING GAS.
NO! NO! IT ISN'T SAFE,
WE DON'T KNOW HOW IT WILL AFFECT HUMAN TISSUE.
LET'S FIND OUT...
NO! PLEASE!
FOR THE LOVE OF ARRRRGH

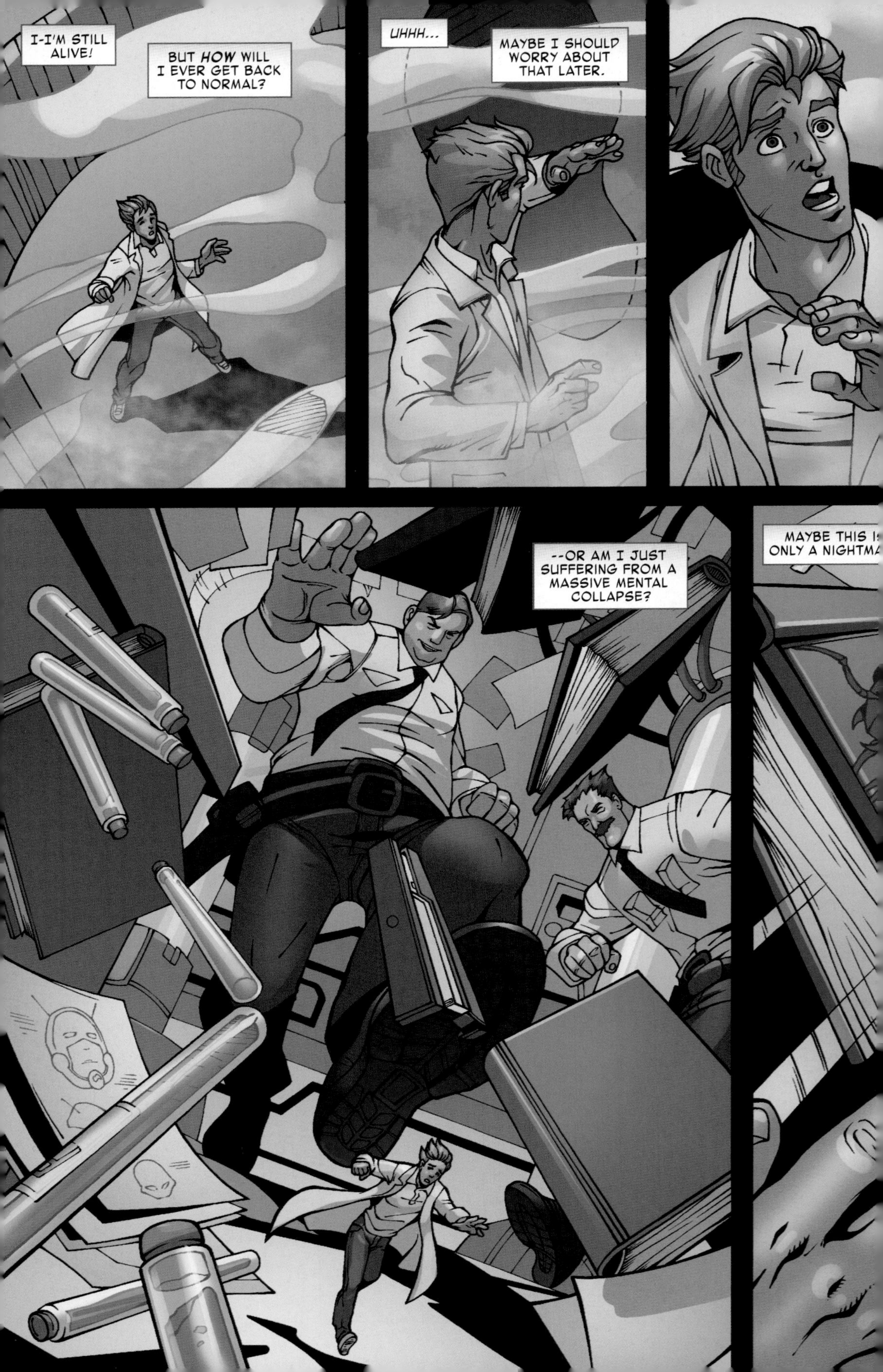
I-I'M STILL ALIVE!
BUT HOW WILL I EVER GET BACK TO NORMAL?
UHHH...
MAYBE I SHOULD WORRY ABOUT THAT LATER.
--OR AM I JUST SUFFERING FROM A MASSIVE MENTAL COLLAPSE?

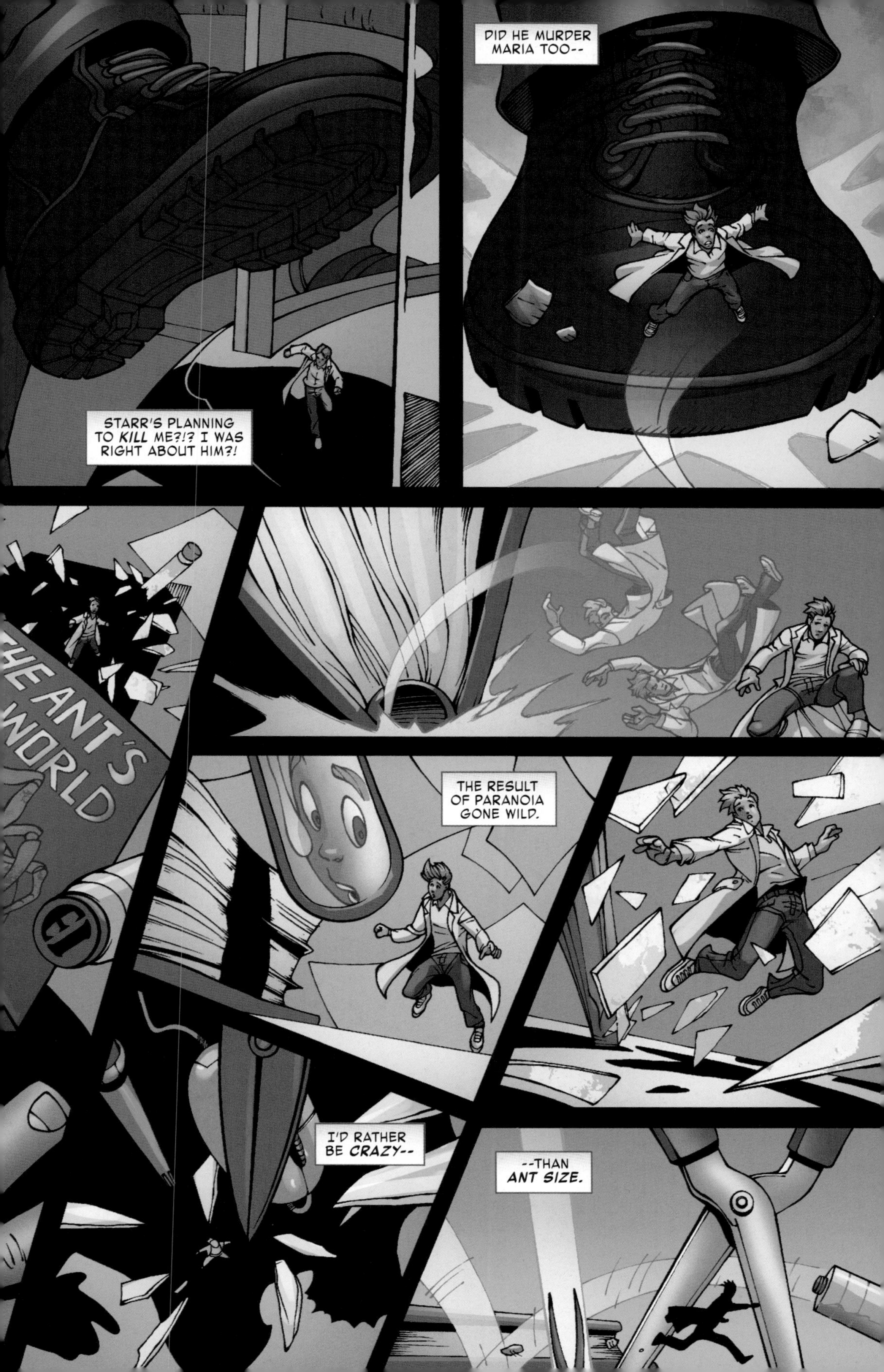
STARR'S PLANNING TO *KILL* ME?!? I WAS RIGHT ABOUT HIM?!
DID HE MURDER MARIA TOO--
THE ANT'S WORLD
THE RESULT OF PARANOIA GONE WILD.
I'D RATHER BE *CRAZY*--
--THAN *ANT SIZE.*

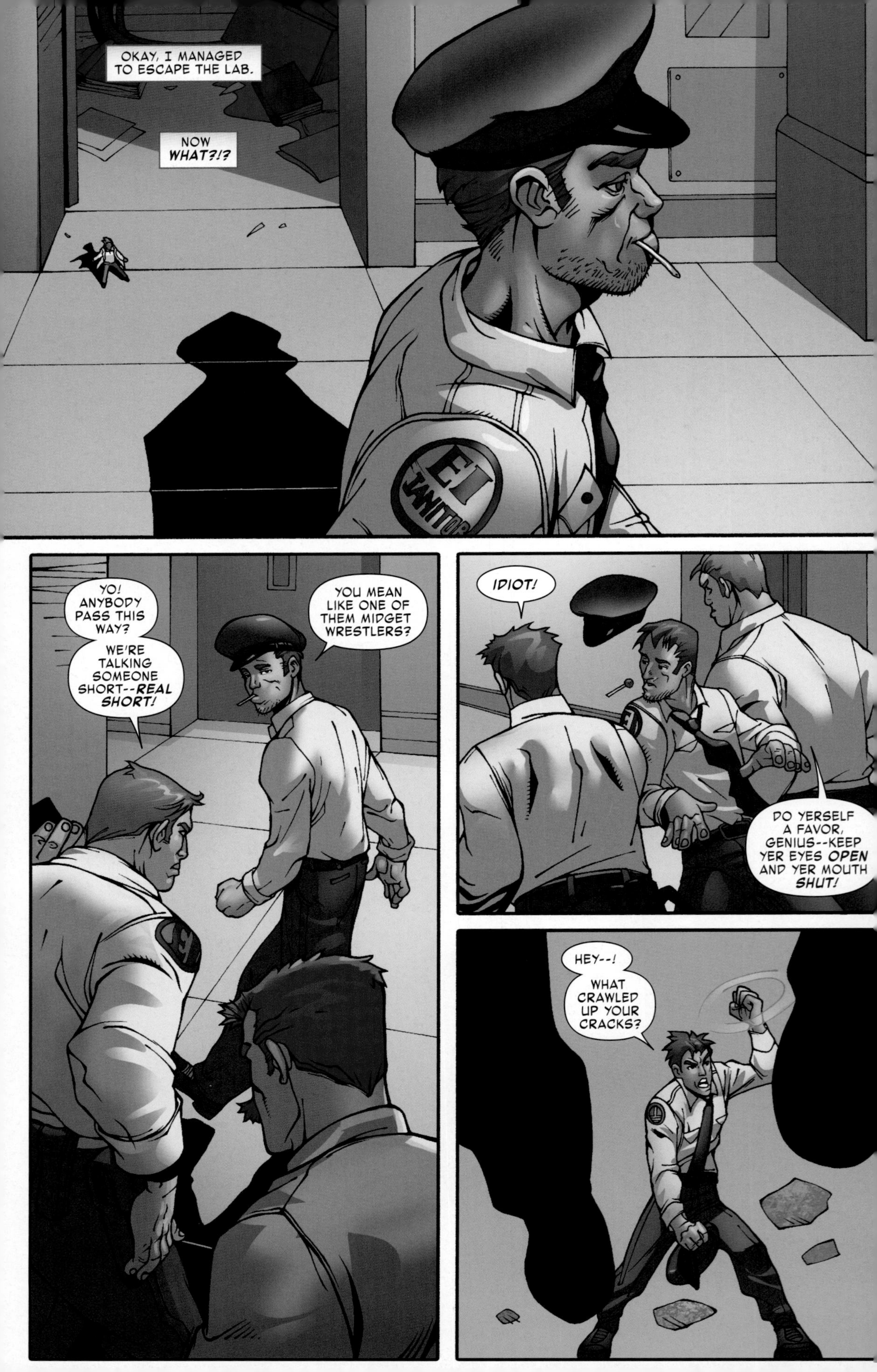

OKAY, I MANAGED TO ESCAPE THE LAB.
NOW WHAT?!?
EI JANITOR
YO! ANYBODY PASS THIS WAY?
WE'RE TALKING SOMEONE SHORT--REAL SHORT!
YOU MEAN LIKE ONE OF THEM MIDGET WRESTLERS?
IDIOT!
DO YERSELF A FAVOR, GENIUS--KEEP YER EYES OPEN AND YER MOUTH SHUT!
HEY--!
WHAT CRAWLED UP YOUR CRACKS?

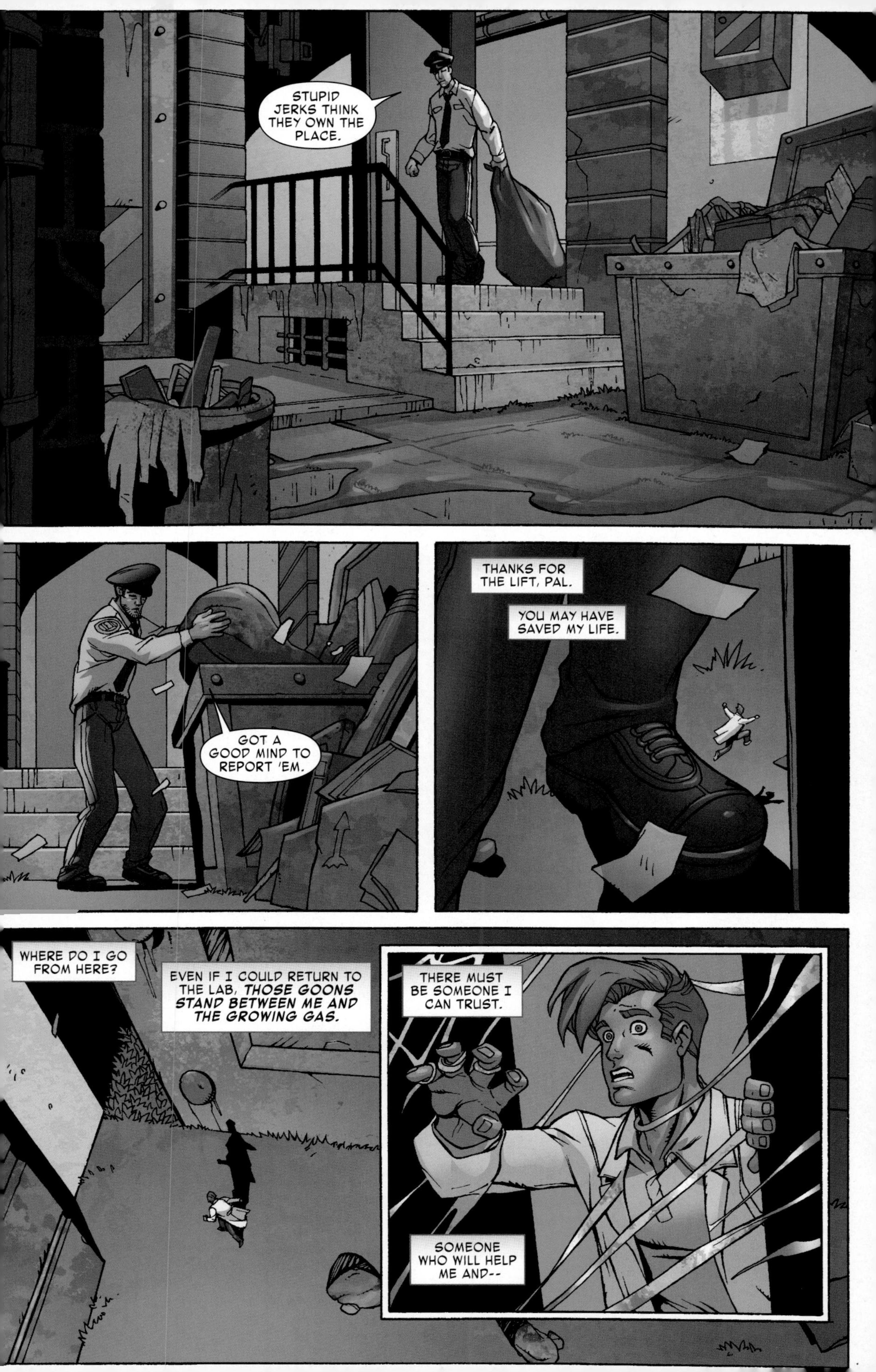
STUPID JERKS THINK THEY OWN THE PLACE.
GOT A GOOD MIND TO REPORT 'EM.
THANKS FOR THE LIFT, PAL.
YOU MAY HAVE SAVED MY LIFE.
WHERE DO I GO FROM HERE?
EVEN IF I COULD RETURN TO THE LAB, THOSE GOONS STAND BETWEEN ME AND THE GROWING GAS.
THERE MUST BE SOMEONE I CAN TRUST.
SOMEONE WHO WILL HELP ME AND--

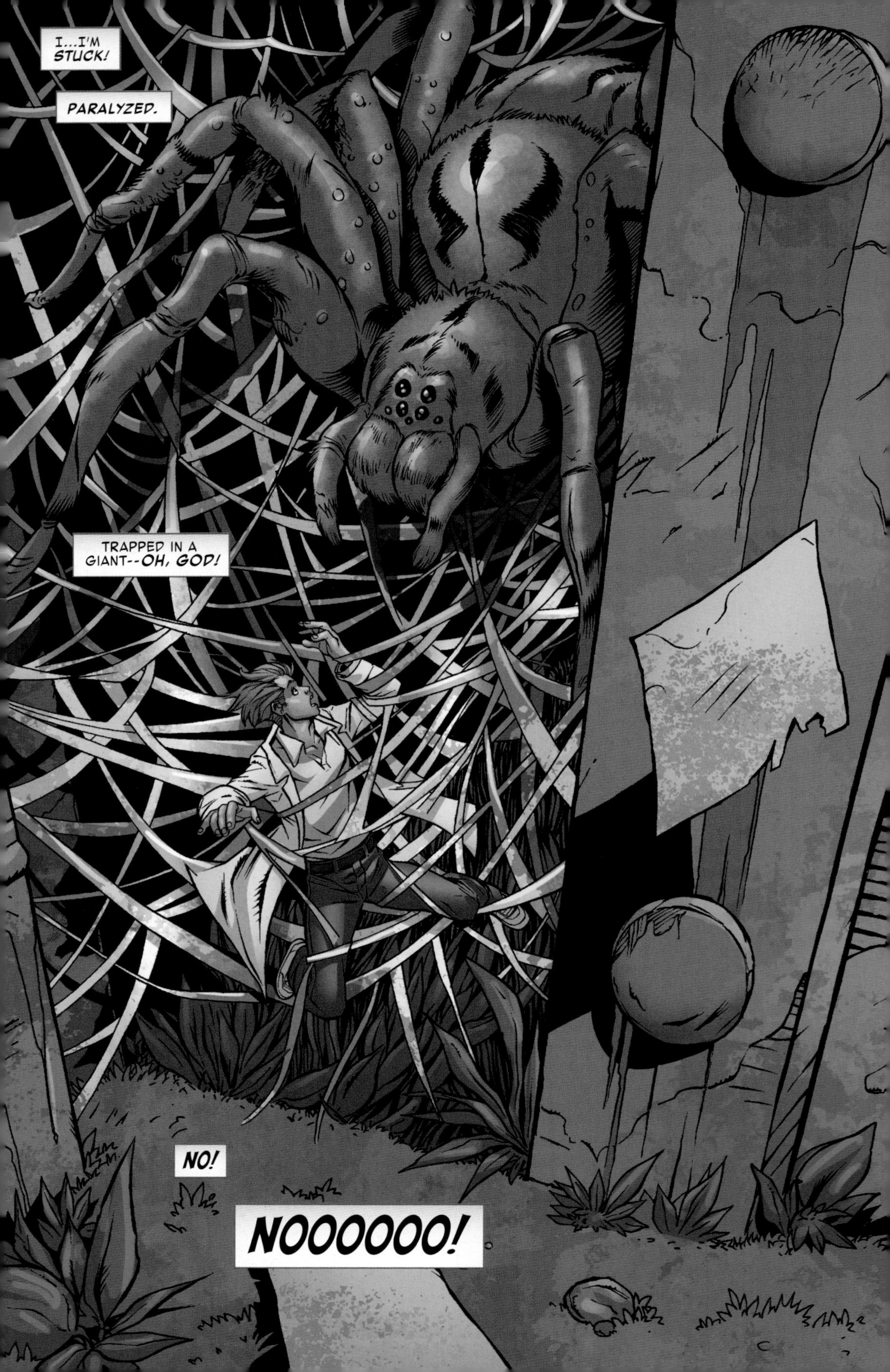

I...I'M STUCK!
PARALYZED.
TRAPPED IN A GIANT--OH, GOD!
NO!
NOOOOOO!

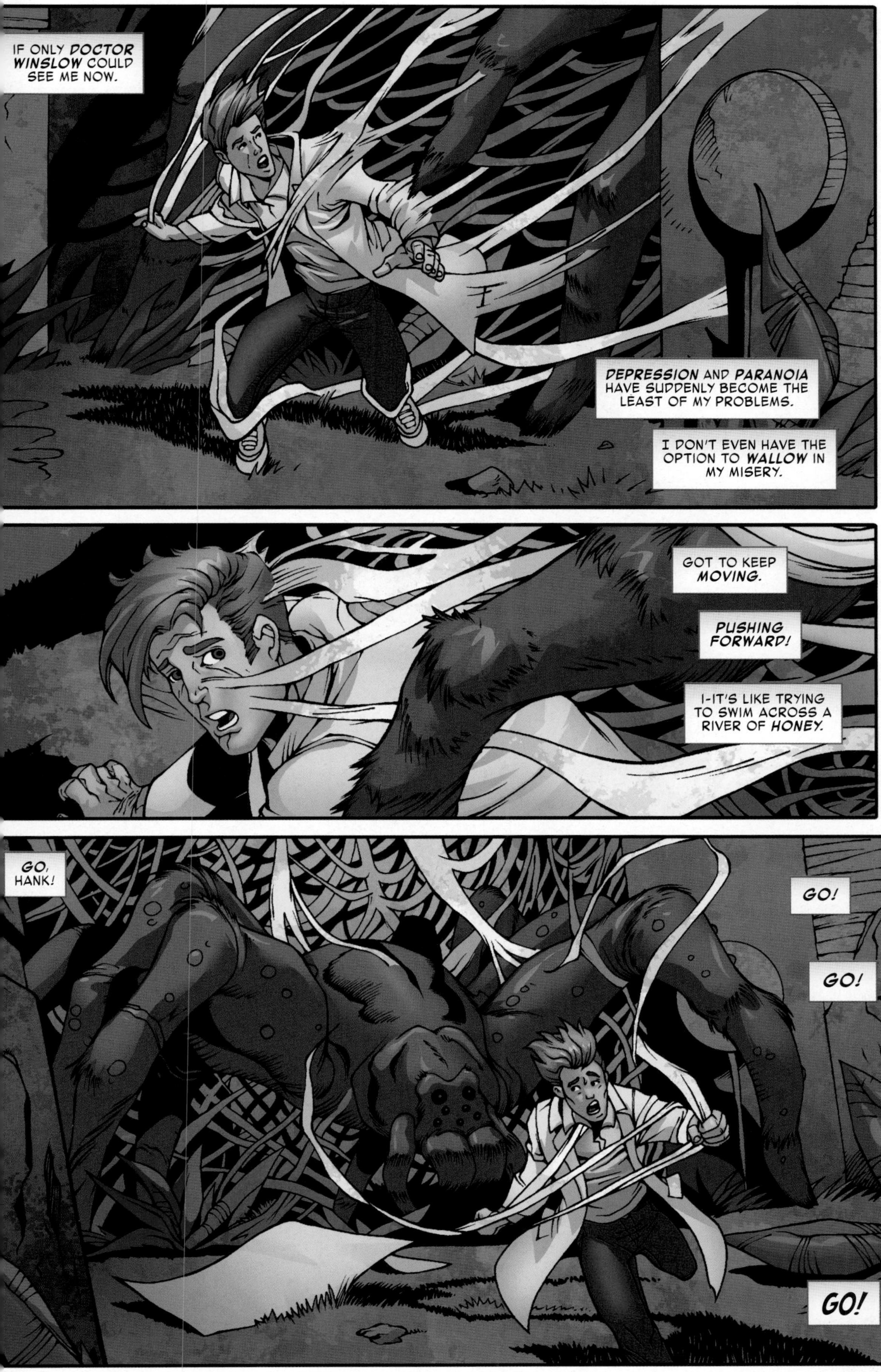
IF ONLY DOCTOR WINSLOW COULD SEE ME NOW.
DEPRESSION AND PARANOIA HAVE SUDDENLY BECOME THE LEAST OF MY PROBLEMS.
I DON'T EVEN HAVE THE OPTION TO WALLOW IN MY MISERY.
GOT TO KEEP MOVING.
PUSHING FORWARD!
I-IT'S LIKE TRYING TO SWIM ACROSS A RIVER OF HONEY.
GO, HANK!
GO!
GO!
GO!

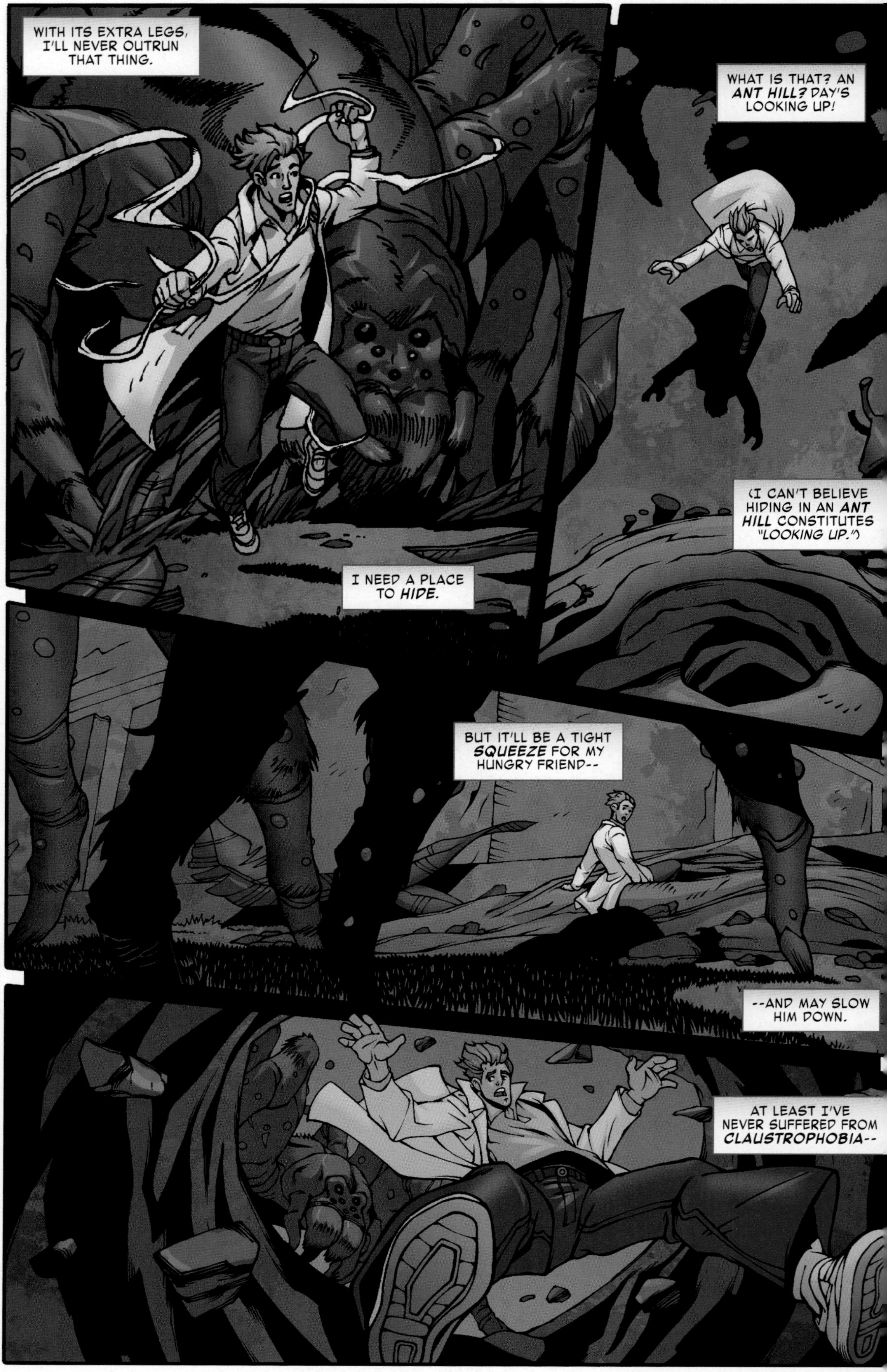
WITH ITS EXTRA LEGS, I'LL NEVER OUTRUN THAT THING.
I NEED A PLACE TO HIDE.
WHAT IS THAT? AN ANT HILL? DAY'S LOOKING UP!
(I CAN'T BELIEVE HIDING IN AN ANT HILL CONSTITUTES "LOOKING UP.")
BUT IT'LL BE A TIGHT SQUEEZE FOR MY HUNGRY FRIEND--
--AND MAY SLOW HIM DOWN.
AT LEAST I'VE NEVER SUFFERED FROM CLAUSTROPHOBIA--

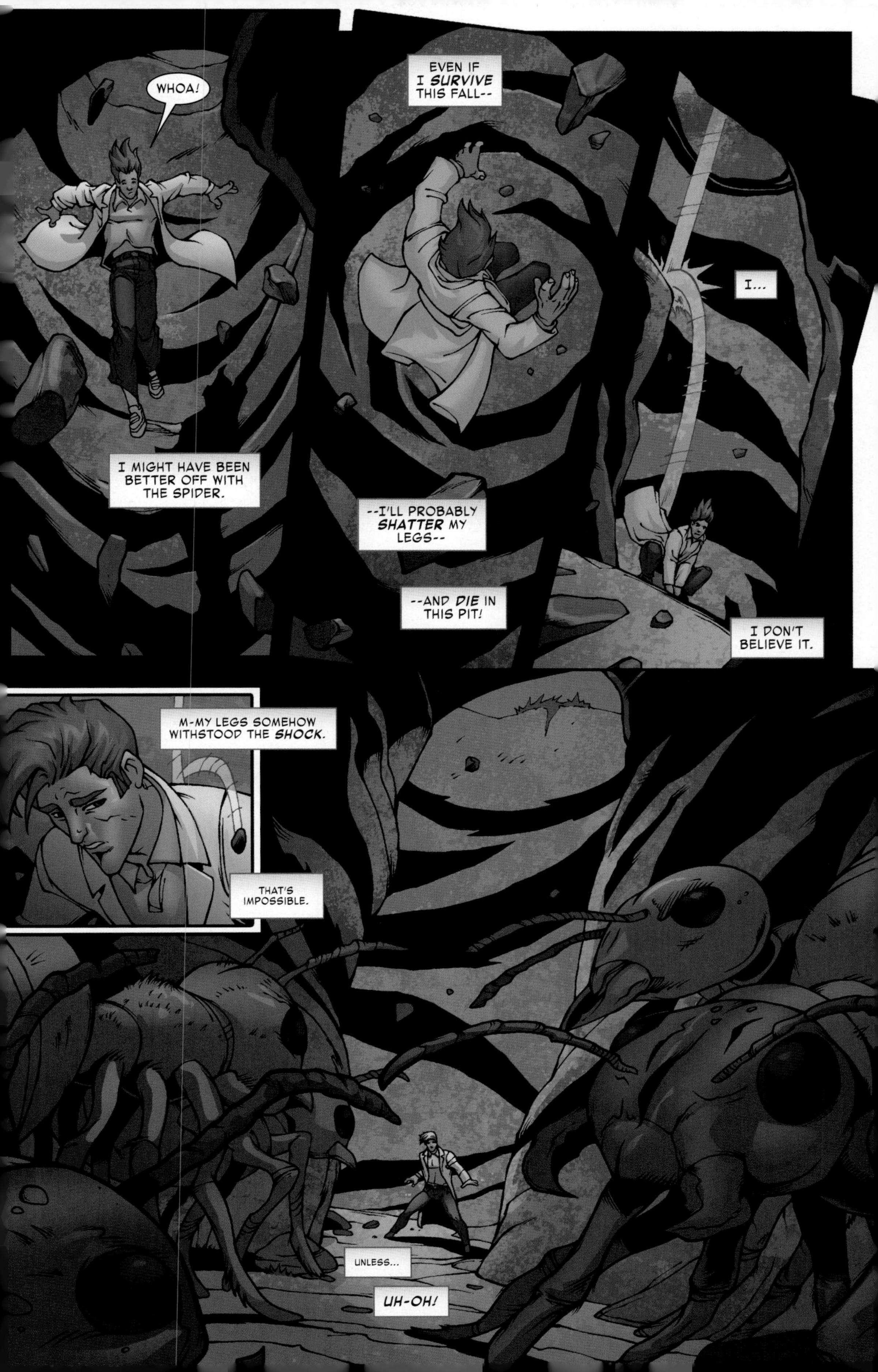
WHOA!
I MIGHT HAVE BEEN BETTER OFF WITH THE SPIDER.
EVEN IF I SURVIVE THIS FALL--
--I'LL PROBABLY SHATTER MY LEGS--
--AND DIE IN THIS PIT!
I...
I DON'T BELIEVE IT.
M-MY LEGS SOMEHOW WITHSTOOD THE SHOCK.
THAT'S IMPOSSIBLE.
UNLESS...
UH-OH!

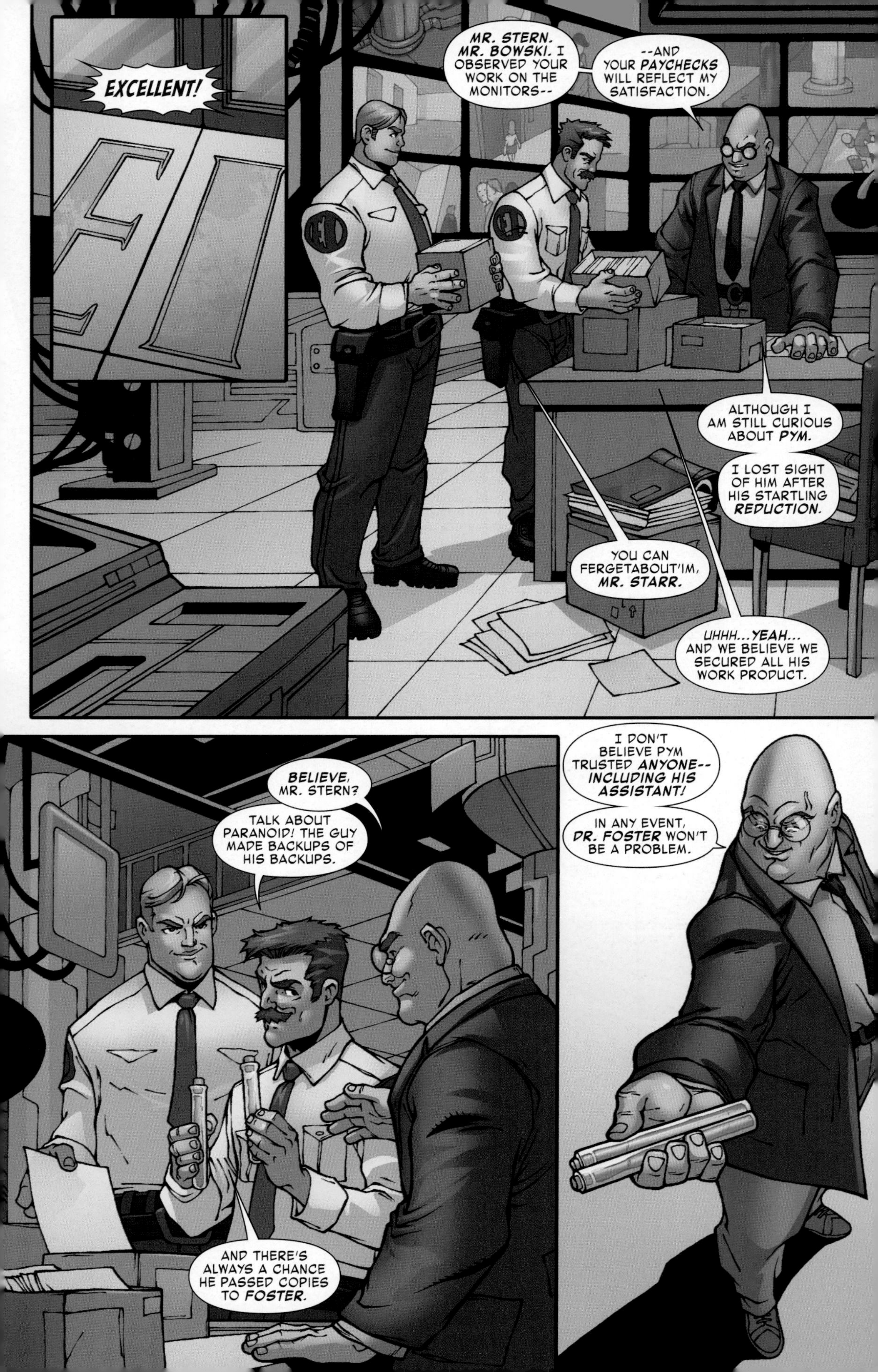
EXCELLENT!
MR. STERN. MR. BOWSKI. I OBSERVED YOUR WORK ON THE MONITORS--
--AND YOUR PAYCHECKS WILL REFLECT MY SATISFACTION.
ALTHOUGH I AM STILL CURIOUS ABOUT PYM.
I LOST SIGHT OF HIM AFTER HIS STARTLING REDUCTION.
YOU CAN FERGETABOUT'IM, MR. STARR.
UHHH...YEAH... AND WE BELIEVE WE SECURED ALL HIS WORK PRODUCT.
BELIEVE, MR. STERN?
TALK ABOUT PARANOID! THE GUY MADE BACKUPS OF HIS BACKUPS.
AND THERE'S ALWAYS A CHANCE HE PASSED COPIES TO FOSTER.
I DON'T BELIEVE PYM TRUSTED ANYONE-- INCLUDING HIS ASSISTANT!
IN ANY EVENT, DR. FOSTER WON'T BE A PROBLEM.

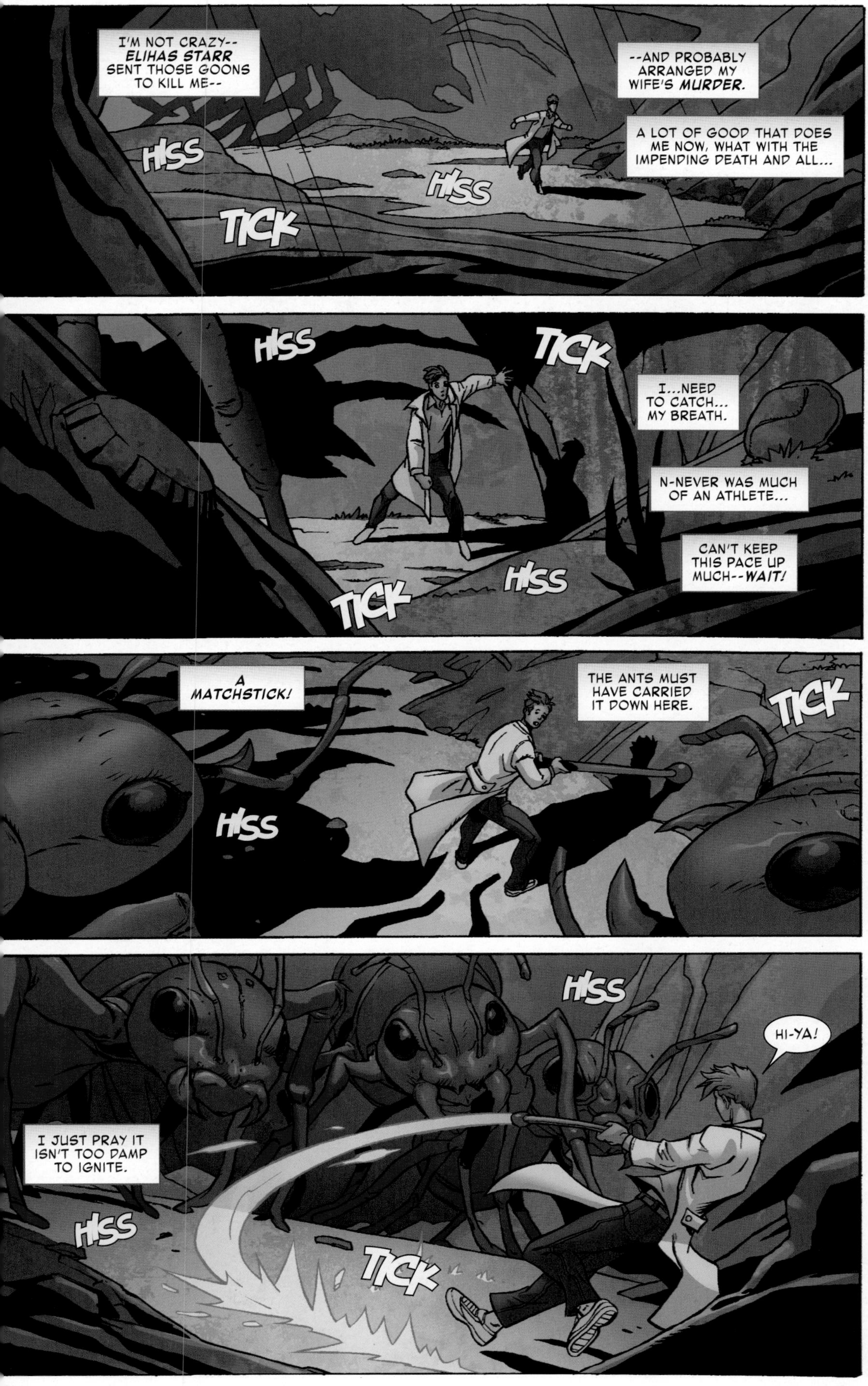
I'M NOT CRAZY--
ELIHAS STARR
SENT THOSE GOONS
TO KILL ME--
--AND PROBABLY ARRANGED MY WIFE'S MURDER.
A LOT OF GOOD THAT DOES ME NOW, WHAT WITH THE IMPENDING DEATH AND ALL...
HISS
HISS
TICK
HISS
TICK
I...NEED TO CATCH... MY BREATH.
N-NEVER WAS MUCH OF AN ATHLETE...
CAN'T KEEP THIS PACE UP MUCH--WAIT!
HISS
TICK
A MATCHSTICK!
THE ANTS MUST HAVE CARRIED IT DOWN HERE.
TICK
HISS
HISS
HI-YA!
I JUST PRAY IT ISN'T TOO DAMP TO IGNITE.
HISS
TICK

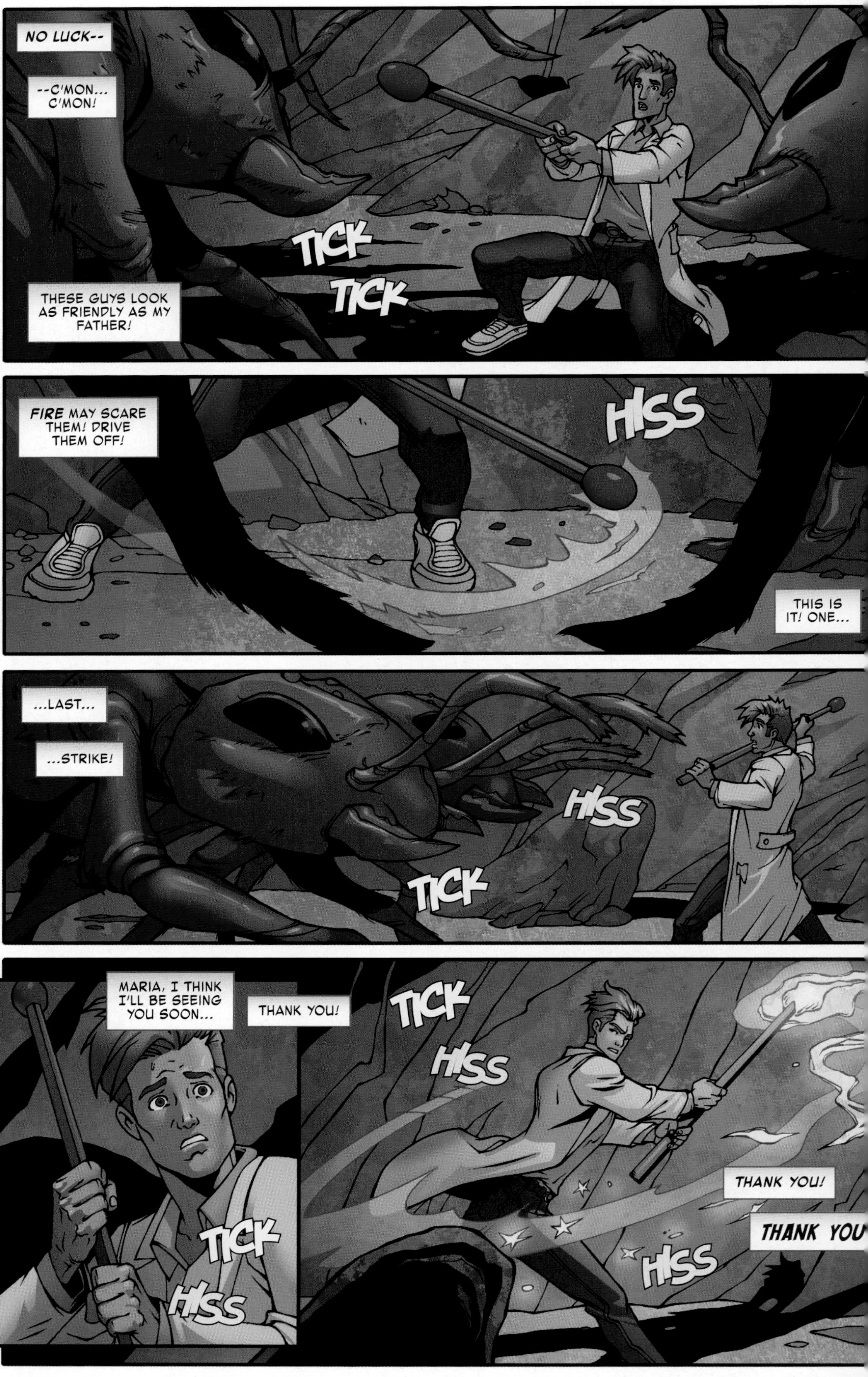
NO LUCK--
--C'MON... C'MON!
TICK
TICK
THESE GUYS LOOK AS FRIENDLY AS MY FATHER!
FIRE MAY SCARE THEM! DRIVE THEM OFF!
HISS
THIS IS IT! ONE...
...LAST...
...STRIKE!
HISS
TICK
MARIA, I THINK I'LL BE SEEING YOU SOON...
THANK YOU!
TICK
HISS
TICK
HISS
THANK YOU!
THANK YOU
HISS

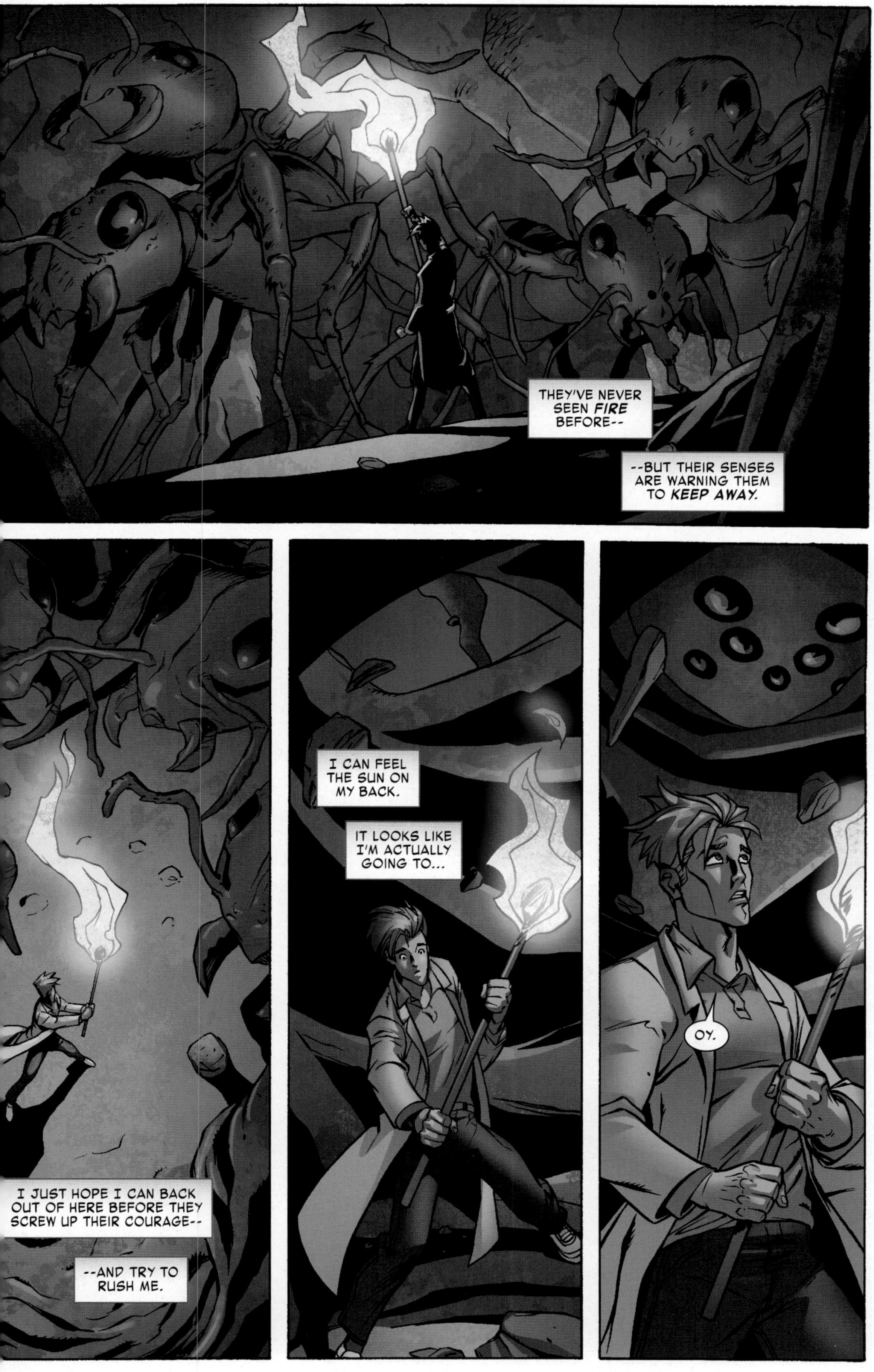

THEY'VE NEVER SEEN *FIRE* BEFORE--
--BUT THEIR SENSES ARE WARNING THEM TO *KEEP AWAY.*
I JUST HOPE I CAN BACK OUT OF HERE BEFORE THEY SCREW UP THEIR COURAGE--
--AND TRY TO RUSH ME.
I CAN FEEL THE SUN ON MY BACK.
IT LOOKS LIKE I'M ACTUALLY GOING TO...
OY.

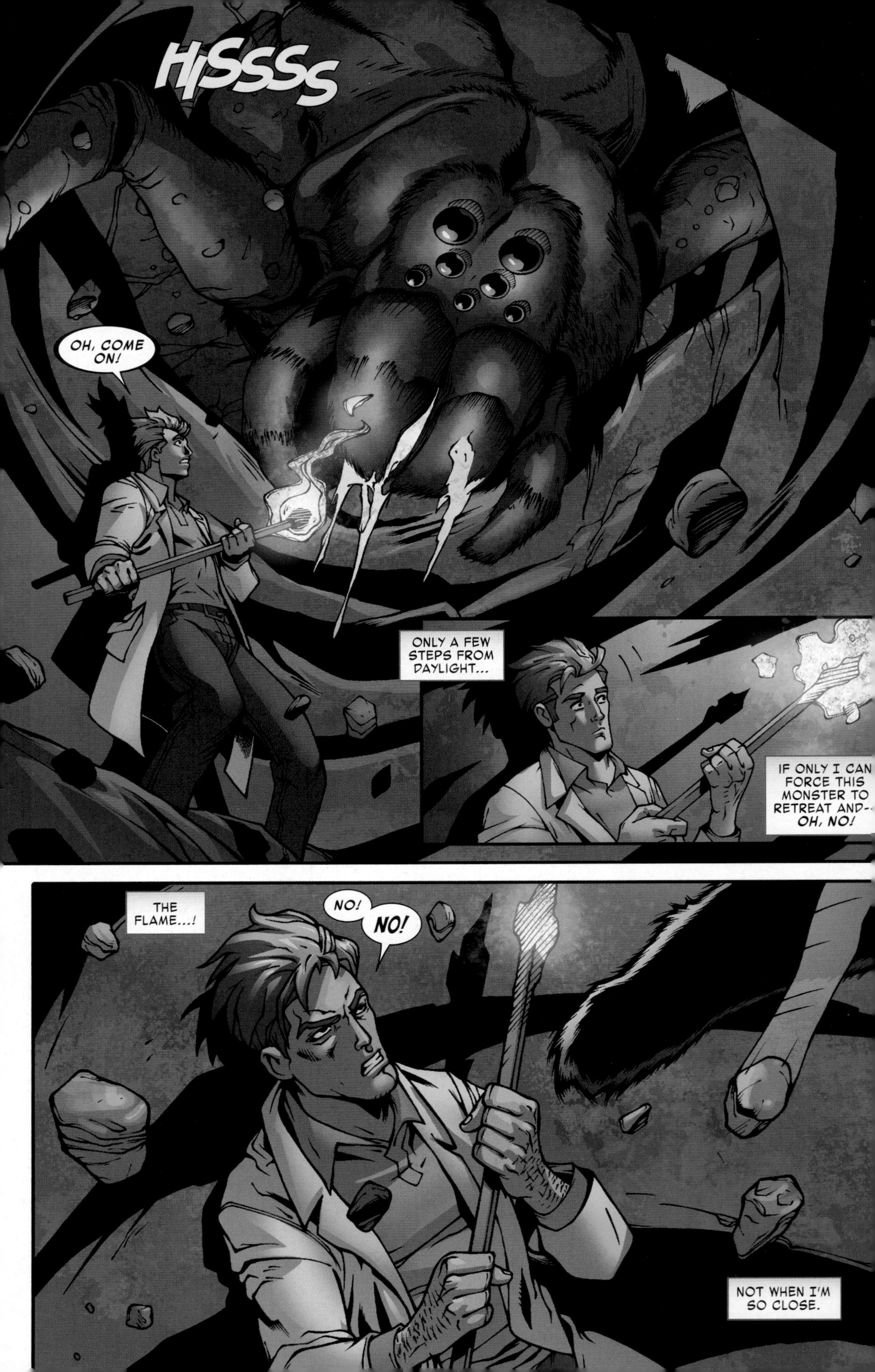
HISSSS
OH, COME ON!
ONLY A FEW STEPS FROM DAYLIGHT...
IF ONLY I CAN FORCE THIS MONSTER TO RETREAT AND-- OH, NO!
THE FLAME...!
NO! NO!
NOT WHEN I'M SO CLOSE.

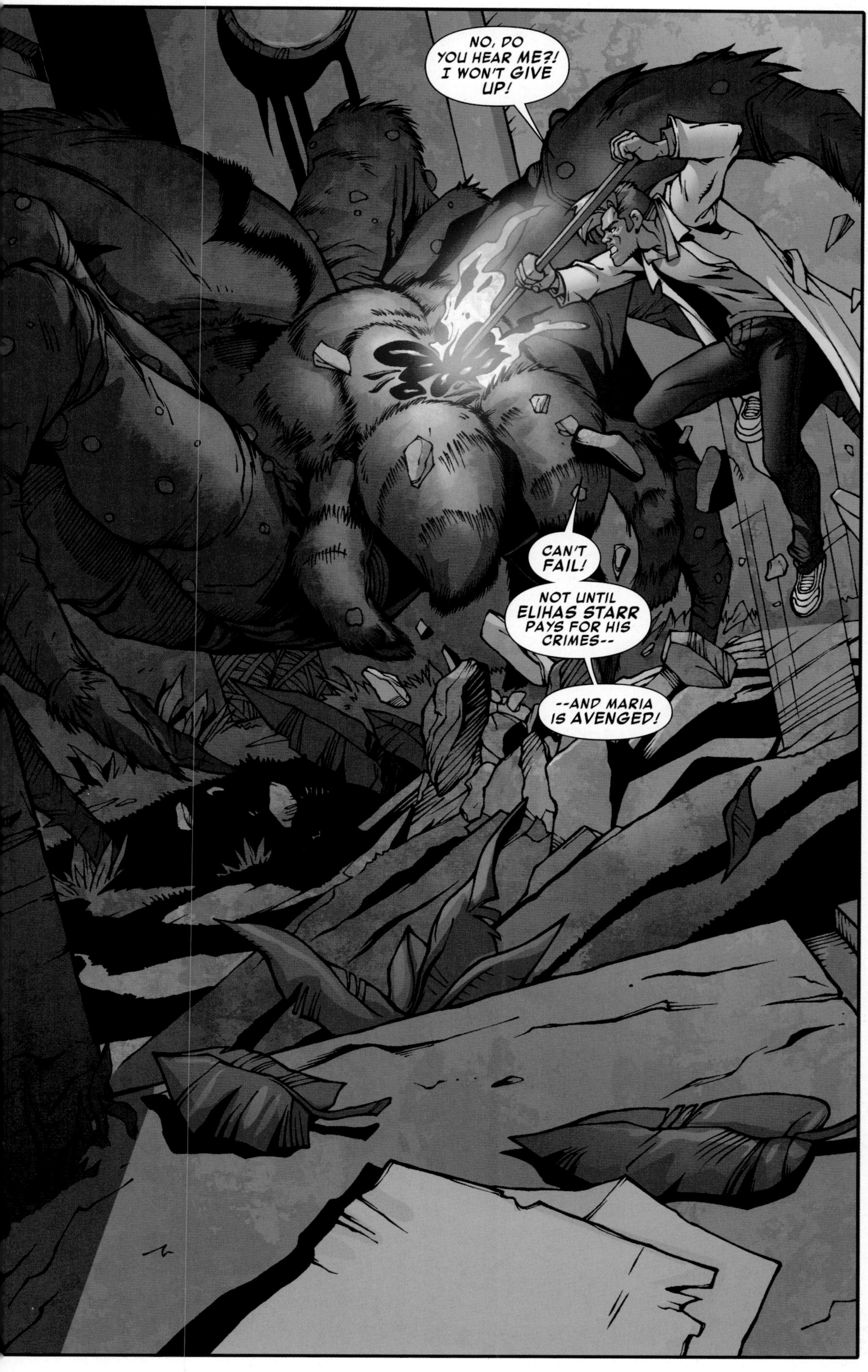
NO, DO YOU HEAR ME?! I WON'T GIVE UP!
CAN'T FAIL!
NOT UNTIL ELIHAS STARR PAYS FOR HIS CRIMES--
--AND MARIA IS AVENGED!

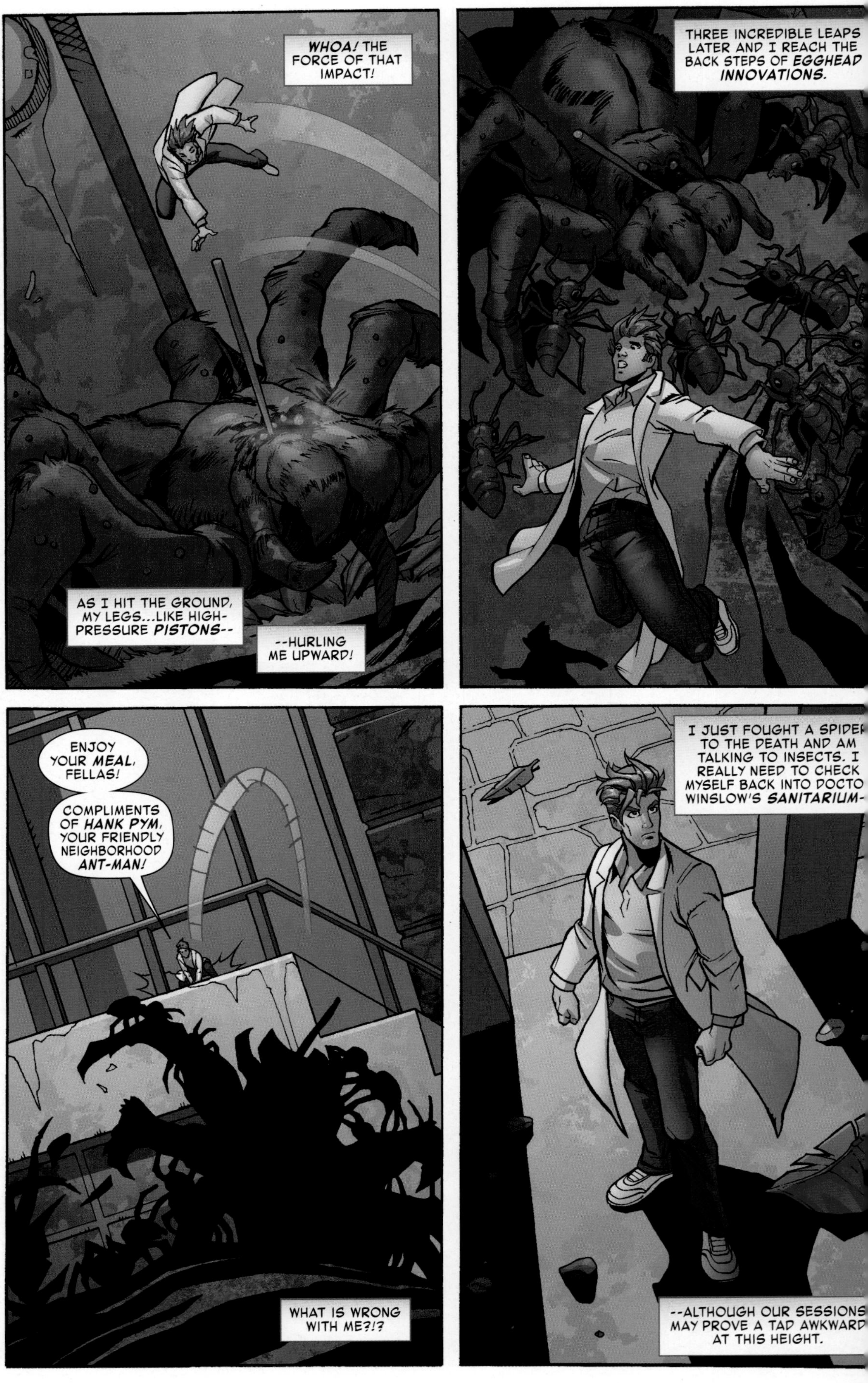
WHOA! THE FORCE OF THAT IMPACT!
AS I HIT THE GROUND, MY LEGS...LIKE HIGH-PRESSURE PISTONS--
--HURLING ME UPWARD!
THREE INCREDIBLE LEAPS LATER AND I REACH THE BACK STEPS OF EGGHEAD INNOVATIONS.
ENJOY YOUR MEAL, FELLAS!
COMPLIMENTS OF HANK PYM, YOUR FRIENDLY NEIGHBORHOOD ANT-MAN!
WHAT IS WRONG WITH ME?!?
I JUST FOUGHT A SPIDER TO THE DEATH AND AM TALKING TO INSECTS. I REALLY NEED TO CHECK MYSELF BACK INTO DOCTO WINSLOW'S SANITARIUM-
--ALTHOUGH OUR SESSIONS MAY PROVE A TAD AWKWARD AT THIS HEIGHT.

DR. FOSTER--?

CAN I HAVE A MOMENT?

I'M AT YOUR DISPOSAL, DR. PYM.

WHAT CAN I DO FOR YOU?

I'M AFRAID I HAVE BAD NEWS.

IT CONCERNS MY SON HENRY.

EVERYONE ALWAYS FOCUSES ON THE NEGATIVE ASPECTS OF PARANOIA.

THERE IS ONE DISTINCT ADVANTAGE--

--YOU PLAN FOR BETRAYAL.

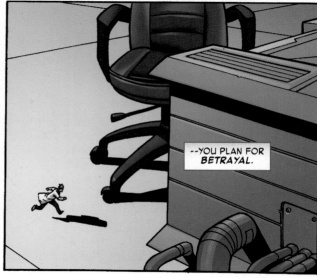

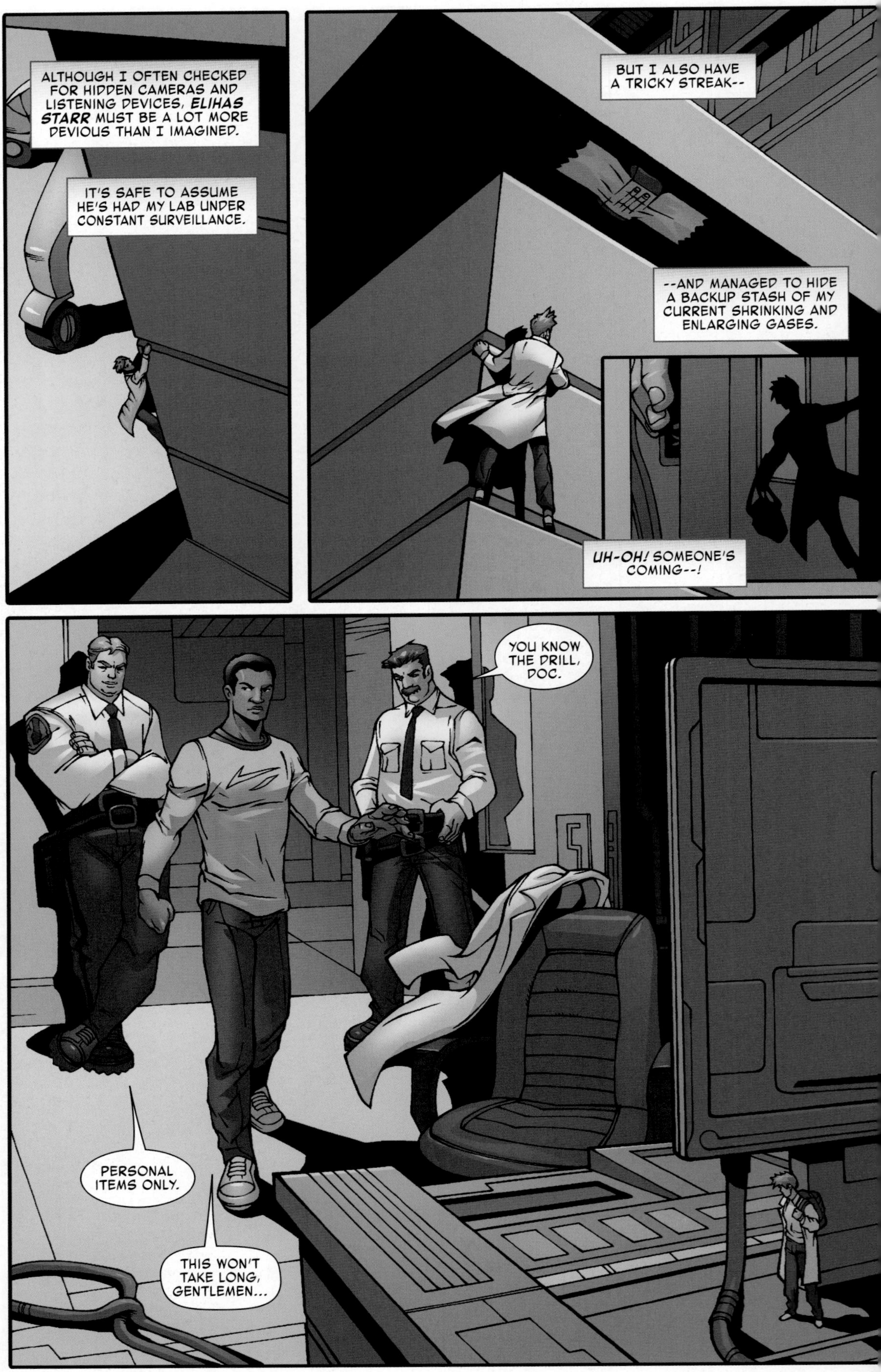
ALTHOUGH I OFTEN CHECKED FOR HIDDEN CAMERAS AND LISTENING DEVICES, *ELIHAS STARR* MUST BE A LOT MORE DEVIOUS THAN I IMAGINED.
IT'S SAFE TO ASSUME HE'S HAD MY LAB UNDER CONSTANT SURVEILLANCE.
BUT I ALSO HAVE A TRICKY STREAK--
--AND MANAGED TO HIDE A BACKUP STASH OF MY CURRENT SHRINKING AND ENLARGING GASES.
UH-OH! SOMEONE'S COMING--!
YOU KNOW THE DRILL, DOC.
PERSONAL ITEMS ONLY.
THIS WON'T TAKE LONG, GENTLEMEN...

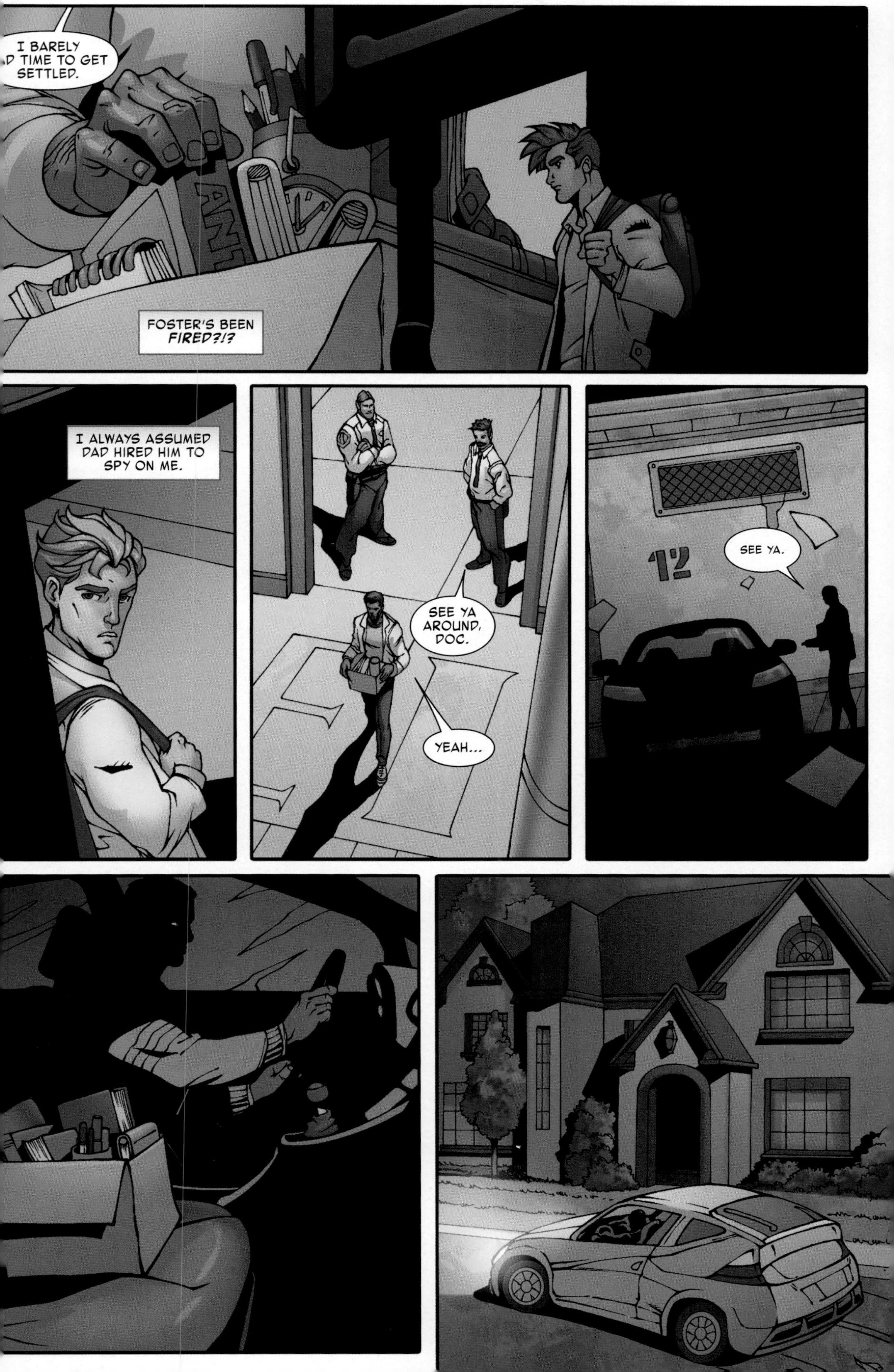
I BARELY
D TIME TO GET SETTLED.
FOSTER'S BEEN *FIRED?!?*
I ALWAYS ASSUMED DAD HIRED HIM TO SPY ON ME.
SEE YA AROUND, DOC.
YEAH...
SEE YA.

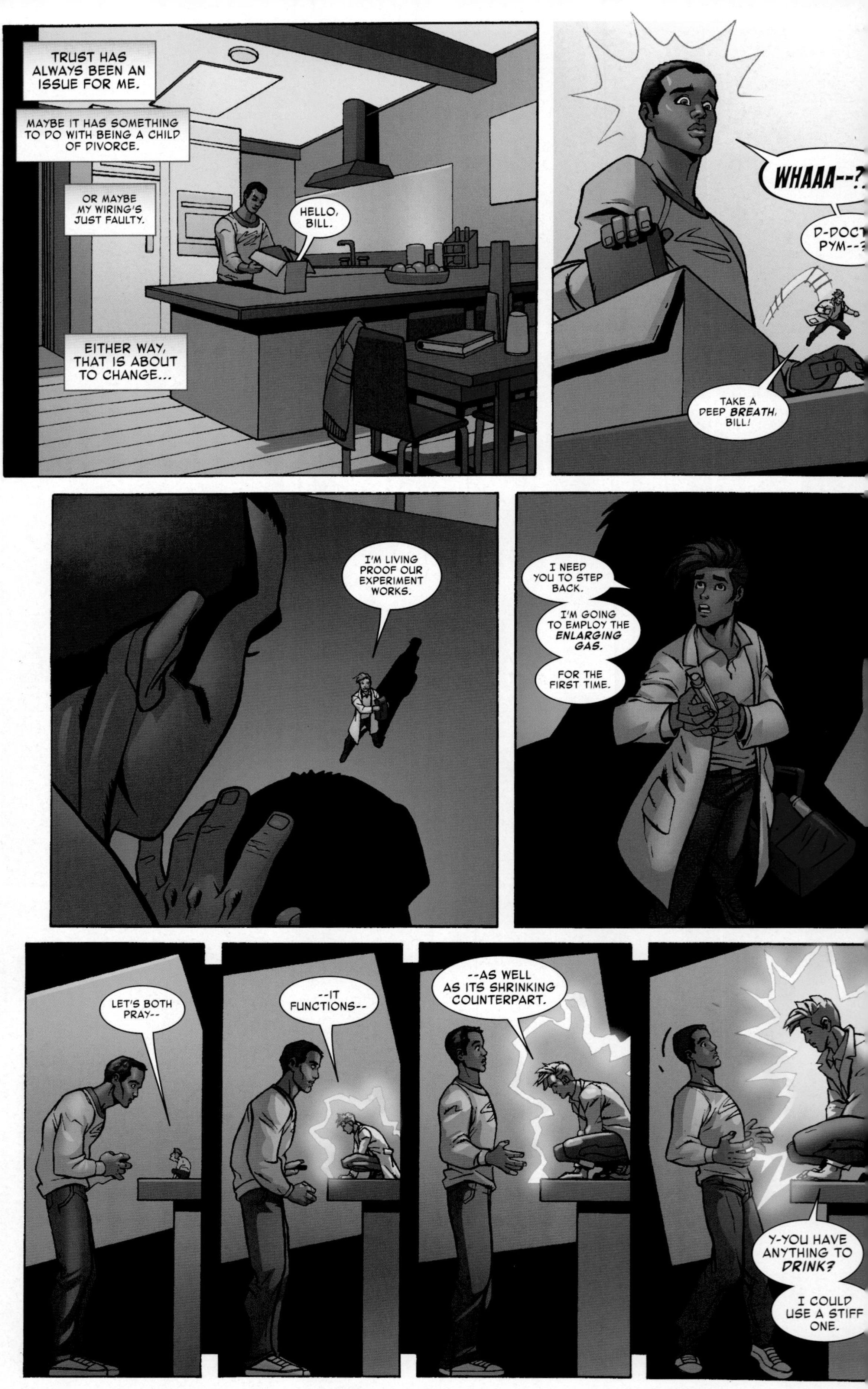
TRUST HAS ALWAYS BEEN AN ISSUE FOR ME.
MAYBE IT HAS SOMETHING TO DO WITH BEING A CHILD OF DIVORCE.
OR MAYBE MY WIRING'S JUST FAULTY.
HELLO, BILL.
EITHER WAY, THAT IS ABOUT TO CHANGE...
WHAAA--?
D-DOCT PYM--?
TAKE A DEEP BREATH, BILL!
I'M LIVING PROOF OUR EXPERIMENT WORKS.
I NEED YOU TO STEP BACK.
I'M GOING TO EMPLOY THE ENLARGING GAS.
FOR THE FIRST TIME.
LET'S BOTH PRAY--
--IT FUNCTIONS--
--AS WELL AS ITS SHRINKING COUNTERPART.
Y-YOU HAVE ANYTHING TO DRINK?
I COULD USE A STIFF ONE.

ELIHAS STARR IS ONE OF THE MOST RESPECTED SCIENTISTS IN THE WORLD.

HARD TO BELIEVE HE'D ORCHESTRATE A CONSPIRACY AGAINST YOU AND YOUR WIFE.

I WAS TOLD YOU HAD SUFFERED ANOTHER MENTAL...

BY WHOM?

YOUR FATHER.

FIGURES.

HE'S ALWAYS BEEN STARR'S TOADY.

ALWAYS CHOSEN HIM OVER ME.

I HATE TO PUT YOU ON THE SPOT, BILL, BUT I NEED HELP TO RECOVER MY RESEARCH FROM STARR.

WHY DON'T YOU JUST GO TO THE POLICE?

WHO DO YOU THINK THEY'LL BELIEVE? THE LOCAL CELEBRITY WHO EMPLOYS THOUSANDS OR ME--

--WITH MY HISTORY OF MENTAL ILLNESS?!

I CAN ALMOST TASTE THE TENSION AS BILL FOSTER STARES OUT THE WINDOW AND THEN...

OKAY, I'M IN.

TERRIFIC! I NEED TO BORROW YOUR LAPTOP.

I HID COPIES OF ALL MY NOTES ON A SECURE SITE AND HAVE TO DOWNLOAD THEM.

MY EXPERIENCE WITH THE ANTS HAS INSPIRED ME TO COMPLETE MARIA'S WORK.

THESE SCHEMATICS ARE INCREDIBLE.

A DEVICE TO COMMUNICATE WITH ANTS THROUGH THEIR *ANTENNAE?!?*

THAT'S RIGHT, BILL. WE'RE ABOUT TO TRANSFORM MY WIFE'S THEORIES--

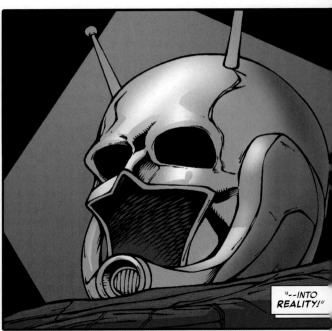

"--INTO *REALITY!*"

IT TOOK LONG ENOUGH, AND THAT DOESN'T COUNT THE TIME WE SPENT CONVERTING MY GARAGE INTO A MAKESHIFT LAB, BUT THE PROTOTYPE'S LOOKING GOOD.

I KNOW THIS IS COMPLETELY OFF-TOPIC, BUT DO THEY REALLY CALL STARR *"EGGHEAD"* BEHIND HIS BACK?

ABSOLUTELY... FOR ALL THE OBVIOUS REASONS.

WHAT DO THEY CALL ME?

MR. PARANOID.

HOW DO YOU PROPOSE WE TEST THIS PROTOTYPE?

ONLY ONE WAY TO DO IT PROPERLY--*IN THE FIELD!*

YOU'RE NOT SERIOUSLY SUGGESTING--

I AM.

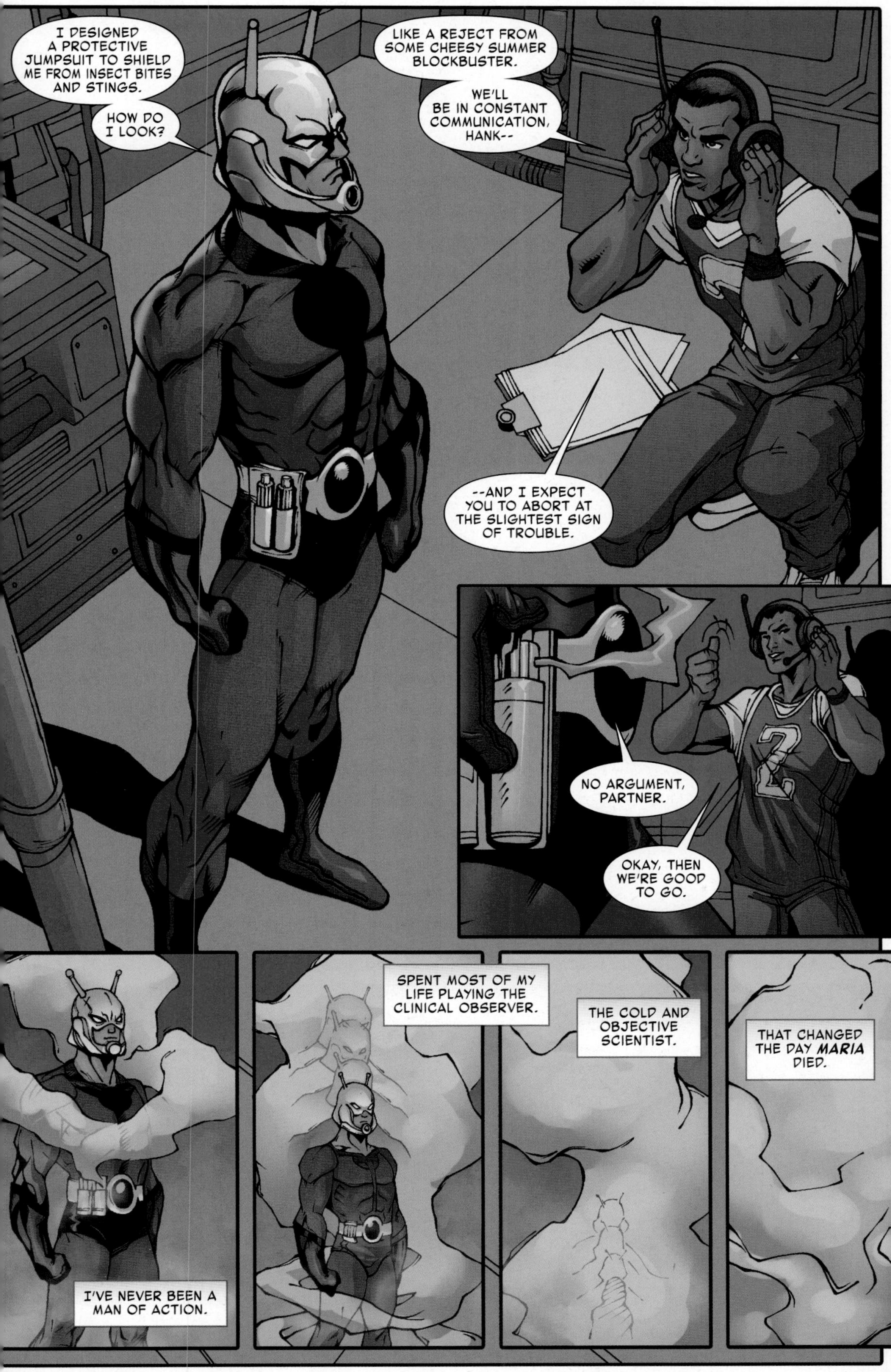
I DESIGNED A PROTECTIVE JUMPSUIT TO SHIELD ME FROM INSECT BITES AND STINGS.
HOW DO I LOOK?
LIKE A REJECT FROM SOME CHEESY SUMMER BLOCKBUSTER.
WE'LL BE IN CONSTANT COMMUNICATION, HANK--
--AND I EXPECT YOU TO ABORT AT THE SLIGHTEST SIGN OF TROUBLE.
NO ARGUMENT, PARTNER.
OKAY, THEN WE'RE GOOD TO GO.
I'VE NEVER BEEN A MAN OF ACTION.
SPENT MOST OF MY LIFE PLAYING THE CLINICAL OBSERVER.
THE COLD AND OBJECTIVE SCIENTIST.
THAT CHANGED THE DAY *MARIA* DIED.

I DON'T KNOW WHY *ELIHAS STARR* ORDERED HER DEATH.

HIS MOTIVATIONS DON'T MATTER.

ONLY HIS *ACTIONS*.

TALK TO ME, HANK.

I CAN'T RECORD SILENCE.

WE NEED TO DOCUMENT YOUR OBSERVATIONS.

I'VE SPOTTED AN ANT HILL.

NO SENSE TAKING ANY NEEDLESS RISKS.

I SUGGEST YOU WAIT AT THE MOUTH UNTIL ONE OF THEM APPEARS.

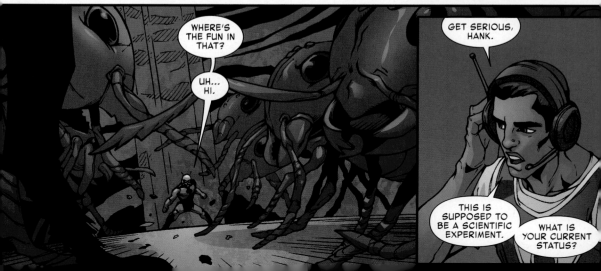

WHERE'S THE FUN IN THAT?

UH... HI.

GET SERIOUS, HANK.

THIS IS SUPPOSED TO BE A SCIENTIFIC EXPERIMENT.

WHAT IS YOUR CURRENT STATUS?

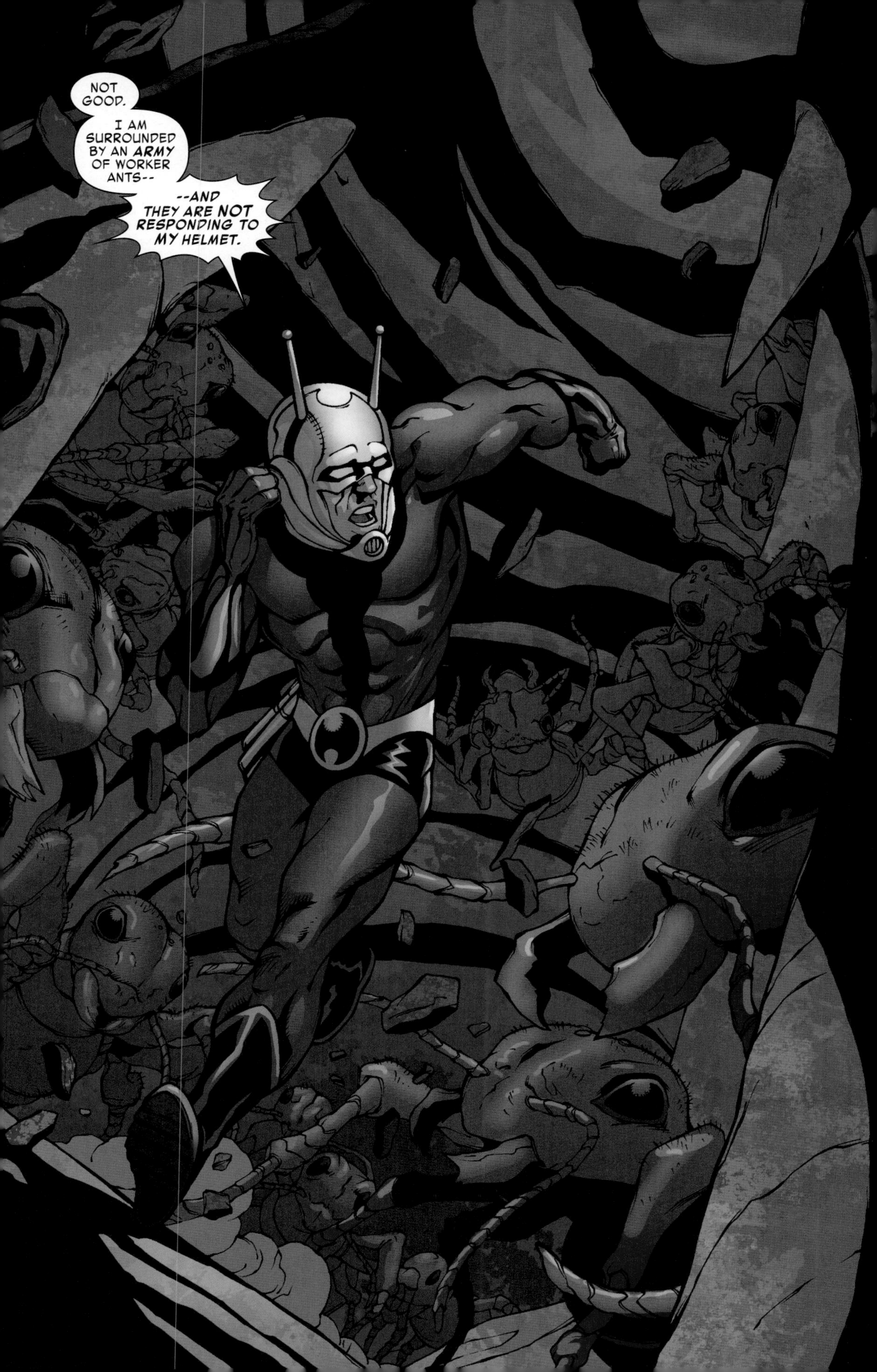
NOT GOOD.
I AM SURROUNDED BY AN ARMY OF WORKER ANTS--
--AND THEY ARE NOT RESPONDING TO MY HELMET.

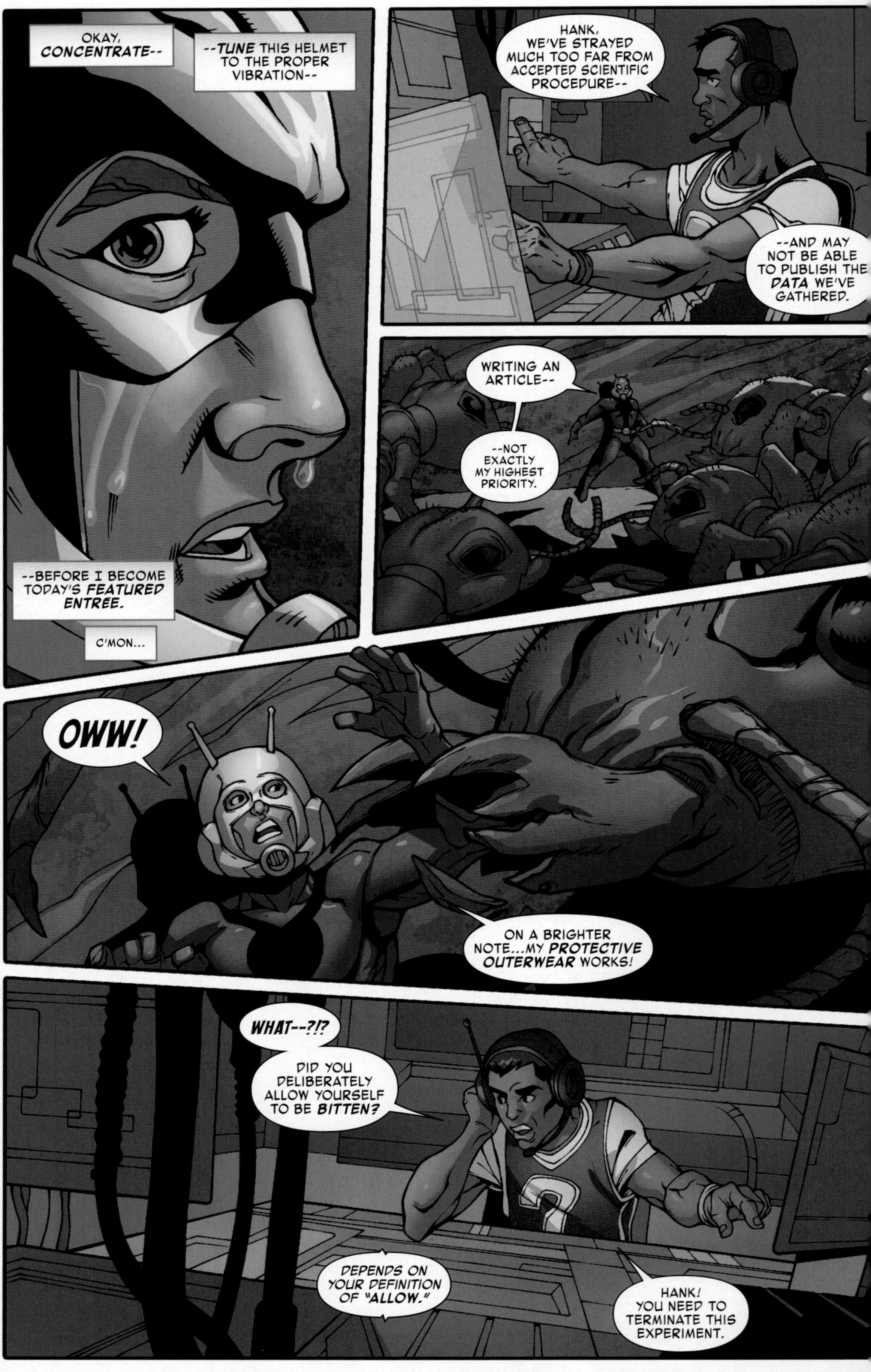
OKAY, CONCENTRATE--
--TUNE THIS HELMET TO THE PROPER VIBRATION--
HANK, WE'VE STRAYED MUCH TOO FAR FROM ACCEPTED SCIENTIFIC PROCEDURE--
--AND MAY NOT BE ABLE TO PUBLISH THE DATA WE'VE GATHERED.
WRITING AN ARTICLE--
--NOT EXACTLY MY HIGHEST PRIORITY.
--BEFORE I BECOME TODAY'S FEATURED ENTREE.
C'MON...
OWW!
ON A BRIGHTER NOTE...MY PROTECTIVE OUTERWEAR WORKS!
WHAT--?!?
DID YOU DELIBERATELY ALLOW YOURSELF TO BE BITTEN?
DEPENDS ON YOUR DEFINITION OF "ALLOW."
HANK! YOU NEED TO TERMINATE THIS EXPERIMENT.

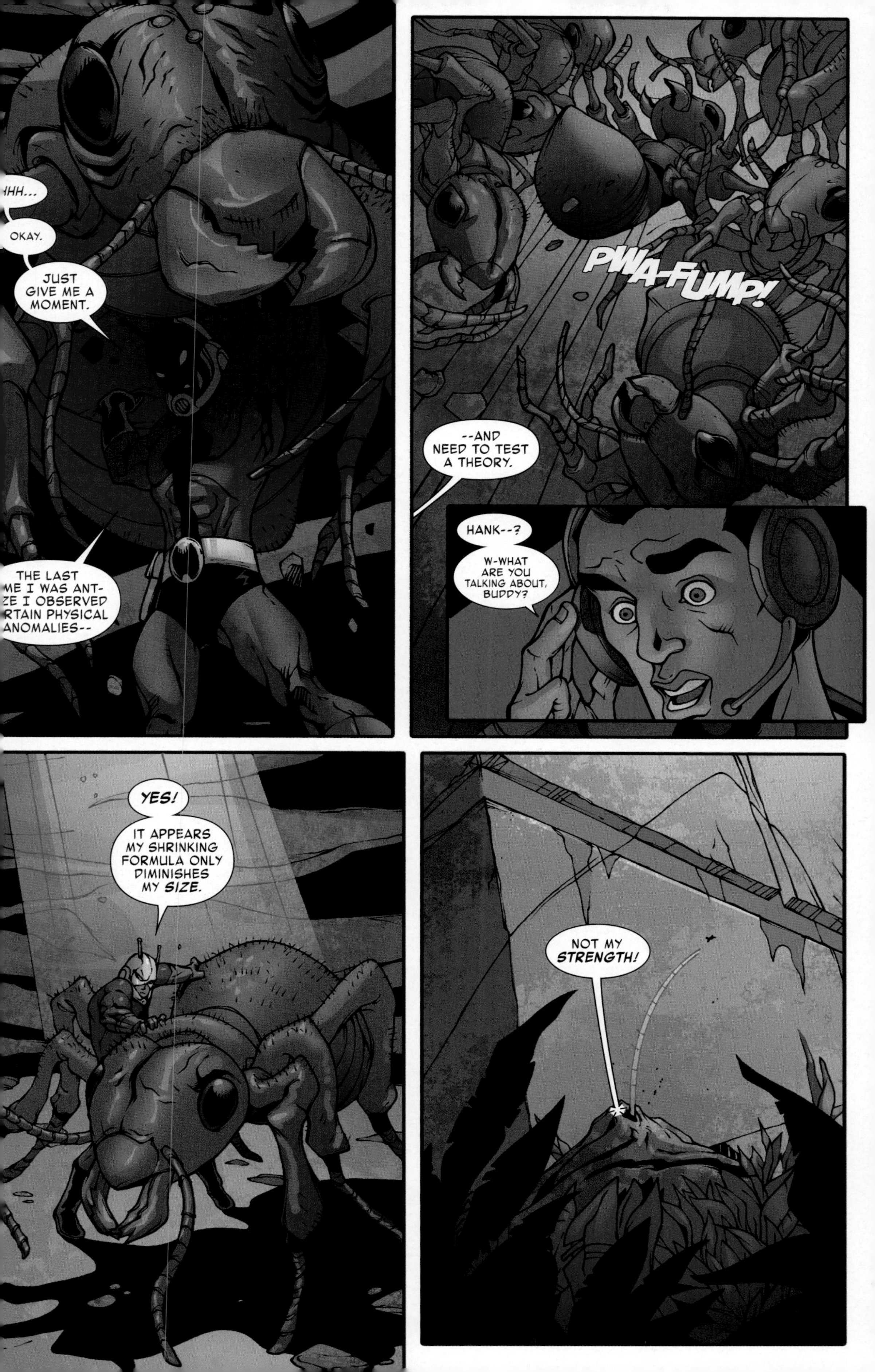

HH...
OKAY.
JUST GIVE ME A MOMENT.
THE LAST ME I WAS ANT- ZE I OBSERVED RTAIN PHYSICAL ANOMALIES--
PWA-FUMP!
--AND NEED TO TEST A THEORY.
HANK--?
W-WHAT ARE YOU TALKING ABOUT, BUDDY?
YES!
IT APPEARS MY SHRINKING FORMULA ONLY DIMINISHES MY SIZE.
NOT MY STRENGTH!

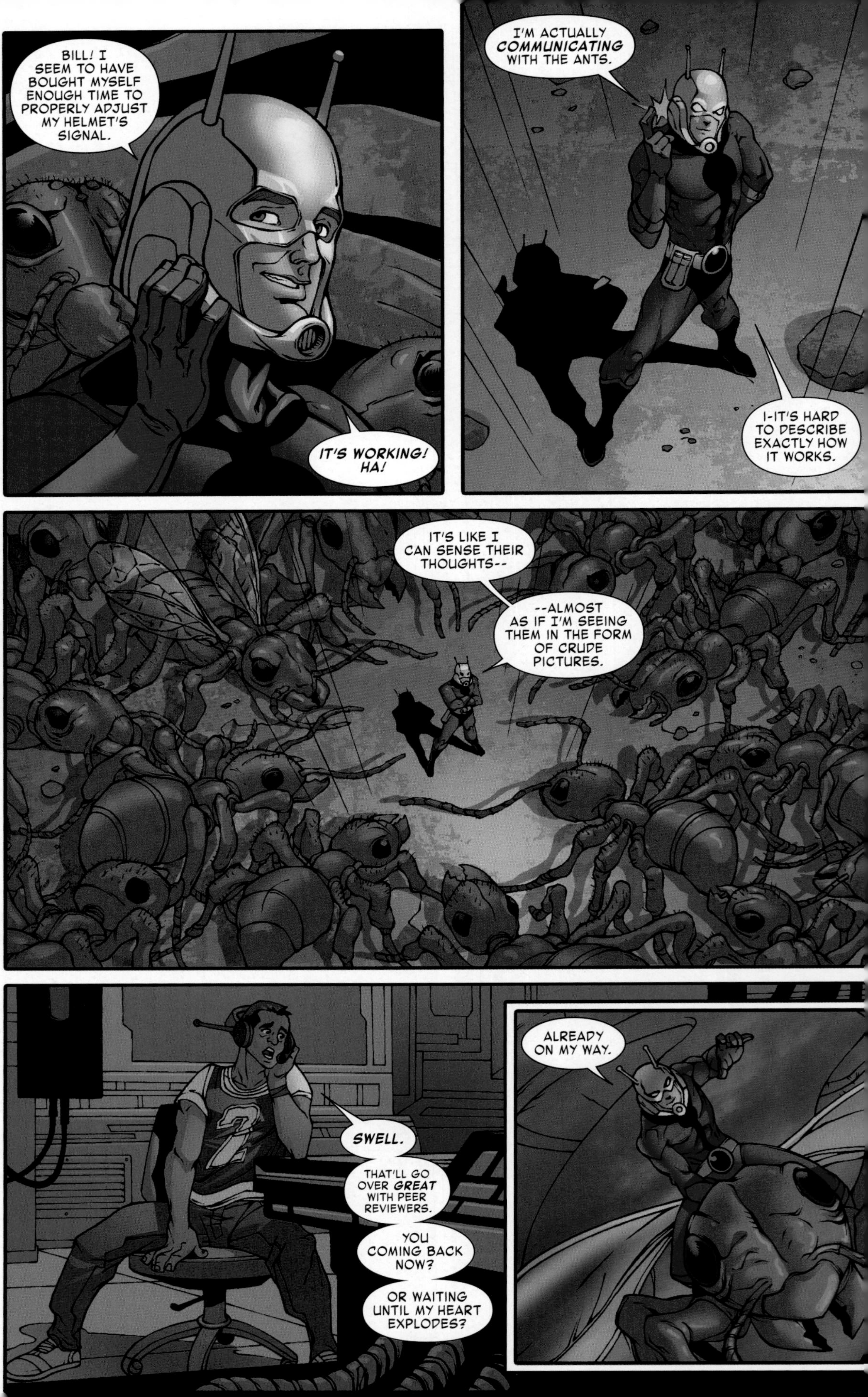
BILL! I SEEM TO HAVE BOUGHT MYSELF ENOUGH TIME TO PROPERLY ADJUST MY HELMET'S SIGNAL.
IT'S WORKING! HA!
I'M ACTUALLY COMMUNICATING WITH THE ANTS.
I-IT'S HARD TO DESCRIBE EXACTLY HOW IT WORKS.
IT'S LIKE I CAN SENSE THEIR THOUGHTS--
--ALMOST AS IF I'M SEEING THEM IN THE FORM OF CRUDE PICTURES.
SWELL.
THAT'LL GO OVER GREAT WITH PEER REVIEWERS.
YOU COMING BACK NOW?
OR WAITING UNTIL MY HEART EXPLODES?
ALREADY ON MY WAY.

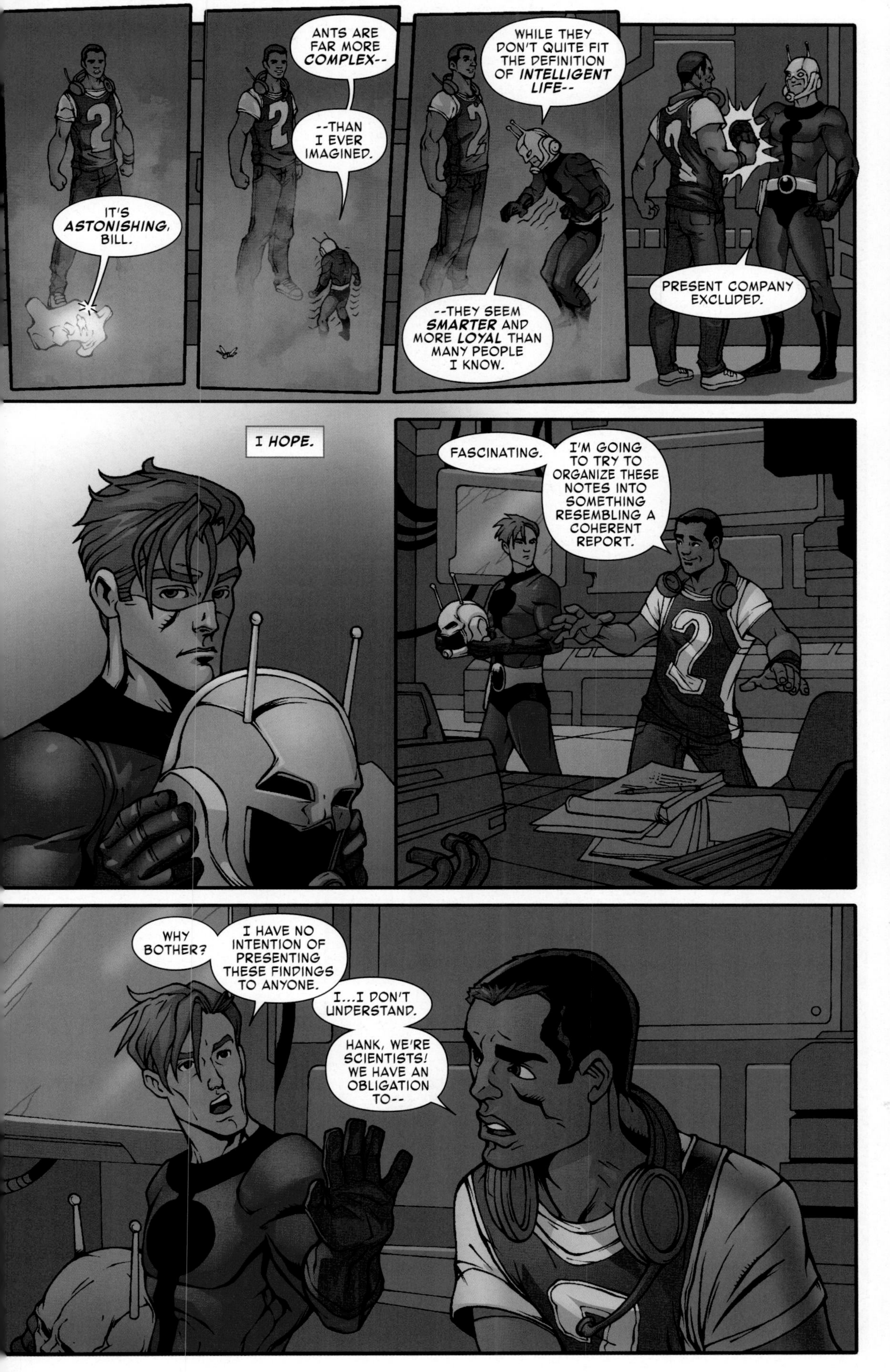
IT'S ASTONISHING, BILL.
ANTS ARE FAR MORE COMPLEX--
--THAN I EVER IMAGINED.
WHILE THEY DON'T QUITE FIT THE DEFINITION OF INTELLIGENT LIFE--
--THEY SEEM SMARTER AND MORE LOYAL THAN MANY PEOPLE I KNOW.
PRESENT COMPANY EXCLUDED.
I HOPE.
FASCINATING.
I'M GOING TO TRY TO ORGANIZE THESE NOTES INTO SOMETHING RESEMBLING A COHERENT REPORT.
WHY BOTHER?
I HAVE NO INTENTION OF PRESENTING THESE FINDINGS TO ANYONE.
I...I DON'T UNDERSTAND.
HANK, WE'RE SCIENTISTS! WE HAVE AN OBLIGATION TO--

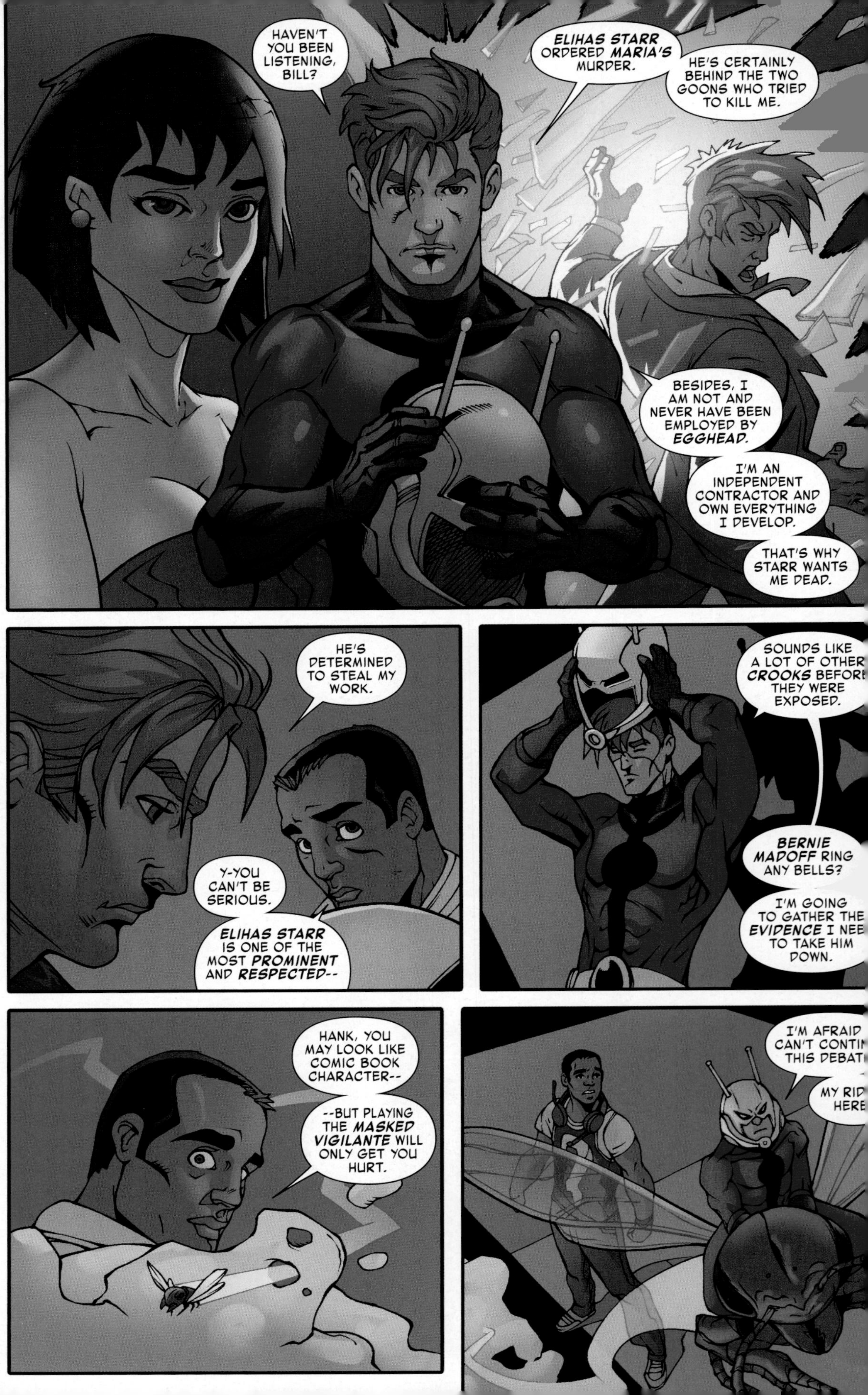
HAVEN'T YOU BEEN LISTENING, BILL?
ELIHAS STARR ORDERED MARIA'S MURDER.
HE'S CERTAINLY BEHIND THE TWO GOONS WHO TRIED TO KILL ME.
BESIDES, I AM NOT AND NEVER HAVE BEEN EMPLOYED BY EGGHEAD.
I'M AN INDEPENDENT CONTRACTOR AND OWN EVERYTHING I DEVELOP.
THAT'S WHY STARR WANTS ME DEAD.
HE'S DETERMINED TO STEAL MY WORK.
Y-YOU CAN'T BE SERIOUS.
ELIHAS STARR IS ONE OF THE MOST PROMINENT AND RESPECTED--
SOUNDS LIKE A LOT OF OTHER CROOKS BEFORE THEY WERE EXPOSED.
BERNIE MADOFF RING ANY BELLS?
I'M GOING TO GATHER THE EVIDENCE I NEE TO TAKE HIM DOWN.
HANK, YOU MAY LOOK LIKE COMIC BOOK CHARACTER--
--BUT PLAYING THE MASKED VIGILANTE WILL ONLY GET YOU HURT.
I'M AFRAID CAN'T CONTI THIS DEBAT
MY RID HERE

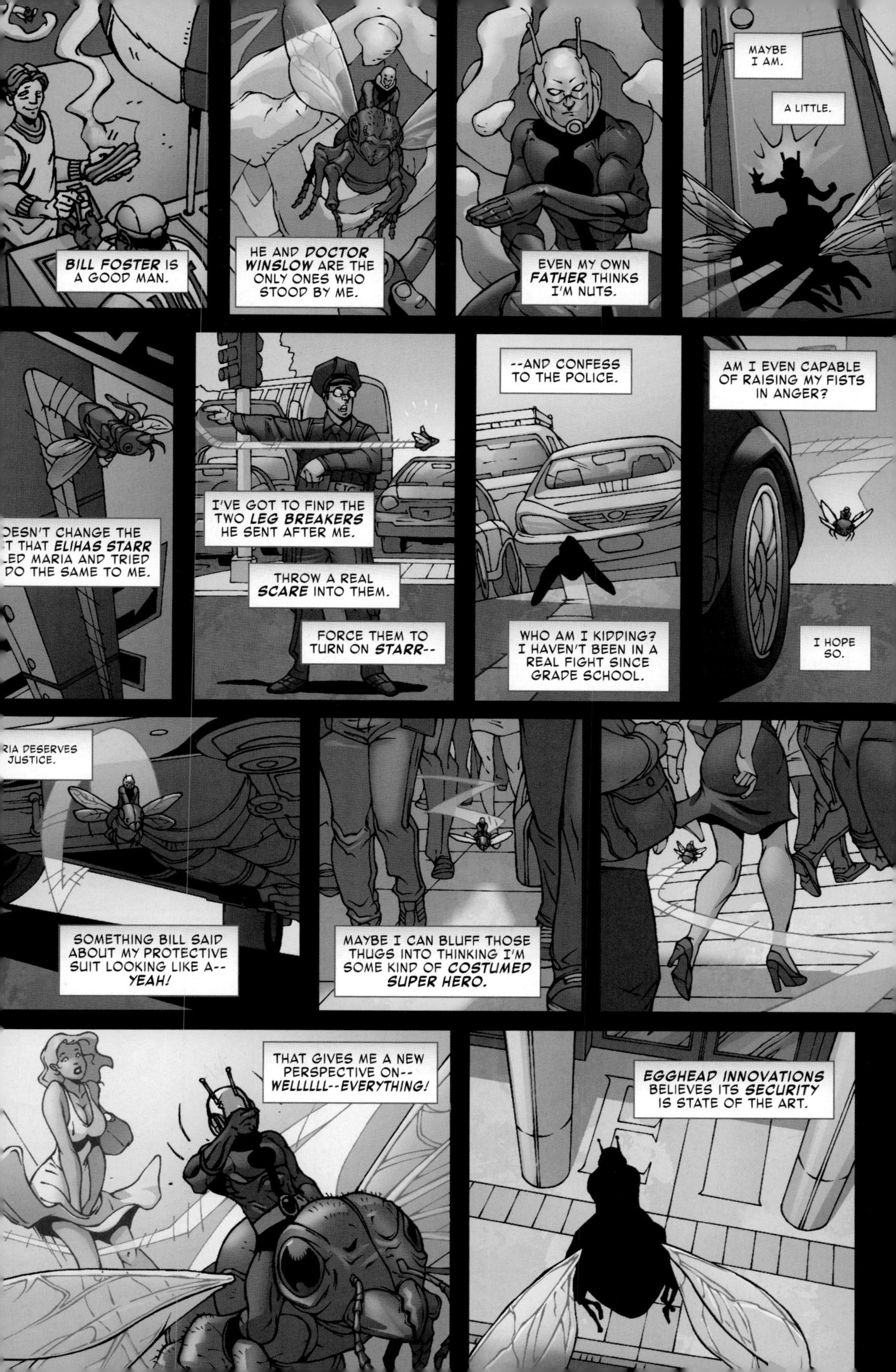

BILL FOSTER IS A GOOD MAN.
HE AND DOCTOR WINSLOW ARE THE ONLY ONES WHO STOOD BY ME.
EVEN MY OWN FATHER THINKS I'M NUTS.
MAYBE I AM.
A LITTLE.
OESN'T CHANGE THE T THAT ELIHAS STARR LED MARIA AND TRIED DO THE SAME TO ME.
I'VE GOT TO FIND THE TWO LEG BREAKERS HE SENT AFTER ME.
THROW A REAL SCARE INTO THEM.
FORCE THEM TO TURN ON STARR--
--AND CONFESS TO THE POLICE.
WHO AM I KIDDING? I HAVEN'T BEEN IN A REAL FIGHT SINCE GRADE SCHOOL.
AM I EVEN CAPABLE OF RAISING MY FISTS IN ANGER?
I HOPE SO.
RIA DESERVES JUSTICE.
SOMETHING BILL SAID ABOUT MY PROTECTIVE SUIT LOOKING LIKE A-- YEAH!
MAYBE I CAN BLUFF THOSE THUGS INTO THINKING I'M SOME KIND OF COSTUMED SUPER HERO.
THAT GIVES ME A NEW PERSPECTIVE ON-- WELLLLLL--EVERYTHING!
EGGHEAD INNOVATIONS BELIEVES ITS SECURITY IS STATE OF THE ART.

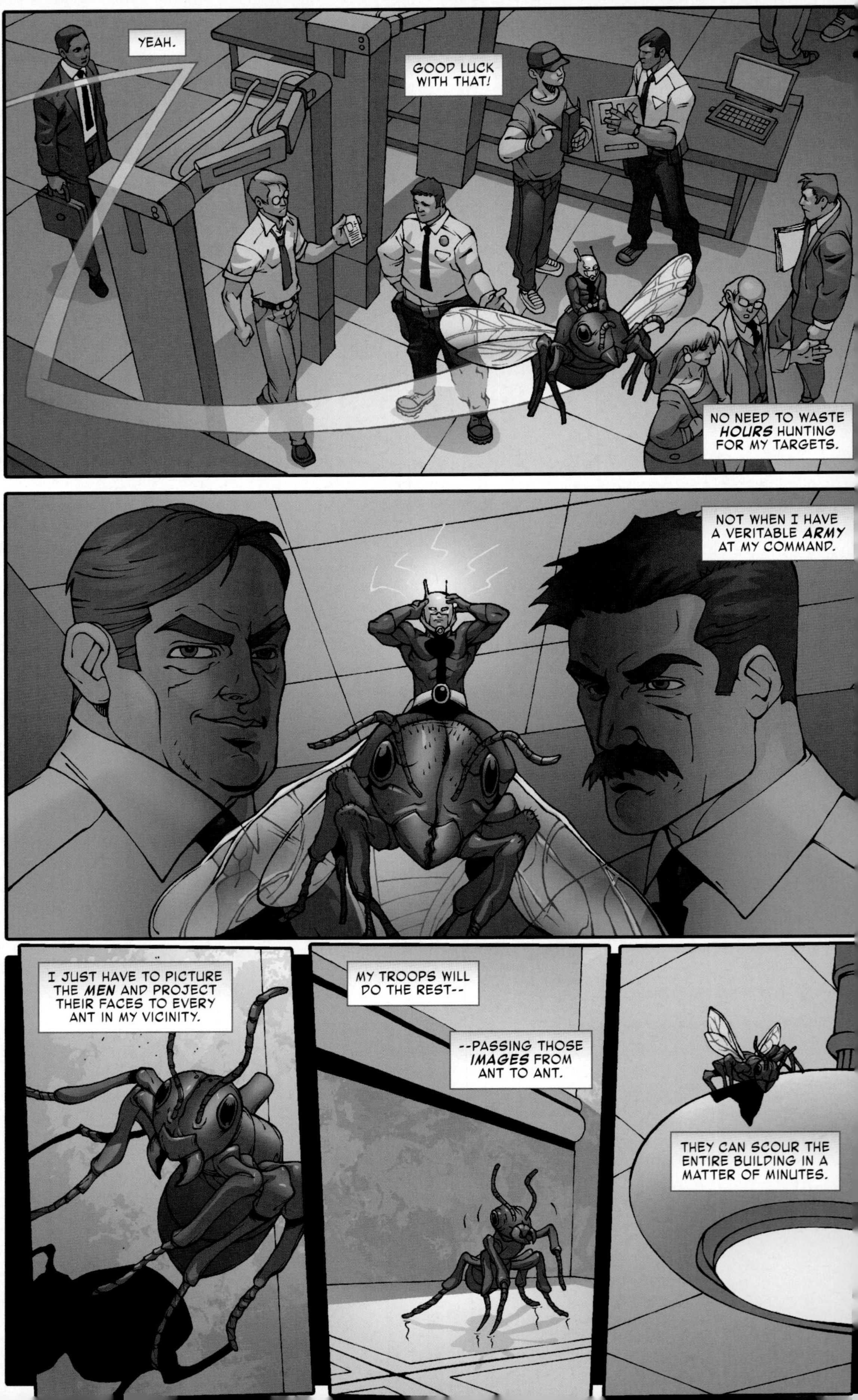
YEAH.
GOOD LUCK WITH THAT!
NO NEED TO WASTE HOURS HUNTING FOR MY TARGETS.
NOT WHEN I HAVE A VERITABLE ARMY AT MY COMMAND.
I JUST HAVE TO PICTURE THE MEN AND PROJECT THEIR FACES TO EVERY ANT IN MY VICINITY.
MY TROOPS WILL DO THE REST--
--PASSING THOSE IMAGES FROM ANT TO ANT.
THEY CAN SCOUR THE ENTIRE BUILDING IN A MATTER OF MINUTES.

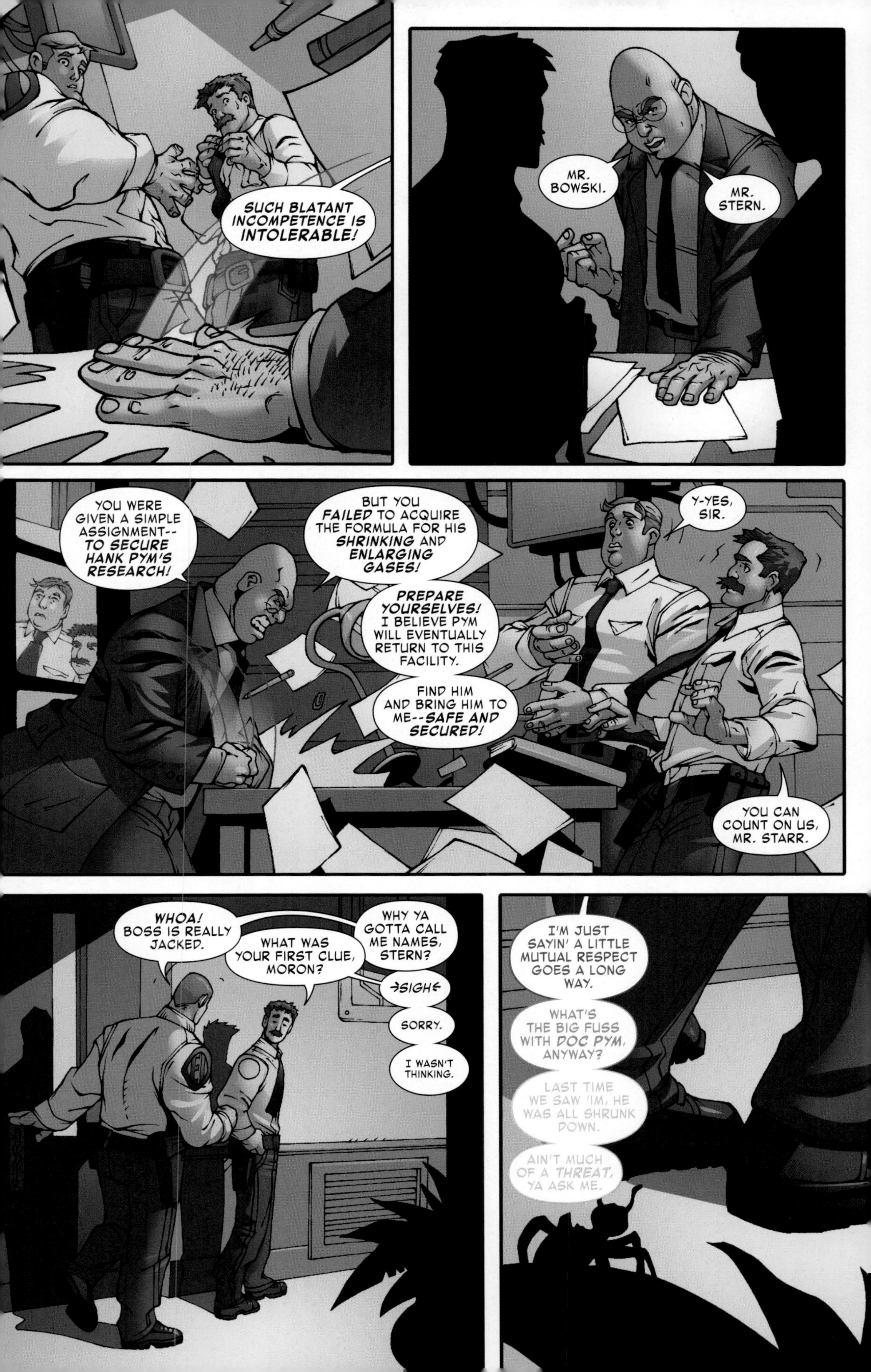
SUCH BLATANT INCOMPETENCE IS INTOLERABLE!
MR. BOWSKI.
MR. STERN.
YOU WERE GIVEN A SIMPLE ASSIGNMENT-- TO SECURE HANK PYM'S RESEARCH!
BUT YOU FAILED TO ACQUIRE THE FORMULA FOR HIS SHRINKING AND ENLARGING GASES!
Y-YES, SIR.
PREPARE YOURSELVES! I BELIEVE PYM WILL EVENTUALLY RETURN TO THIS FACILITY.
FIND HIM AND BRING HIM TO ME--SAFE AND SECURED!
YOU CAN COUNT ON US, MR. STARR.
WHOA! BOSS IS REALLY JACKED.
WHAT WAS YOUR FIRST CLUE, MORON?
WHY YA GOTTA CALL ME NAMES, STERN?
SIGH
SORRY.
I WASN'T THINKING.
I'M JUST SAYIN' A LITTLE MUTUAL RESPECT GOES A LONG WAY.
WHAT'S THE BIG FUSS WITH DOC PYM, ANYWAY?
LAST TIME WE SAW 'IM, HE WAS ALL SHRUNK DOWN.
AIN'T MUCH OF A THREAT, YA ASK ME.

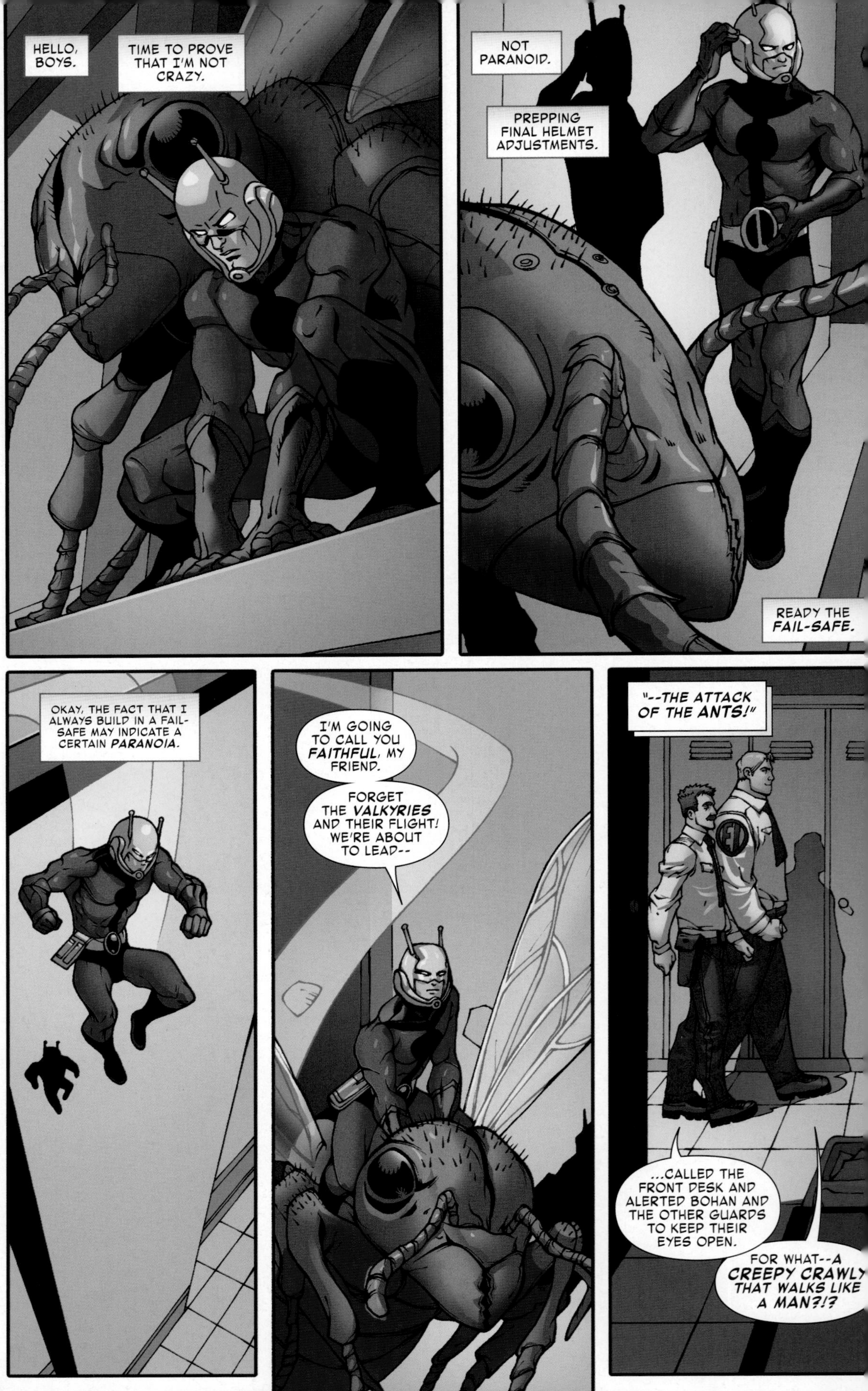
HELLO, BOYS.
TIME TO PROVE THAT I'M NOT CRAZY.
NOT PARANOID.
PREPPING FINAL HELMET ADJUSTMENTS.
READY THE FAIL-SAFE.
OKAY, THE FACT THAT I ALWAYS BUILD IN A FAIL-SAFE MAY INDICATE A CERTAIN PARANOIA.
I'M GOING TO CALL YOU FAITHFUL, MY FRIEND.
FORGET THE VALKYRIES AND THEIR FLIGHT! WE'RE ABOUT TO LEAD--
"--THE ATTACK OF THE ANTS!"
...CALLED THE FRONT DESK AND ALERTED BOHAN AND THE OTHER GUARDS TO KEEP THEIR EYES OPEN.
FOR WHAT--A CREEPY CRAWLY THAT WALKS LIKE A MAN?!?

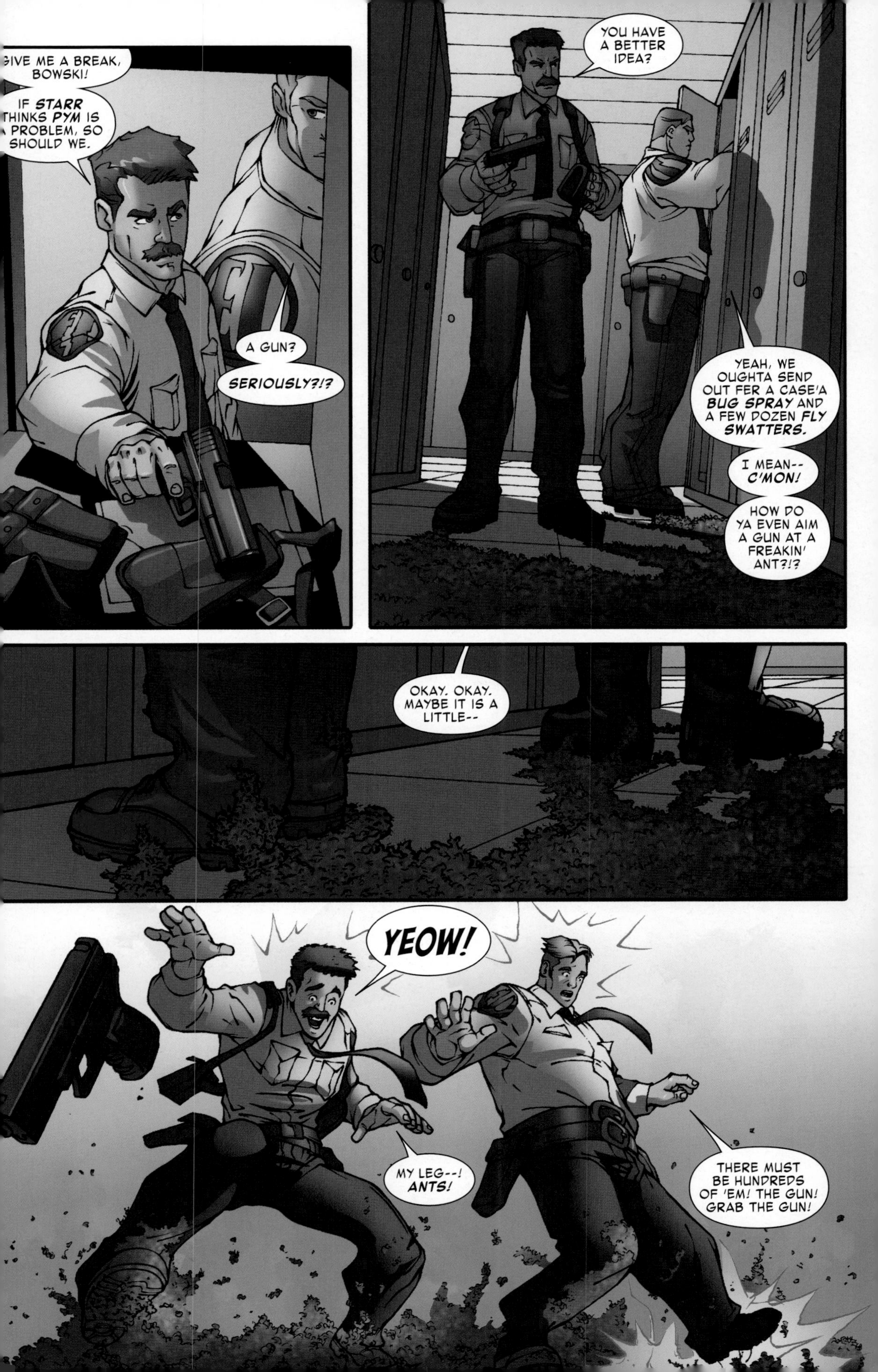
GIVE ME A BREAK, BOWSKI!
IF STARR THINKS PYM IS A PROBLEM, SO SHOULD WE.
A GUN?
SERIOUSLY?!?
YOU HAVE A BETTER IDEA?
YEAH, WE OUGHTA SEND OUT FER A CASE'A BUG SPRAY AND A FEW DOZEN FLY SWATTERS.
I MEAN-- C'MON!
HOW DO YA EVEN AIM A GUN AT A FREAKIN' ANT?!?
OKAY. OKAY. MAYBE IT IS A LITTLE--
YEOW!
MY LEG--! ANTS!
THERE MUST BE HUNDREDS OF 'EM! THE GUN! GRAB THE GUN!

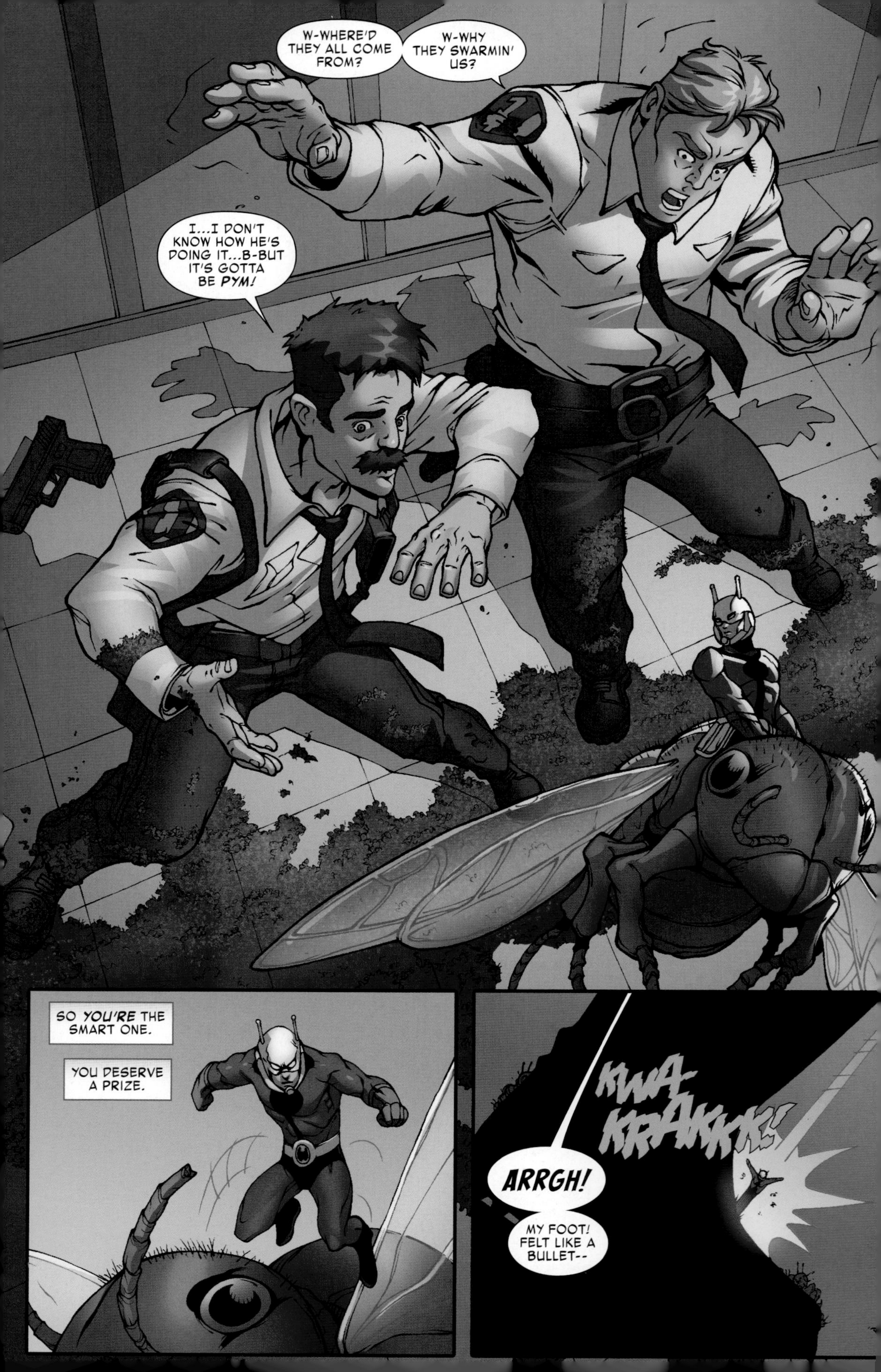
W-WHERE'D THEY ALL COME FROM?
W-WHY THEY SWARMIN' US?
I...I DON'T KNOW HOW HE'S DOING IT...B-BUT IT'S GOTTA BE *PYM!*
SO *YOU'RE* THE SMART ONE.
YOU DESERVE A PRIZE.
KWA-KRAKKK!
ARRGH!
MY FOOT! FELT LIKE A BULLET--

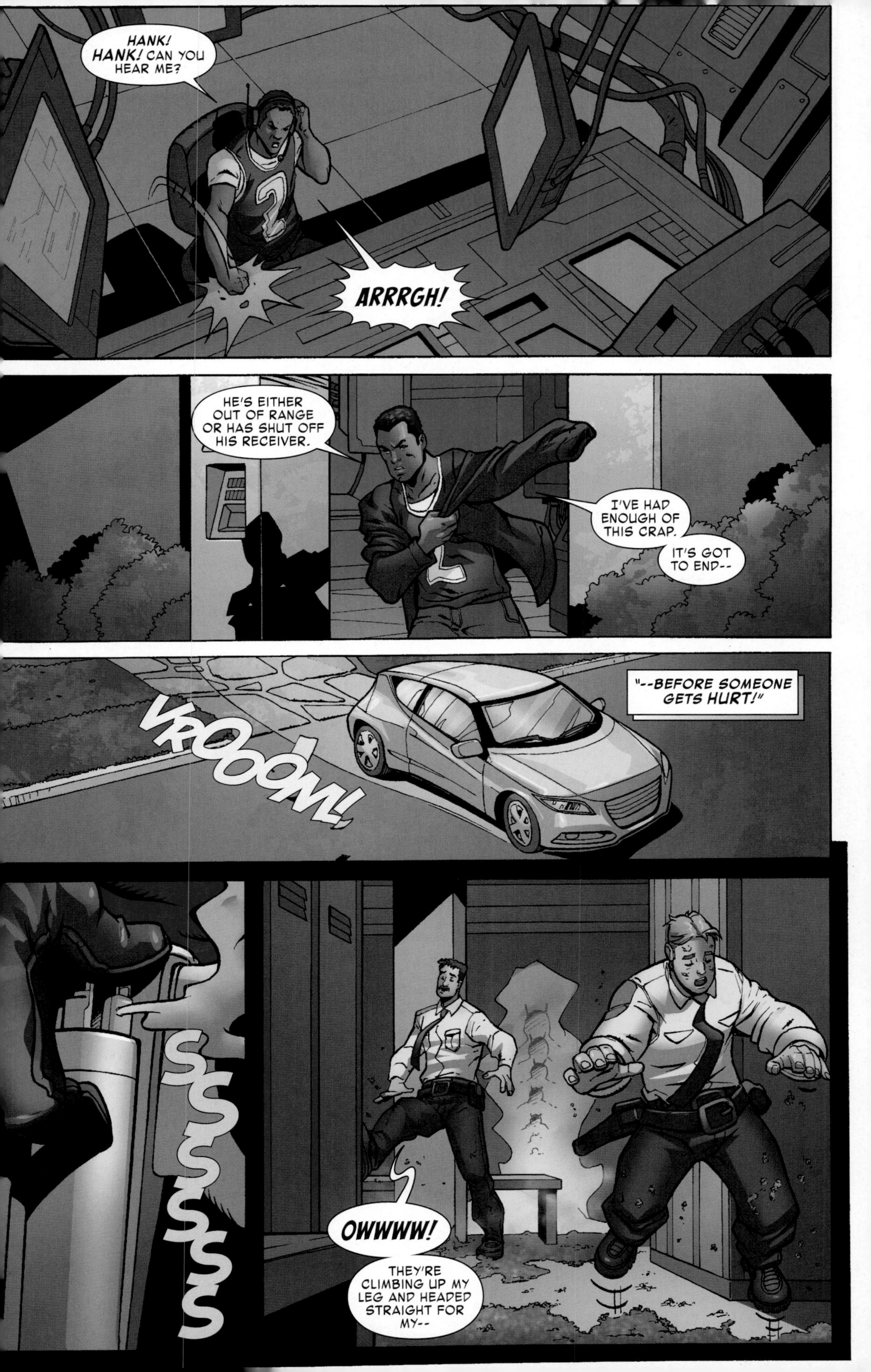
HANK! HANK! CAN YOU HEAR ME?
ARRRGH!
HE'S EITHER OUT OF RANGE OR HAS SHUT OFF HIS RECEIVER.
I'VE HAD ENOUGH OF THIS CRAP.
IT'S GOT TO END--
"--BEFORE SOMEONE GETS HURT!"
VROOOM!
SSSSSS
OWWWW!
THEY'RE CLIMBING UP MY LEG AND HEADED STRAIGHT FOR MY--

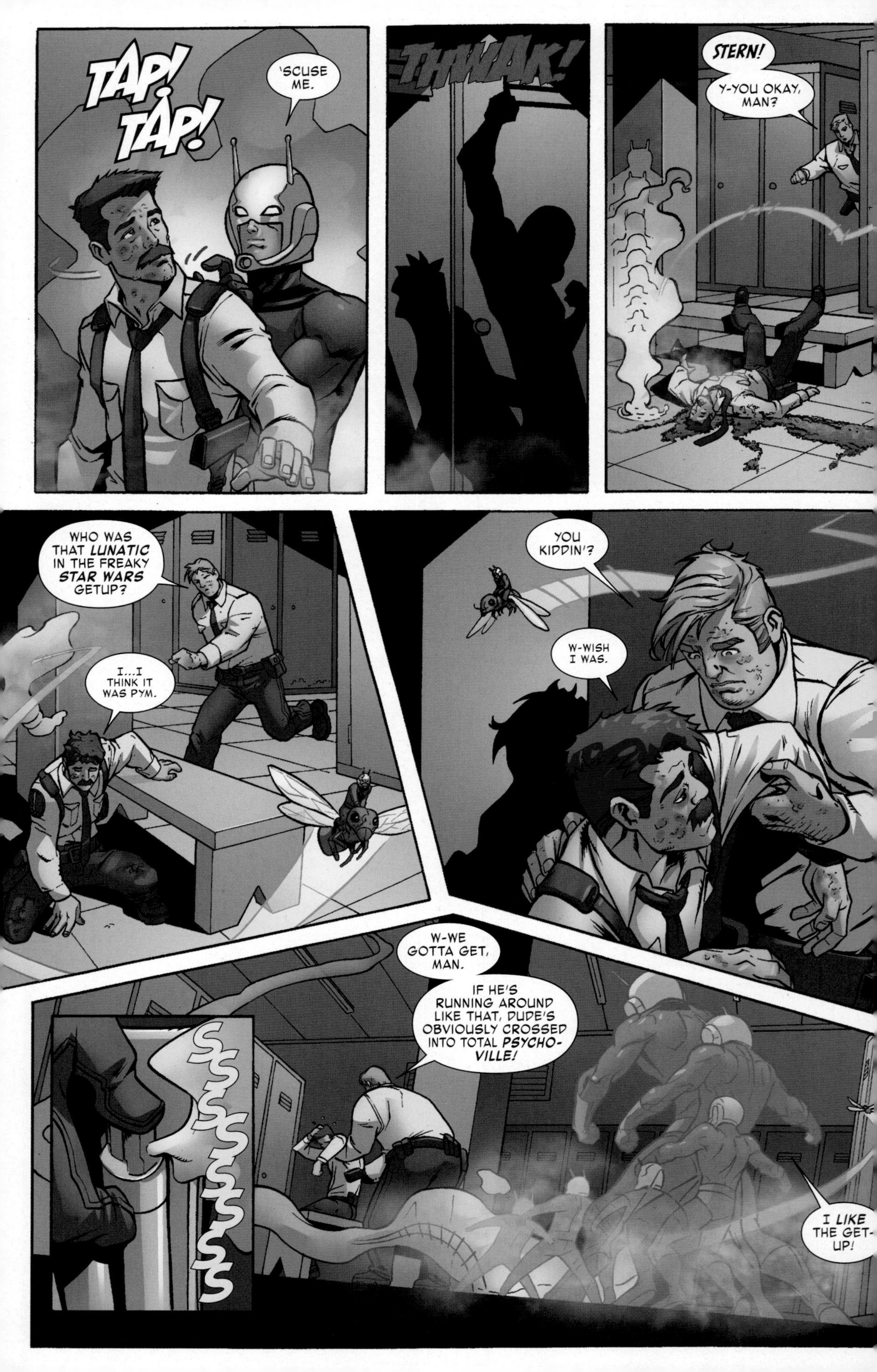
TAP! TAP!
'SCUSE ME.
THWAK!
STERN!
Y-YOU OKAY, MAN?
WHO WAS THAT LUNATIC IN THE FREAKY STAR WARS GETUP?
I...I THINK IT WAS PYM.
YOU KIDDIN'?
W-WISH I WAS.
W-WE GOTTA GET, MAN.
IF HE'S RUNNING AROUND LIKE THAT, DUDE'S OBVIOUSLY CROSSED INTO TOTAL PSYCHO-VILLE!
SSSSSSSSS
I LIKE THE GET-UP!

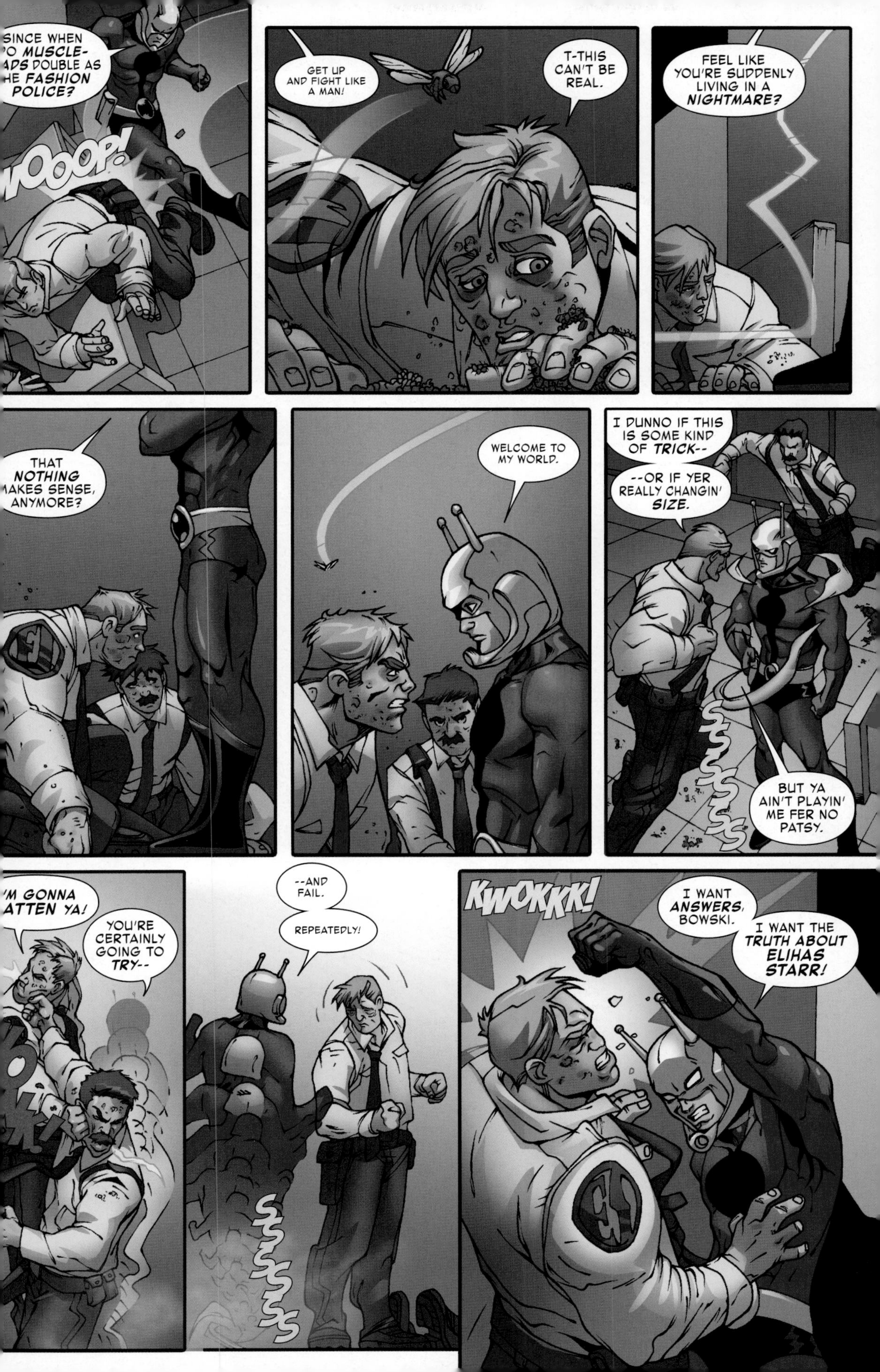

SINCE WHEN
'O MUSCLE-
ADS DOUBLE AS
HE FASHION
POLICE?
WOOOP!
GET UP AND FIGHT LIKE A MAN!
T-THIS CAN'T BE REAL.
FEEL LIKE YOU'RE SUDDENLY LIVING IN A NIGHTMARE?
THAT NOTHING
MAKES SENSE, ANYMORE?
WELCOME TO MY WORLD.
I DUNNO IF THIS IS SOME KIND OF TRICK--
--OR IF YER REALLY CHANGIN' SIZE.
BUT YA AIN'T PLAYIN' ME FER NO PATSY.
'M GONNA
ATTEN YA!
YOU'RE CERTAINLY GOING TO TRY--
--AND FAIL.
REPEATEDLY!
KWOKKK!
I WANT ANSWERS, BOWSKI.
I WANT THE TRUTH ABOUT ELIHAS STARR!

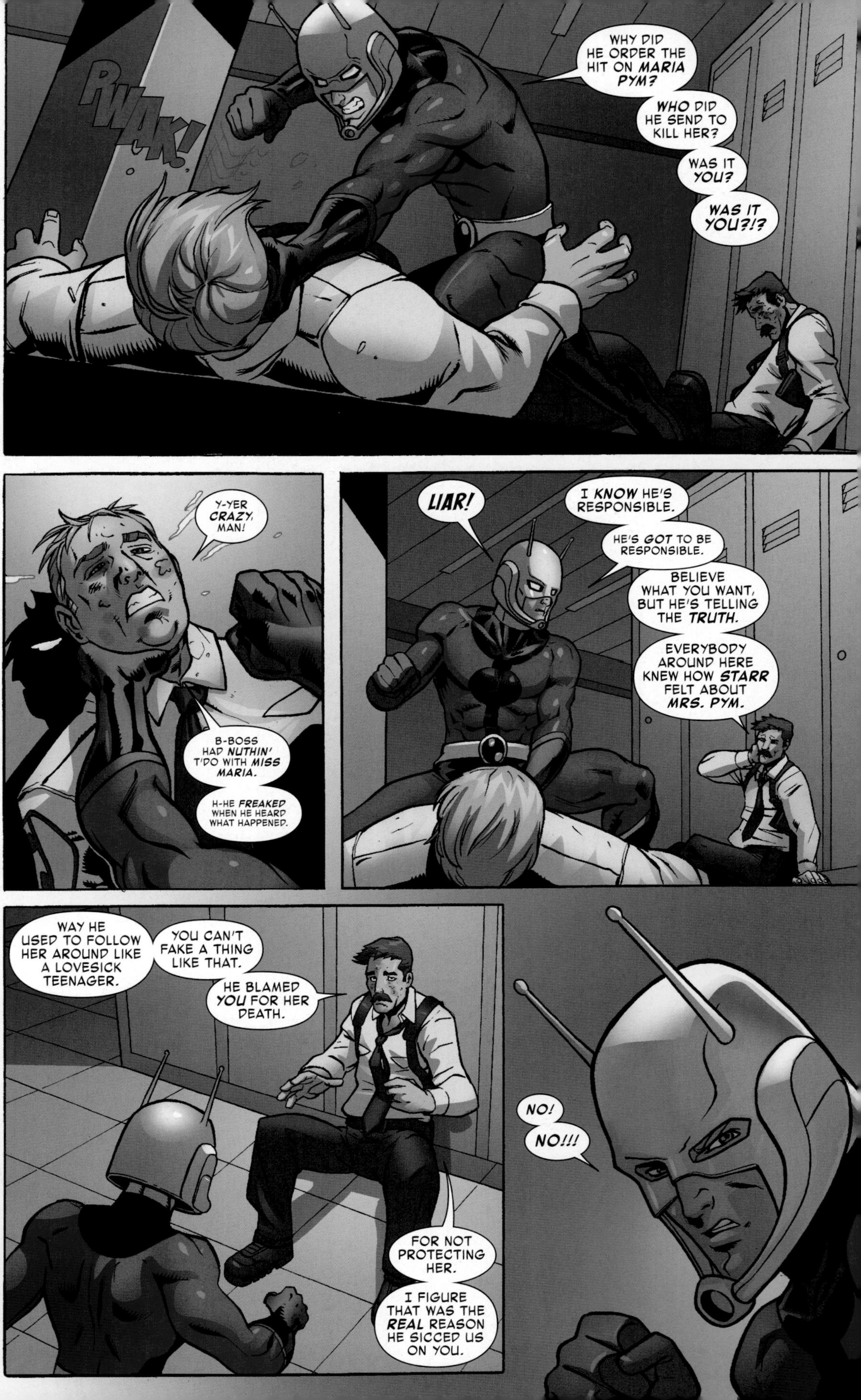
PWAK!
WHY DID HE ORDER THE HIT ON MARIA PYM?
WHO DID HE SEND TO KILL HER?
WAS IT YOU?
WAS IT YOU?!?
Y-YER CRAZY, MAN!
B-BOSS HAD NUTHIN' T'DO WITH MISS MARIA.
H-HE FREAKED WHEN HE HEARD WHAT HAPPENED.
LIAR!
I KNOW HE'S RESPONSIBLE.
HE'S GOT TO BE RESPONSIBLE.
BELIEVE WHAT YOU WANT, BUT HE'S TELLING THE TRUTH.
EVERYBODY AROUND HERE KNEW HOW STARR FELT ABOUT MRS. PYM.
WAY HE USED TO FOLLOW HER AROUND LIKE A LOVESICK TEENAGER.
YOU CAN'T FAKE A THING LIKE THAT.
HE BLAMED YOU FOR HER DEATH.
FOR NOT PROTECTING HER.
I FIGURE THAT WAS THE REAL REASON HE SICCED US ON YOU.
NO!
NO!!!

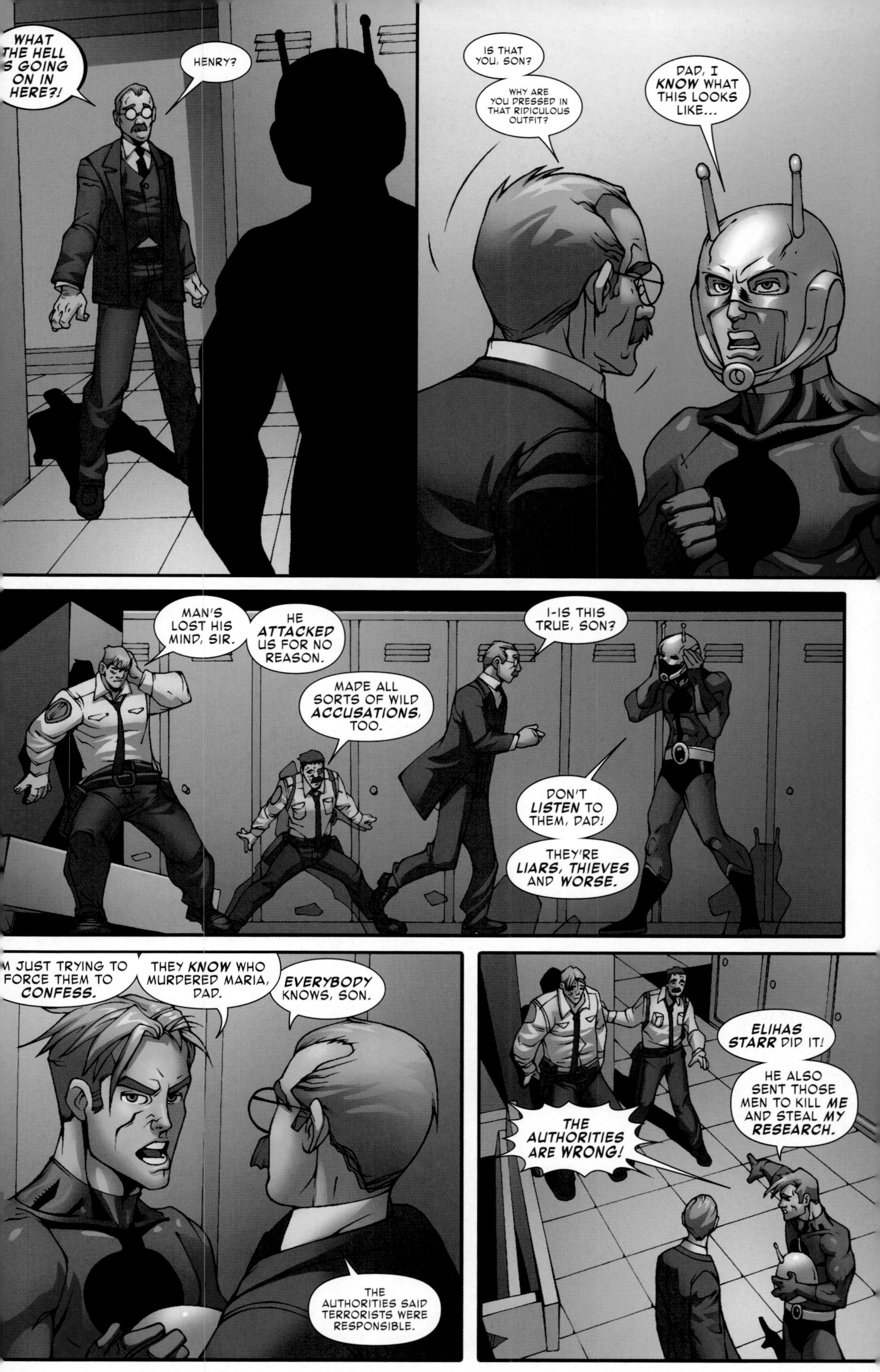
WHAT THE HELL 'S GOING ON IN HERE?!
HENRY?
IS THAT YOU, SON?
WHY ARE YOU DRESSED IN THAT RIDICULOUS OUTFIT?
DAD, I KNOW WHAT THIS LOOKS LIKE...
MAN'S LOST HIS MIND, SIR.
HE ATTACKED US FOR NO REASON.
MADE ALL SORTS OF WILD ACCUSATIONS, TOO.
I-IS THIS TRUE, SON?
DON'T LISTEN TO THEM, DAD!
THEY'RE LIARS, THIEVES AND WORSE.
'M JUST TRYING TO FORCE THEM TO CONFESS.
THEY KNOW WHO MURDERED MARIA, DAD.
EVERYBODY KNOWS, SON.
THE AUTHORITIES SAID TERRORISTS WERE RESPONSIBLE.
THE AUTHORITIES ARE WRONG!
ELIHAS STARR DID IT!
HE ALSO SENT THOSE MEN TO KILL ME AND STEAL MY RESEARCH.

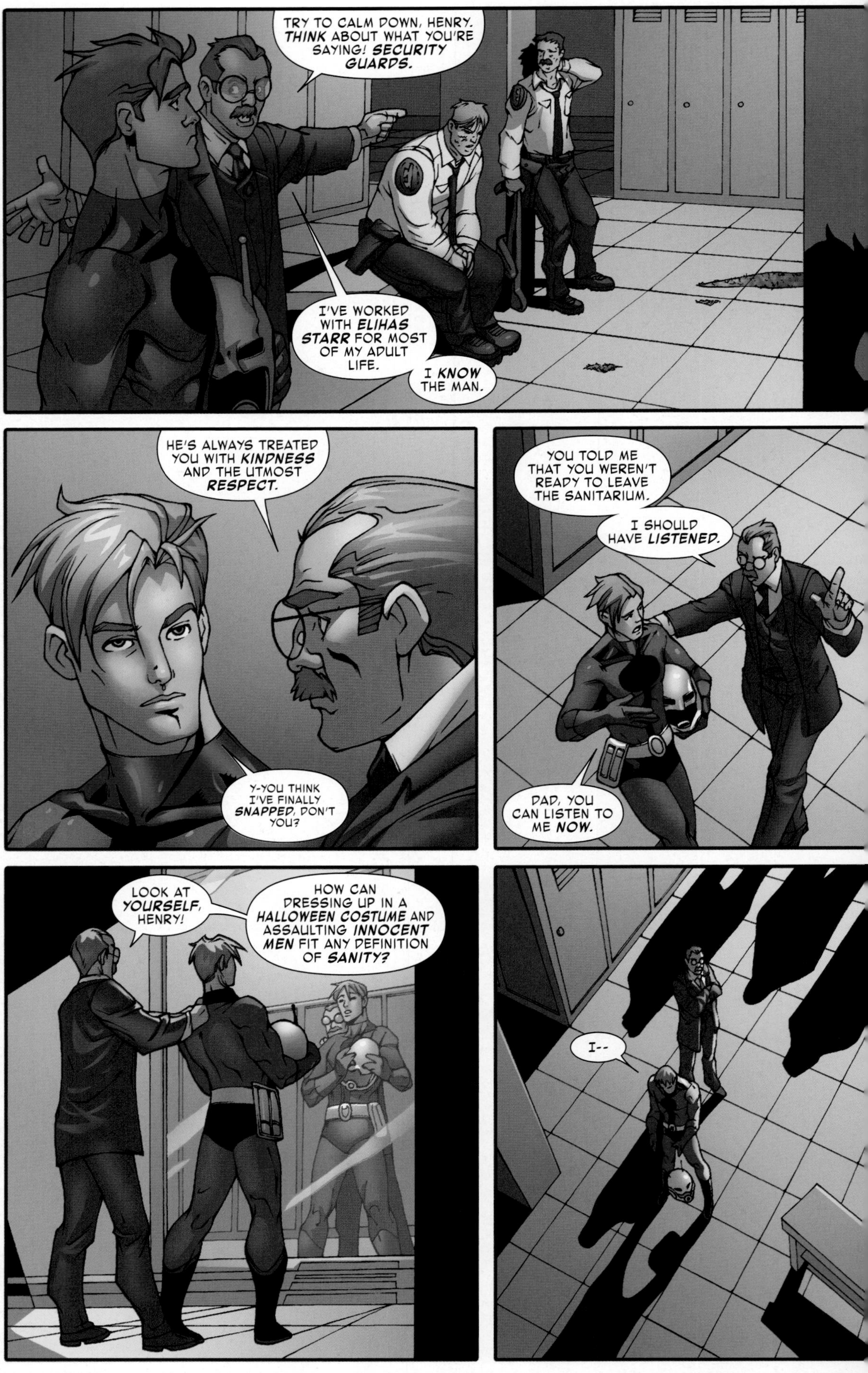
TRY TO CALM DOWN, HENRY. THINK ABOUT WHAT YOU'RE SAYING! SECURITY GUARDS.
I'VE WORKED WITH ELIHAS STARR FOR MOST OF MY ADULT LIFE.
I KNOW THE MAN.
HE'S ALWAYS TREATED YOU WITH KINDNESS AND THE UTMOST RESPECT.
Y-YOU THINK I'VE FINALLY SNAPPED, DON'T YOU?
YOU TOLD ME THAT YOU WEREN'T READY TO LEAVE THE SANITARIUM.
I SHOULD HAVE LISTENED.
DAD, YOU CAN LISTEN TO ME NOW.
LOOK AT YOURSELF, HENRY!
HOW CAN DRESSING UP IN A HALLOWEEN COSTUME AND ASSAULTING INNOCENT MEN FIT ANY DEFINITION OF SANITY?
I--

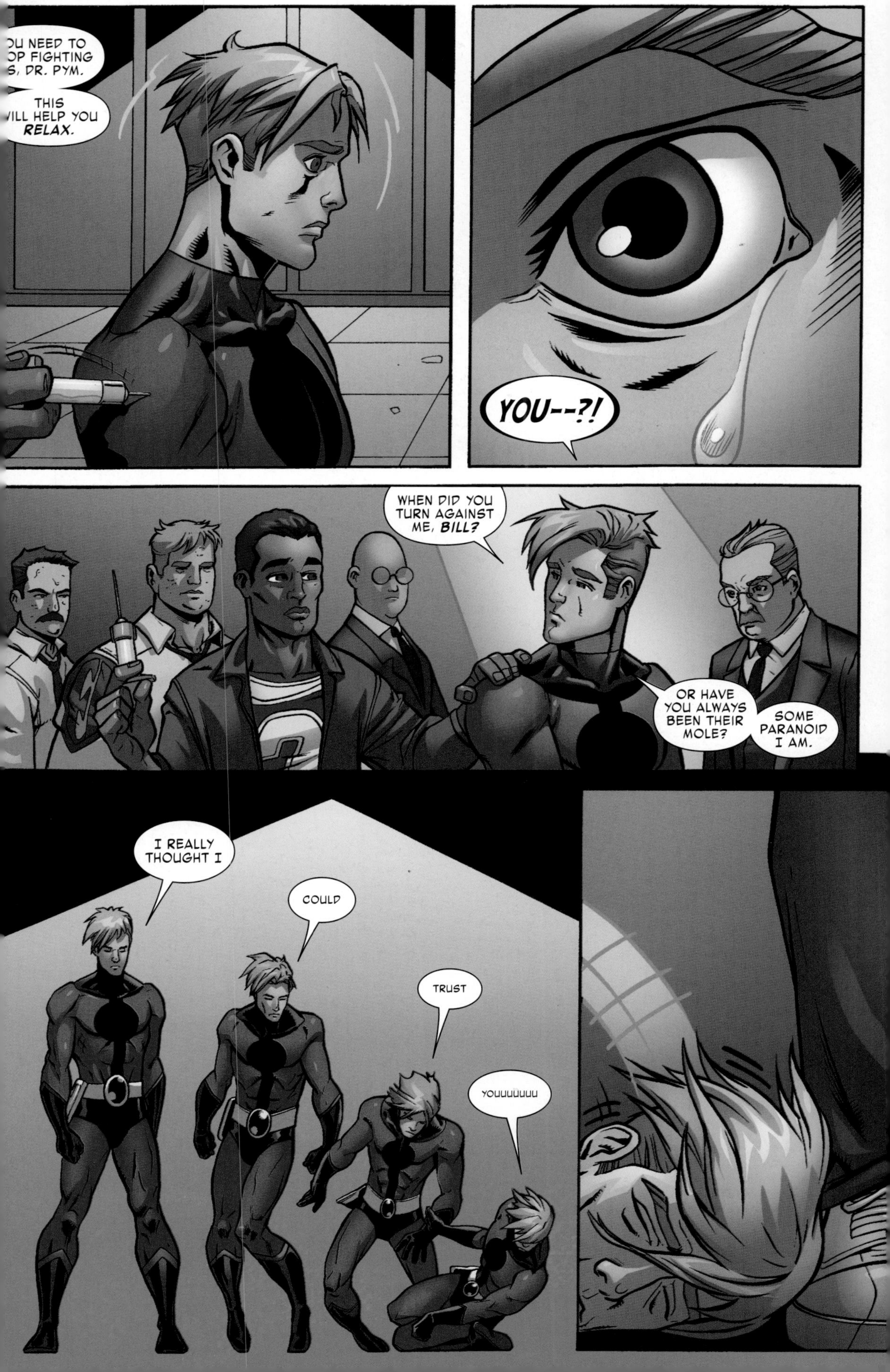

OU NEED TO
OP FIGHTING
S, DR. PYM.
THIS
ILL HELP YOU
RELAX.
YOU--?!
WHEN DID YOU
TURN AGAINST
ME, BILL?
OR HAVE
YOU ALWAYS
BEEN THEIR
MOLE?
SOME
PARANOID
I AM.
I REALLY
THOUGHT I
COULD
TRUST
YOUUUUUUU

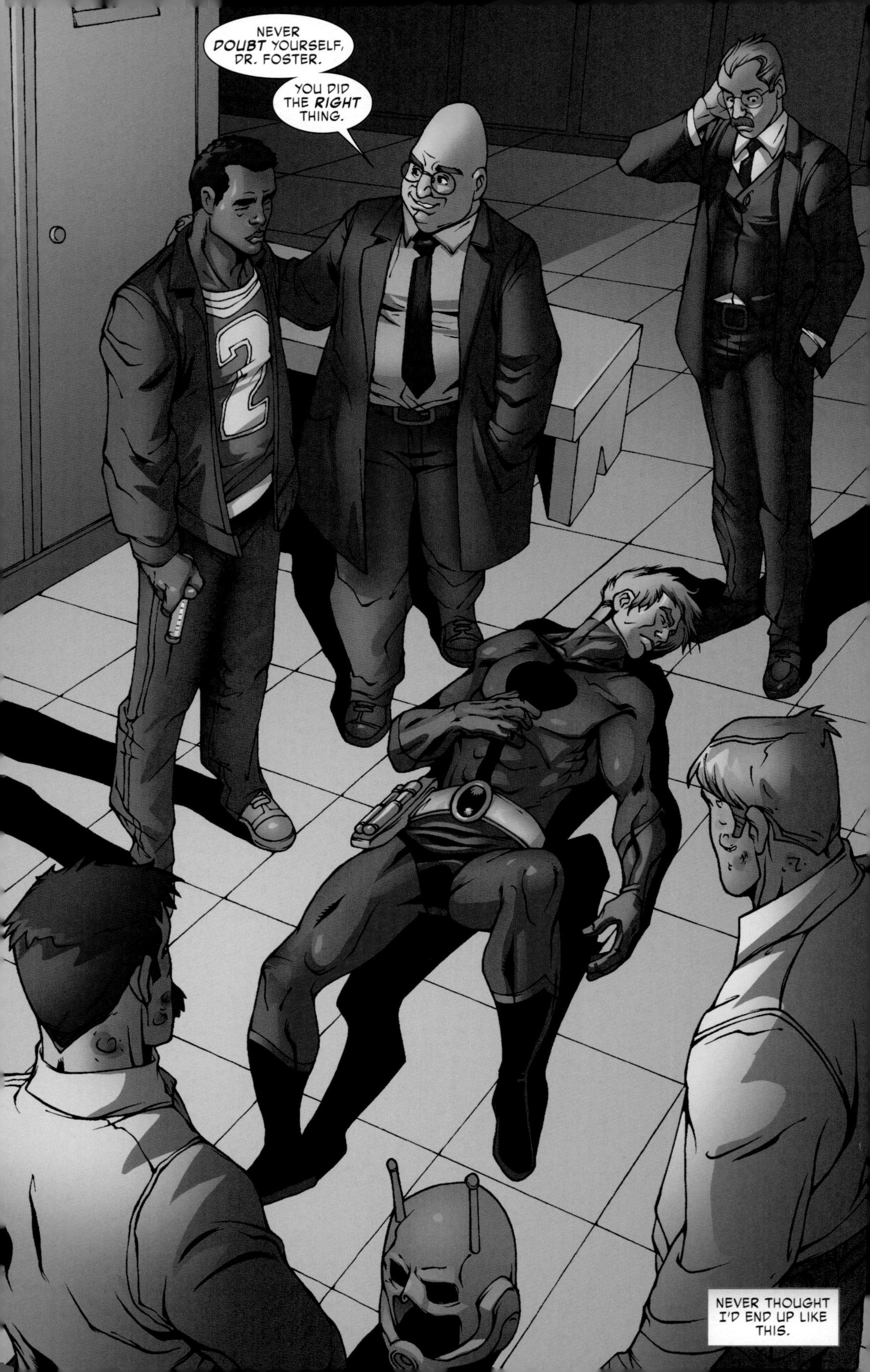
NEVER DOUBT YOURSELF, DR. FOSTER.
YOU DID THE RIGHT THING.
NEVER THOUGHT I'D END UP LIKE THIS.

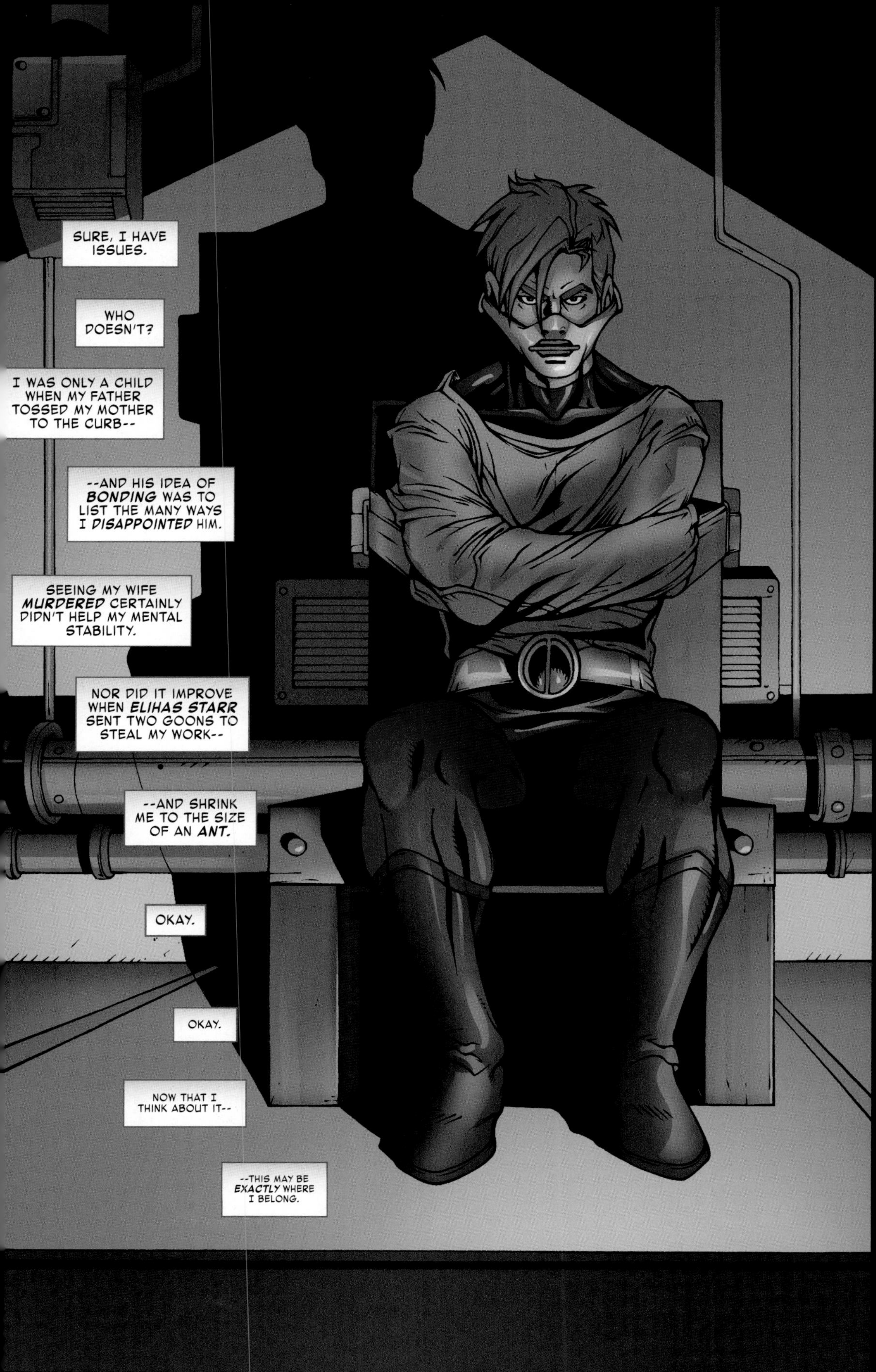
SURE, I HAVE ISSUES.
WHO DOESN'T?
I WAS ONLY A CHILD WHEN MY FATHER TOSSED MY MOTHER TO THE CURB--
--AND HIS IDEA OF BONDING WAS TO LIST THE MANY WAYS I DISAPPOINTED HIM.
SEEING MY WIFE MURDERED CERTAINLY DIDN'T HELP MY MENTAL STABILITY.
NOR DID IT IMPROVE WHEN ELIHAS STARR SENT TWO GOONS TO STEAL MY WORK--
--AND SHRINK ME TO THE SIZE OF AN ANT.
OKAY.
OKAY.
NOW THAT I THINK ABOUT IT--
--THIS MAY BE EXACTLY WHERE I BELONG.

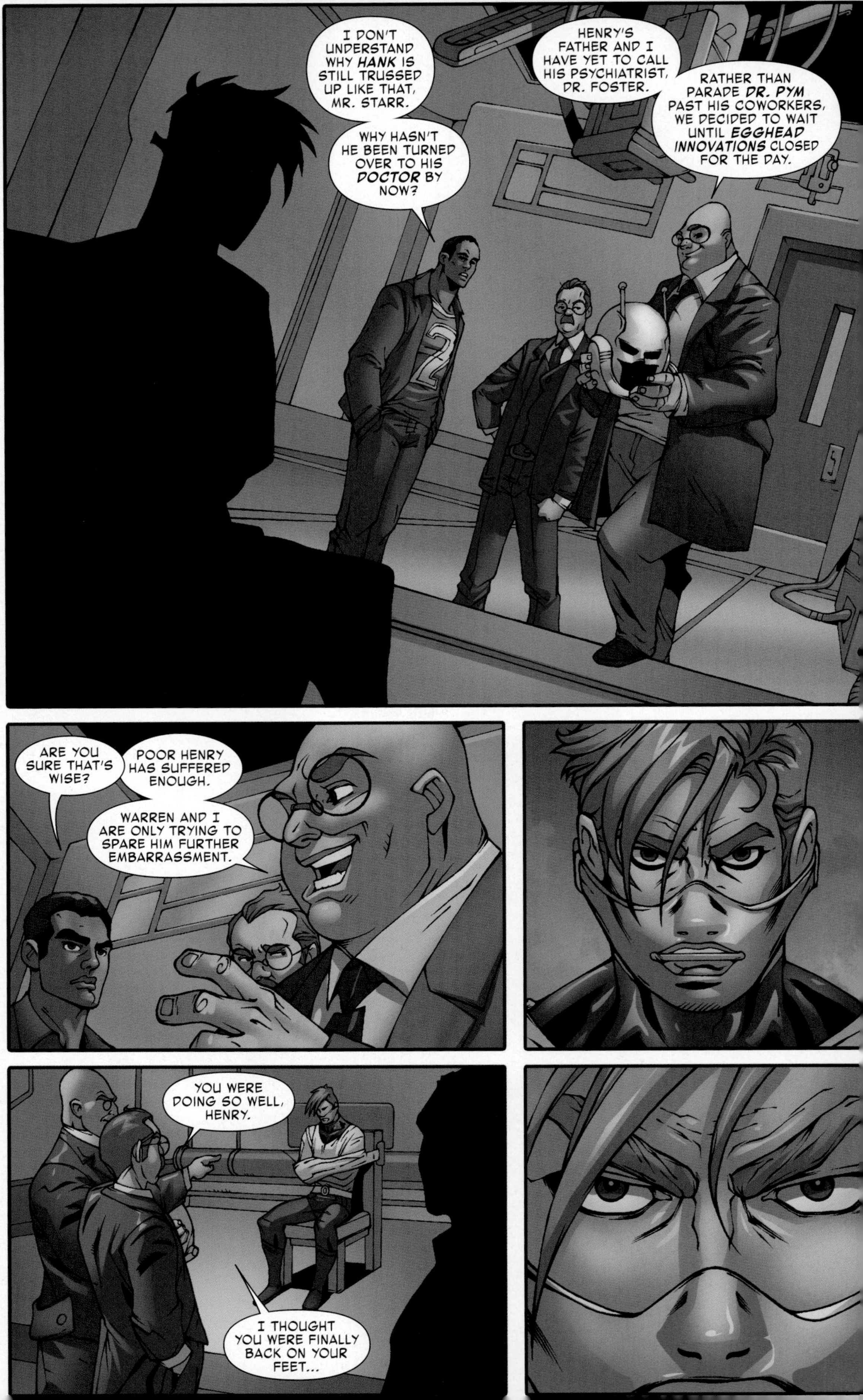
I DON'T UNDERSTAND WHY HANK IS STILL TRUSSED UP LIKE THAT, MR. STARR.
WHY HASN'T HE BEEN TURNED OVER TO HIS DOCTOR BY NOW?
HENRY'S FATHER AND I HAVE YET TO CALL HIS PSYCHIATRIST, DR. FOSTER.
RATHER THAN PARADE DR. PYM PAST HIS COWORKERS, WE DECIDED TO WAIT UNTIL EGGHEAD INNOVATIONS CLOSED FOR THE DAY.
ARE YOU SURE THAT'S WISE?
POOR HENRY HAS SUFFERED ENOUGH.
WARREN AND I ARE ONLY TRYING TO SPARE HIM FURTHER EMBARRASSMENT.
YOU WERE DOING SO WELL, HENRY.
I THOUGHT YOU WERE FINALLY BACK ON YOUR FEET...

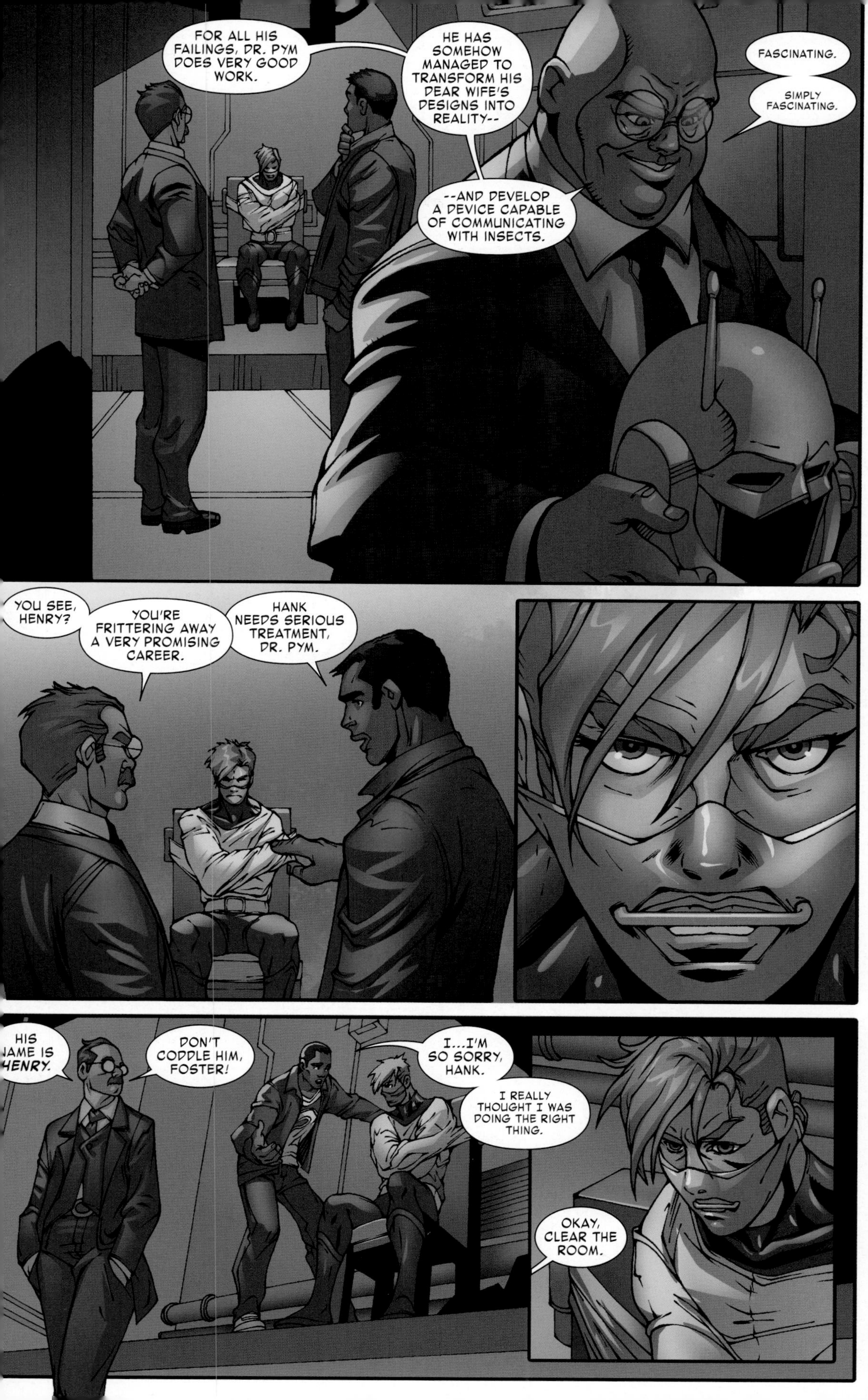
FOR ALL HIS FAILINGS, DR. PYM DOES VERY GOOD WORK.
HE HAS SOMEHOW MANAGED TO TRANSFORM HIS DEAR WIFE'S DESIGNS INTO REALITY--
--AND DEVELOP A DEVICE CAPABLE OF COMMUNICATING WITH INSECTS.
FASCINATING.
SIMPLY FASCINATING.
YOU SEE, HENRY?
YOU'RE FRITTERING AWAY A VERY PROMISING CAREER.
HANK NEEDS SERIOUS TREATMENT, DR. PYM.
HIS NAME IS HENRY.
DON'T CODDLE HIM, FOSTER!
I...I'M SO SORRY, HANK.
I REALLY THOUGHT I WAS DOING THE RIGHT THING.
OKAY, CLEAR THE ROOM.

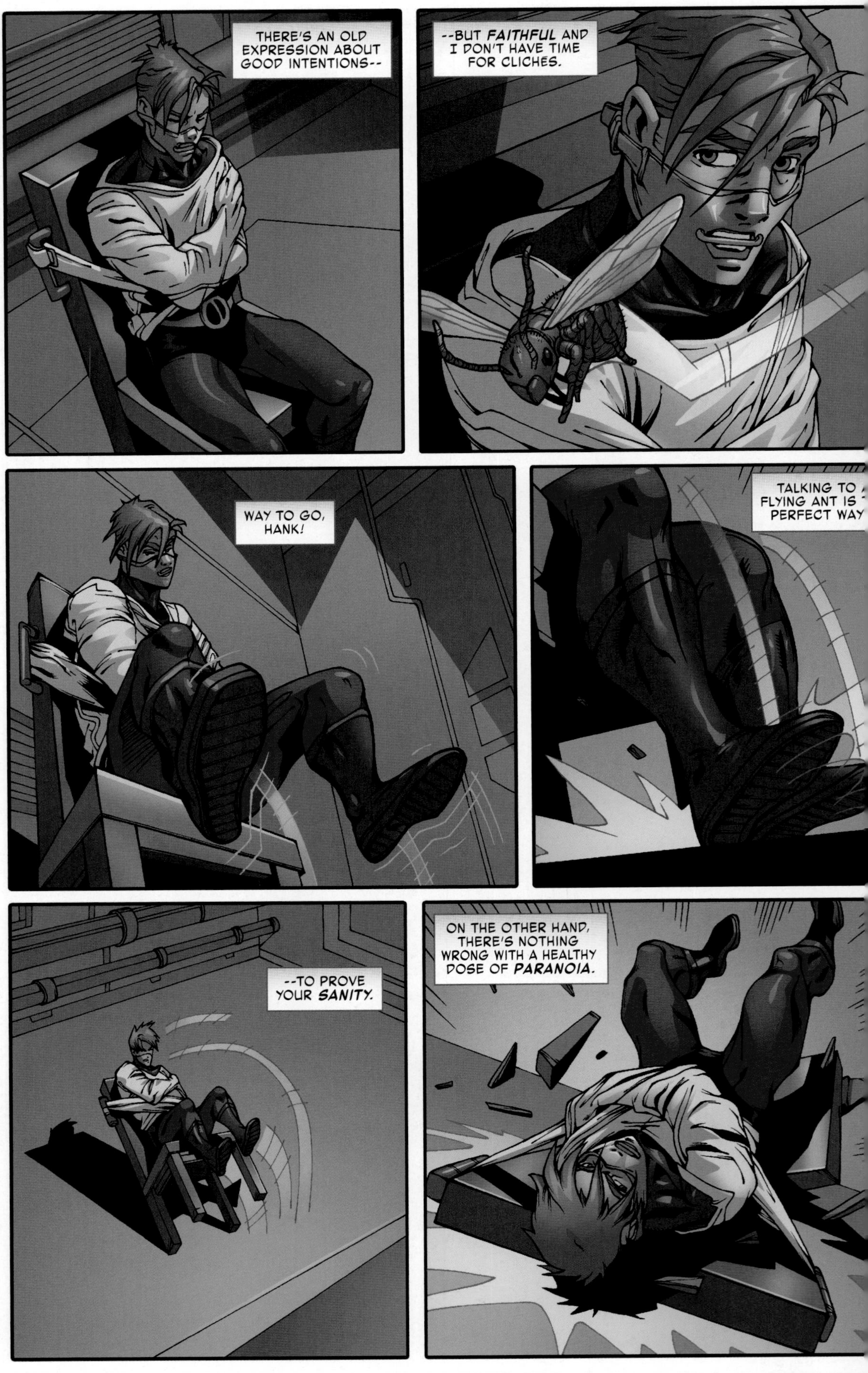
THERE'S AN OLD EXPRESSION ABOUT GOOD INTENTIONS--
--BUT FAITHFUL AND I DON'T HAVE TIME FOR CLICHES.
WAY TO GO, HANK!
TALKING TO
FLYING ANT IS
PERFECT WAY
--TO PROVE YOUR SANITY.
ON THE OTHER HAND, THERE'S NOTHING WRONG WITH A HEALTHY DOSE OF PARANOIA.

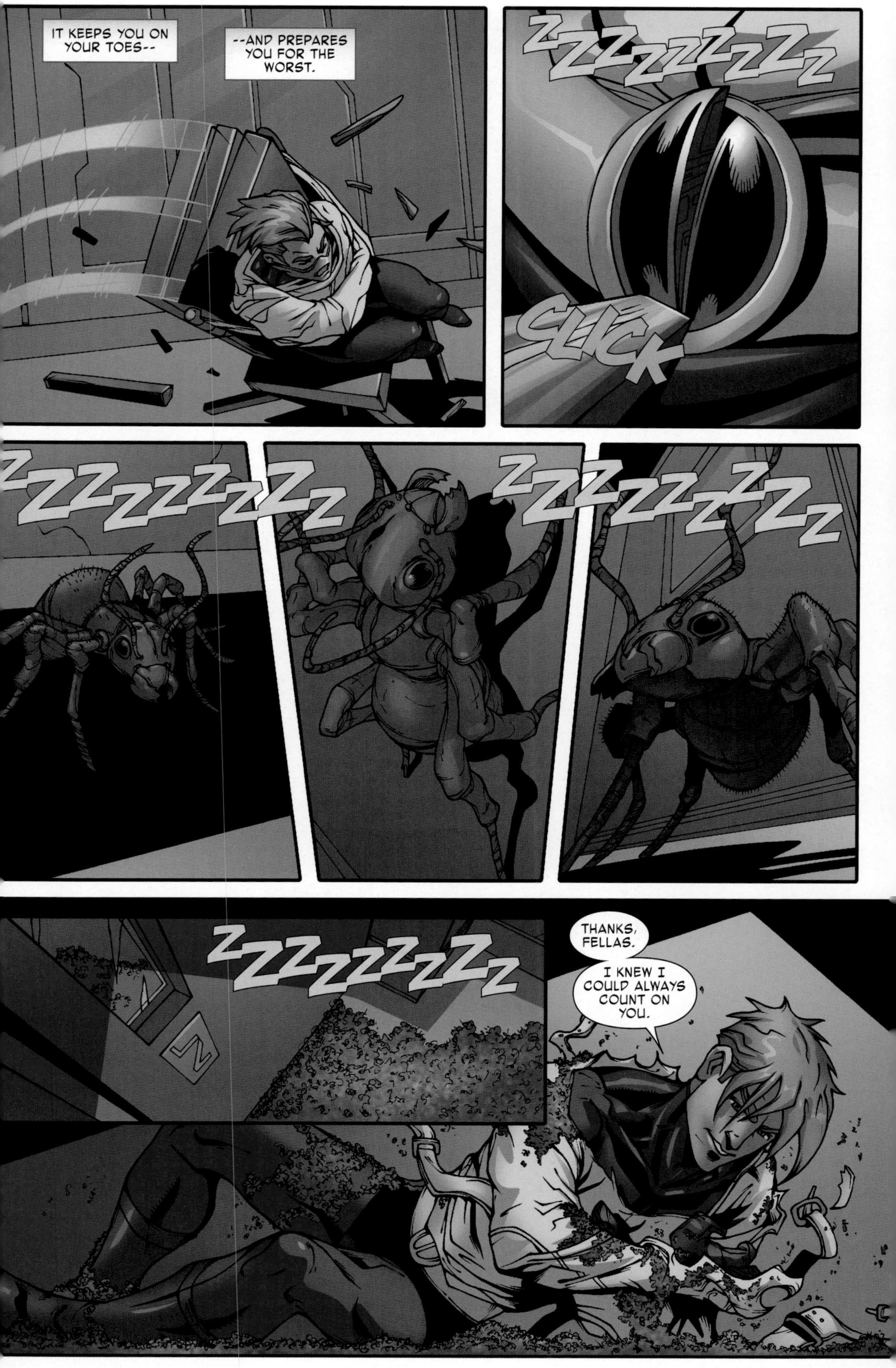

IT KEEPS YOU ON YOUR TOES--
--AND PREPARES YOU FOR THE WORST.
ZZZZZZZZZZZ
SLICK
ZZZZZZZZZZ
ZZZZZZZZZZZ
ZZZZZZZZZZ
THANKS, FELLAS.
I KNEW I COULD ALWAYS COUNT ON YOU.

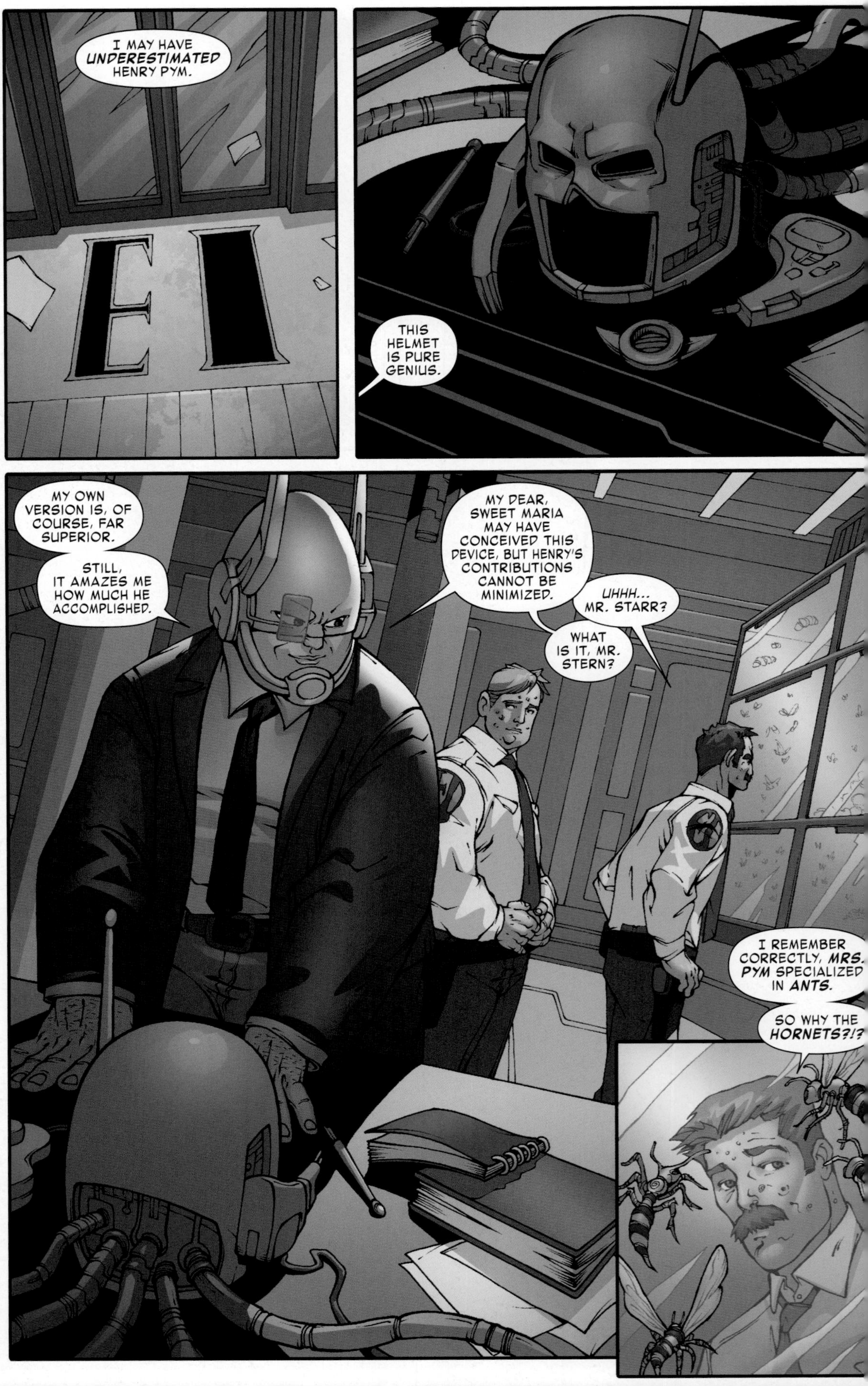
I MAY HAVE *UNDERESTIMATED* HENRY PYM.
THIS HELMET IS PURE GENIUS.
MY OWN VERSION IS, OF COURSE, FAR SUPERIOR.
STILL, IT AMAZES ME HOW MUCH HE ACCOMPLISHED.
MY DEAR, SWEET MARIA MAY HAVE CONCEIVED THIS DEVICE, BUT HENRY'S CONTRIBUTIONS CANNOT BE MINIMIZED.
UHHH... MR. STARR?
WHAT IS IT, MR. STERN?
I REMEMBER CORRECTLY, *MRS. PYM* SPECIALIZED IN *ANTS*.
SO WHY THE *HORNETS?!?*

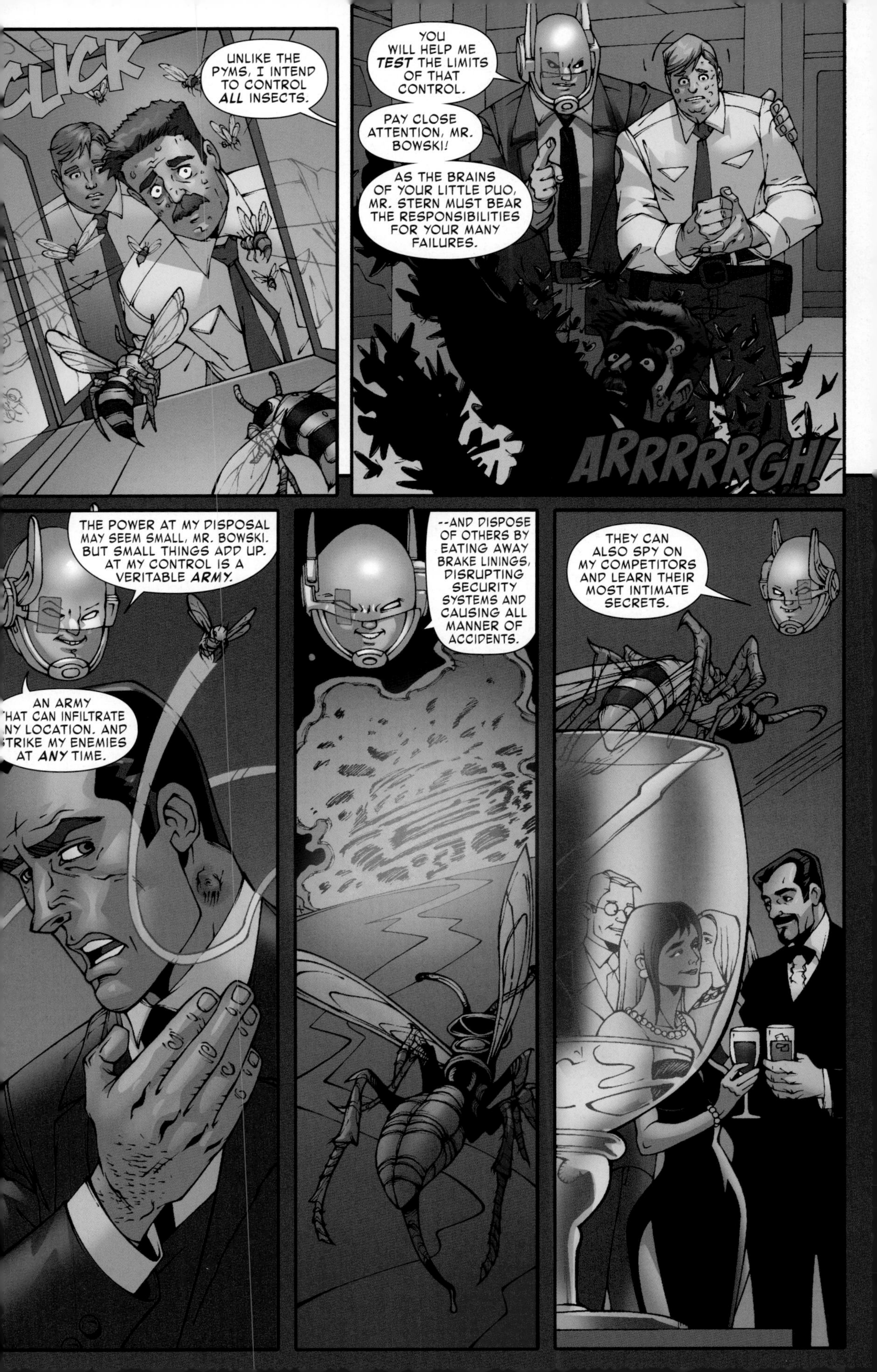
CLICK
UNLIKE THE PYMS, I INTEND TO CONTROL ALL INSECTS.
YOU WILL HELP ME TEST THE LIMITS OF THAT CONTROL.
PAY CLOSE ATTENTION, MR. BOWSKI!
AS THE BRAINS OF YOUR LITTLE DUO, MR. STERN MUST BEAR THE RESPONSIBILITIES FOR YOUR MANY FAILURES.
ARRRRRGH!
THE POWER AT MY DISPOSAL MAY SEEM SMALL, MR. BOWSKI. BUT SMALL THINGS ADD UP. AT MY CONTROL IS A VERITABLE ARMY.
AN ARMY THAT CAN INFILTRATE NY LOCATION. AND STRIKE MY ENEMIES AT ANY TIME.
--AND DISPOSE OF OTHERS BY EATING AWAY BRAKE LININGS, DISRUPTING SECURITY SYSTEMS AND CAUSING ALL MANNER OF ACCIDENTS.
THEY CAN ALSO SPY ON MY COMPETITORS AND LEARN THEIR MOST INTIMATE SECRETS.

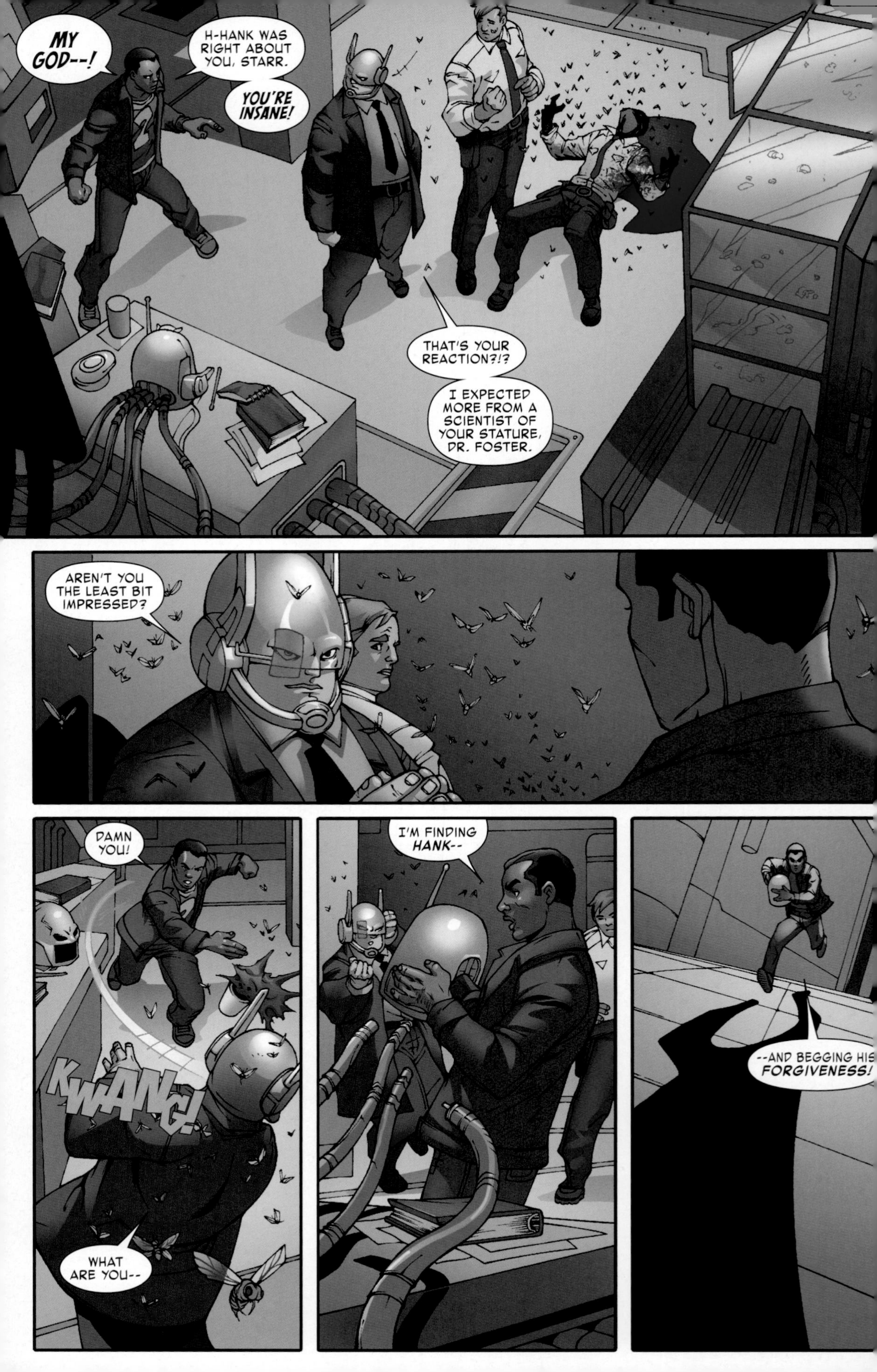
MY GOD--!
H-HANK WAS RIGHT ABOUT YOU, STARR.
YOU'RE INSANE!
THAT'S YOUR REACTION?!?
I EXPECTED MORE FROM A SCIENTIST OF YOUR STATURE, DR. FOSTER.
AREN'T YOU THE LEAST BIT IMPRESSED?
DAMN YOU!
KWANG!
WHAT ARE YOU--
I'M FINDING HANK--
--AND BEGGING HIS FORGIVENESS!

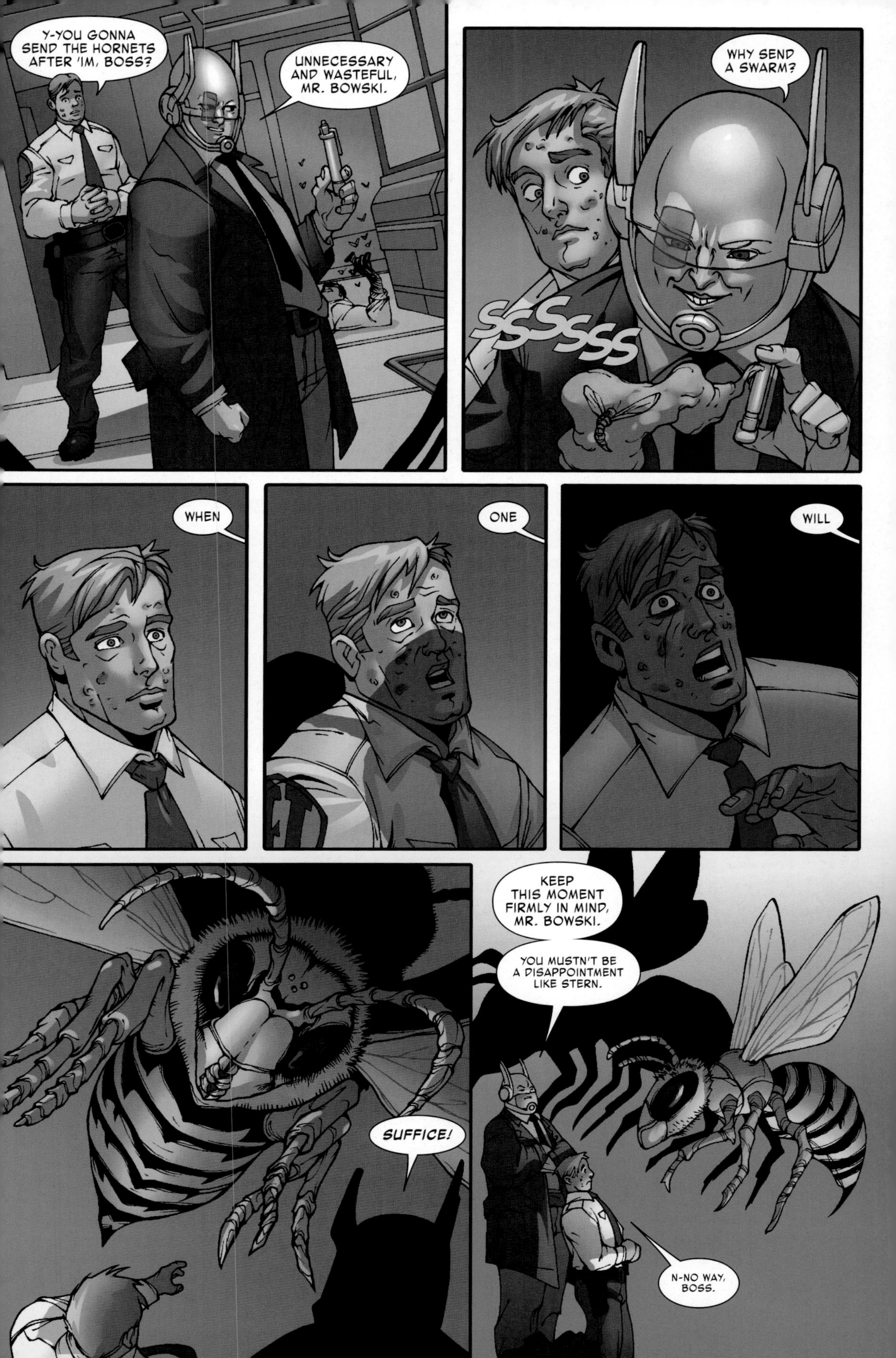
Y-YOU GONNA SEND THE HORNETS AFTER 'IM, BOSS?
UNNECESSARY AND WASTEFUL, MR. BOWSKI.
WHY SEND A SWARM?
SSSSSSS
WHEN
ONE
WILL
SUFFICE!
KEEP THIS MOMENT FIRMLY IN MIND, MR. BOWSKI.
YOU MUSTN'T BE A DISAPPOINTMENT LIKE STERN.
N-NO WAY, BOSS.

YES!

I DON'T CARE WHAT *DR. WINSLOW* SAYS.

I'M PROUD TO EMBRACE A *PARANOIAC LIFESTYLE*.

I'LL ADMIT IT CAN BE RATHER DEPRESSING TO GO THROUGH LIFE ALWAYS EXPECTING TO GET SHAFTED.

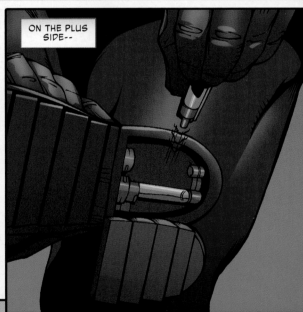

ON THE PLUS SIDE--

--I DO TAKE THE NECESSARY PRECAUTIONS.

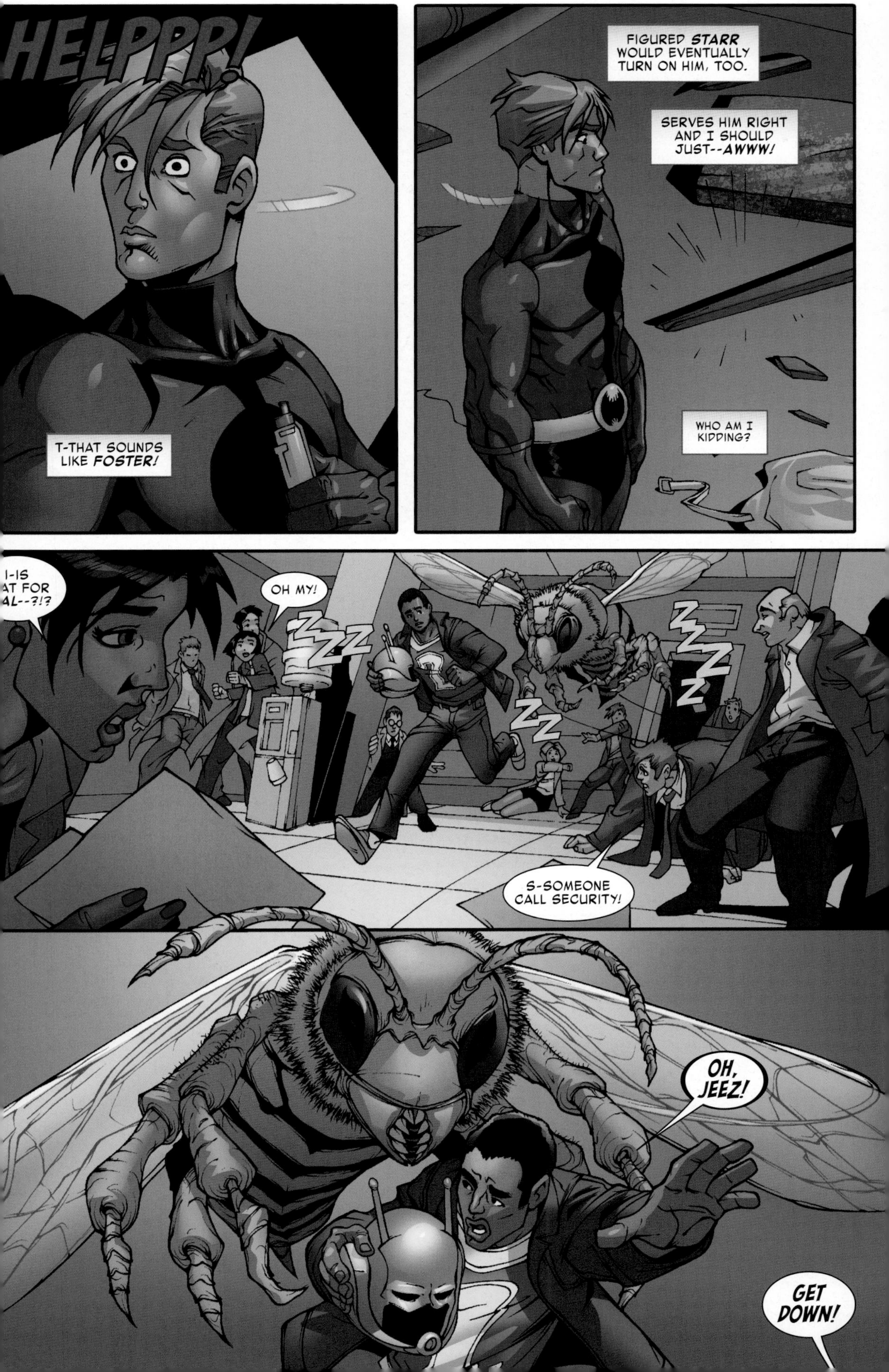
HELPPP!
T-THAT SOUNDS LIKE FOSTER!
FIGURED STARR WOULD EVENTUALLY TURN ON HIM, TOO.
SERVES HIM RIGHT AND I SHOULD JUST--AWWW!
WHO AM I KIDDING?
I-IS AT FOR AL--?!?
OH MY!
ZZZ
ZZZZ
ZZ
S-SOMEONE CALL SECURITY!
OH, JEEZ!
GET DOWN!

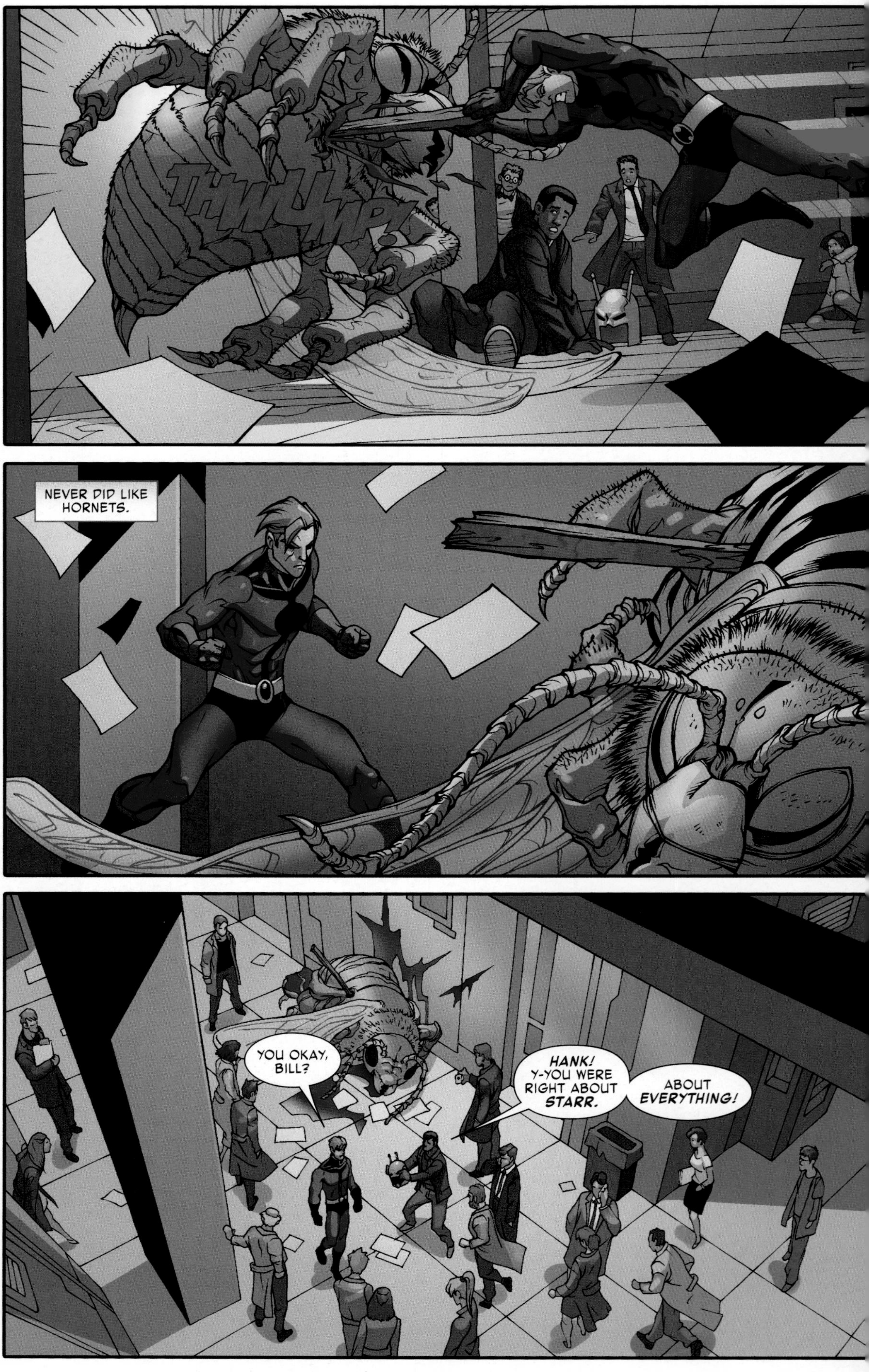
THWUMP!
NEVER DID LIKE HORNETS.
YOU OKAY, BILL?
HANK! Y-YOU WERE RIGHT ABOUT STARR.
ABOUT EVERYTHING!

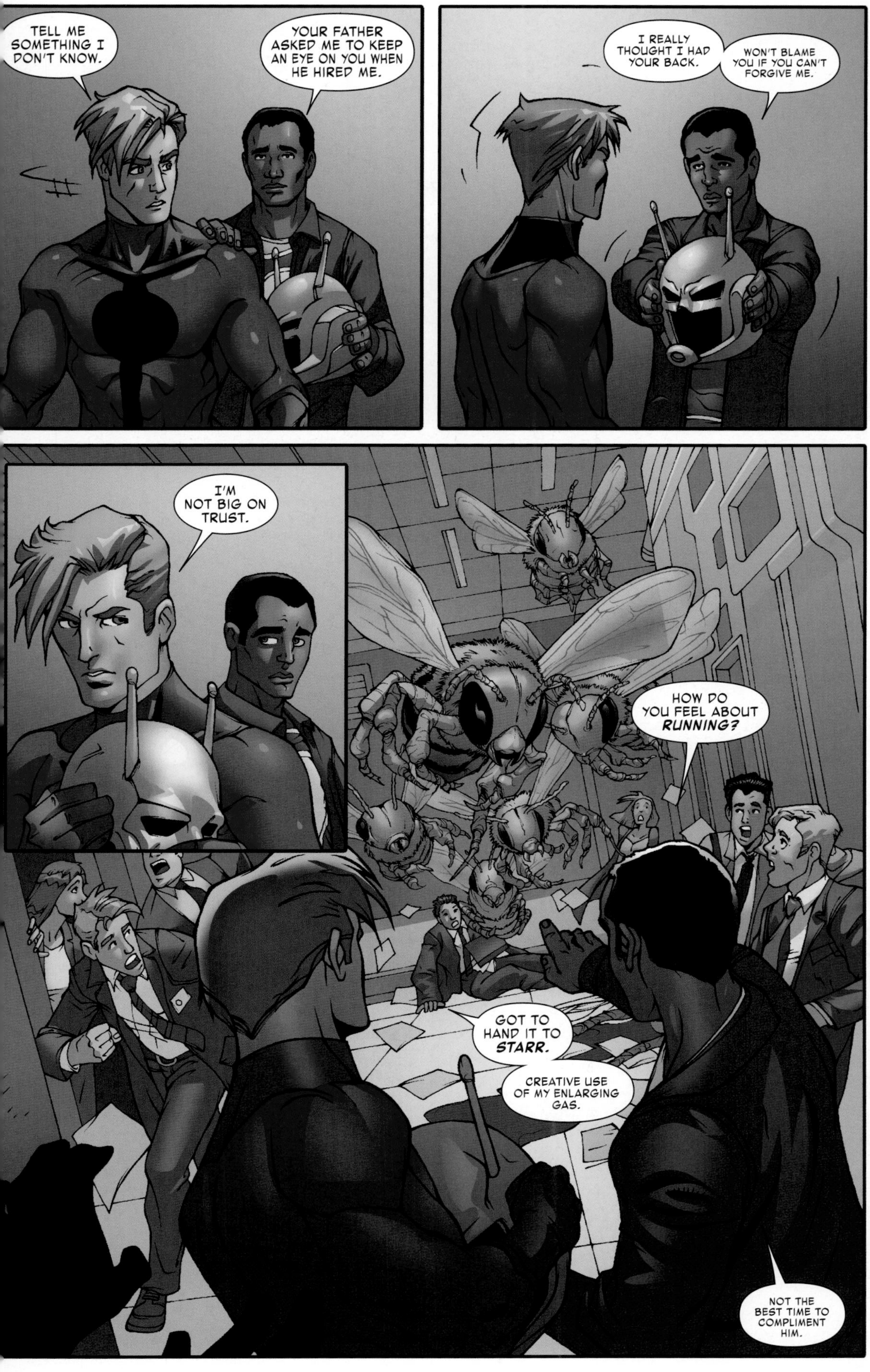
TELL ME SOMETHING I DON'T KNOW.
YOUR FATHER ASKED ME TO KEEP AN EYE ON YOU WHEN HE HIRED ME.
I REALLY THOUGHT I HAD YOUR BACK.
WON'T BLAME YOU IF YOU CAN'T FORGIVE ME.
I'M NOT BIG ON TRUST.
HOW DO YOU FEEL ABOUT RUNNING?
GOT TO HAND IT TO STARR.
CREATIVE USE OF MY ENLARGING GAS.
NOT THE BEST TIME TO COMPLIMENT HIM.

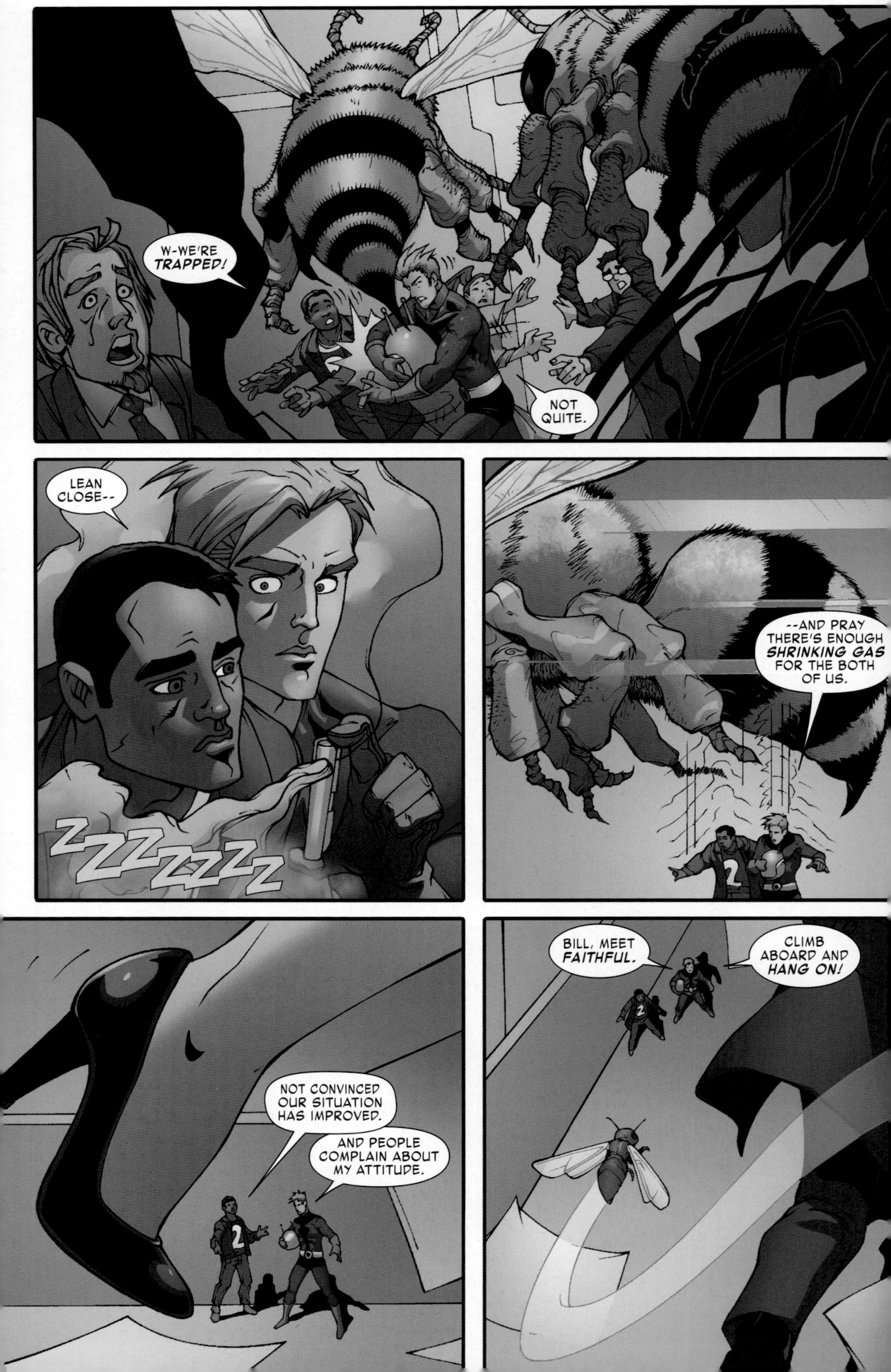
W-WE'RE TRAPPED!
NOT QUITE.
LEAN CLOSE--
ZZZZZZZZ
--AND PRAY THERE'S ENOUGH SHRINKING GAS FOR THE BOTH OF US.
NOT CONVINCED OUR SITUATION HAS IMPROVED.
AND PEOPLE COMPLAIN ABOUT MY ATTITUDE.
BILL, MEET FAITHFUL.
CLIMB ABOARD AND HANG ON!

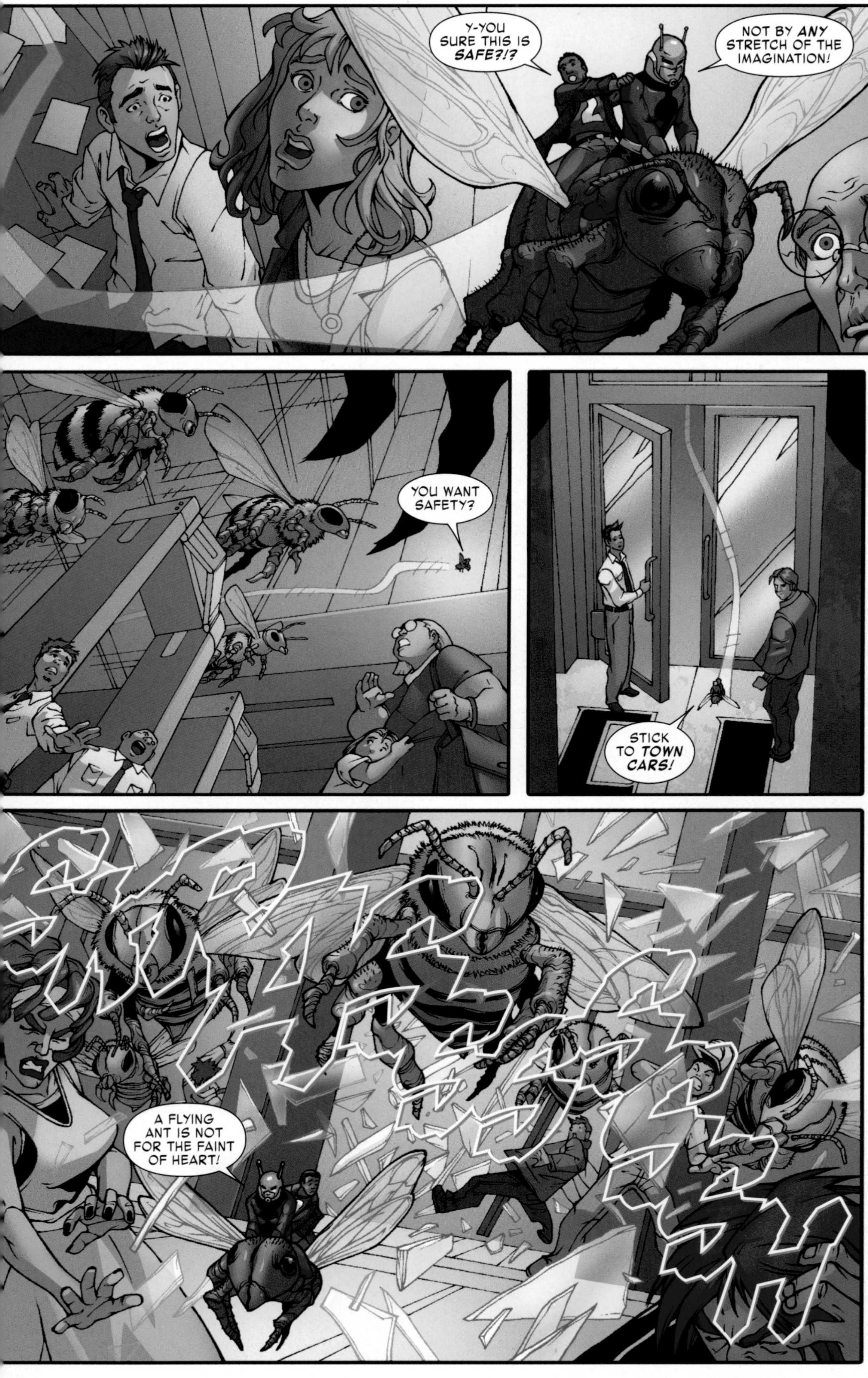

Y-YOU SURE THIS IS SAFE?!?
NOT BY ANY STRETCH OF THE IMAGINATION!
YOU WANT SAFETY?
STICK TO TOWN CARS!
A FLYING ANT IS NOT FOR THE FAINT OF HEART!

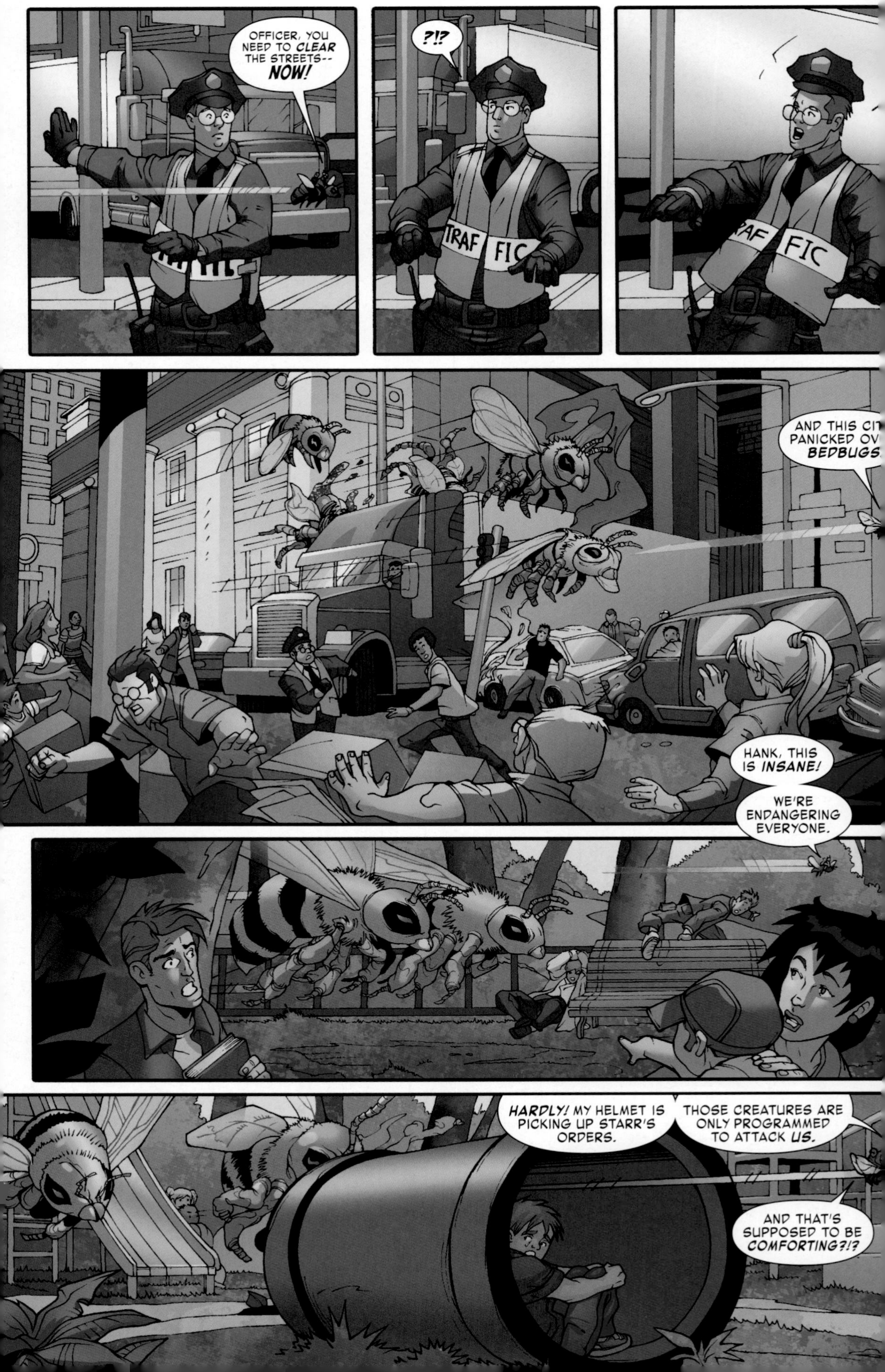

OFFICER, YOU NEED TO CLEAR THE STREETS-- NOW!
?!?
TRAF FIC
TRAF FIC
AND THIS CIT PANICKED OV BEDBUGS.
HANK, THIS IS INSANE!
WE'RE ENDANGERING EVERYONE.
HARDLY! MY HELMET IS PICKING UP STARR'S ORDERS.
THOSE CREATURES ARE ONLY PROGRAMMED TO ATTACK US.
AND THAT'S SUPPOSED TO BE COMFORTING?!?

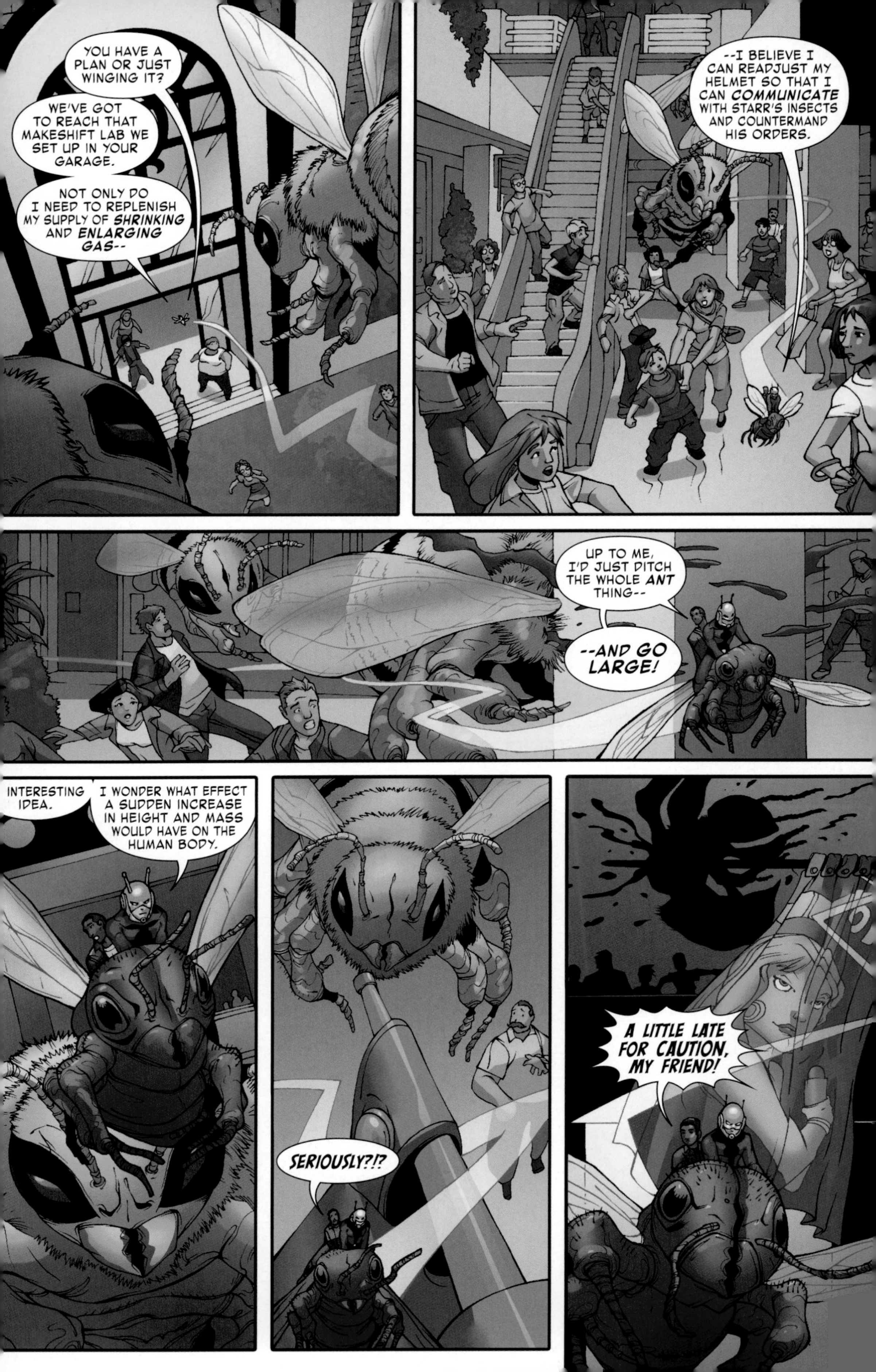
YOU HAVE A PLAN OR JUST WINGING IT?
WE'VE GOT TO REACH THAT MAKESHIFT LAB WE SET UP IN YOUR GARAGE.
NOT ONLY DO I NEED TO REPLENISH MY SUPPLY OF SHRINKING AND ENLARGING GAS--
--I BELIEVE I CAN READJUST MY HELMET SO THAT I CAN COMMUNICATE WITH STARR'S INSECTS AND COUNTERMAND HIS ORDERS.
UP TO ME, I'D JUST DITCH THE WHOLE ANT THING--
--AND GO LARGE!
INTERESTING IDEA.
I WONDER WHAT EFFECT A SUDDEN INCREASE IN HEIGHT AND MASS WOULD HAVE ON THE HUMAN BODY.
SERIOUSLY?!?
A LITTLE LATE FOR CAUTION, MY FRIEND!

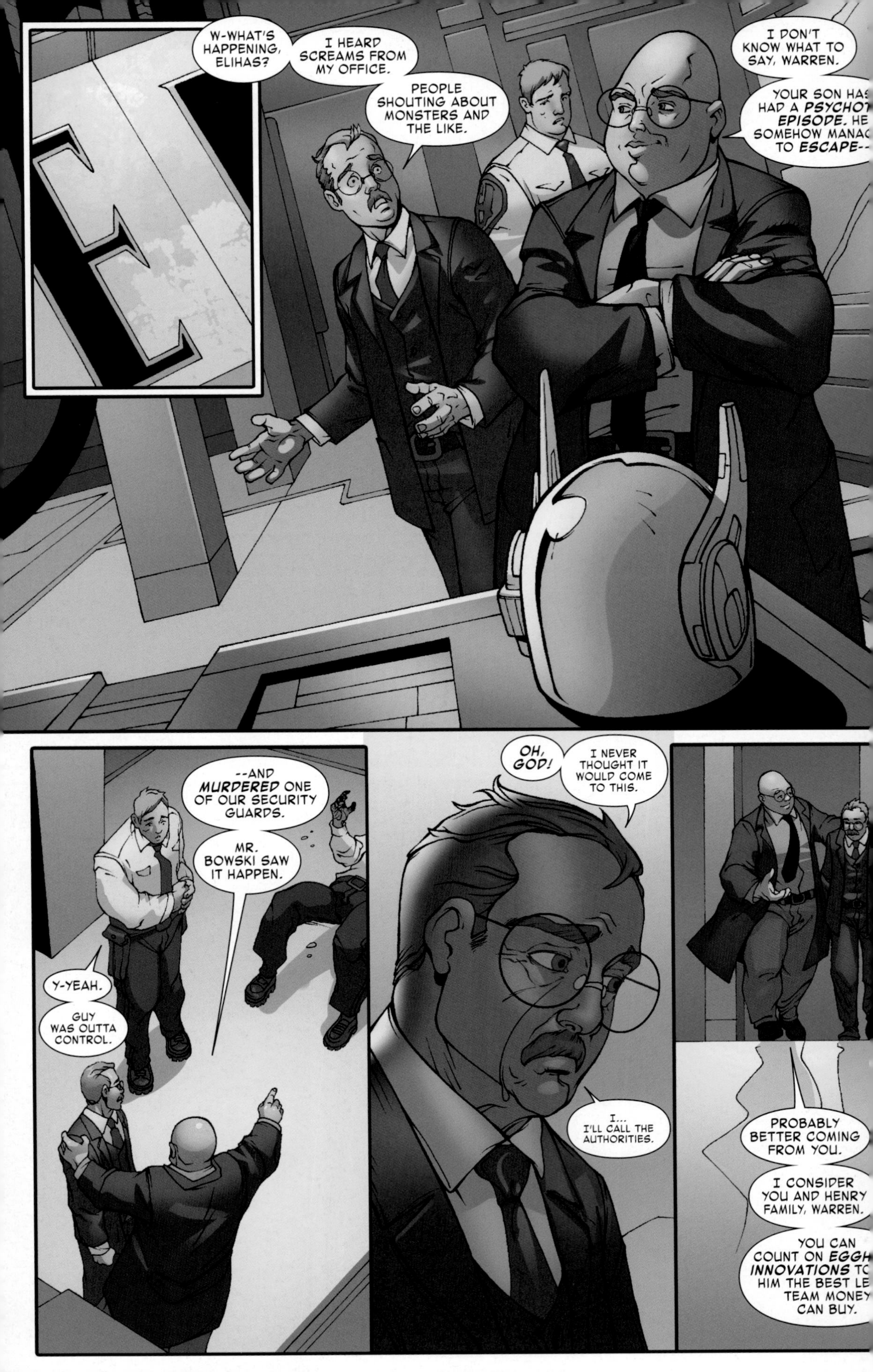
W-WHAT'S HAPPENING, ELIHAS?
I HEARD SCREAMS FROM MY OFFICE.
PEOPLE SHOUTING ABOUT MONSTERS AND THE LIKE.
I DON'T KNOW WHAT TO SAY, WARREN.
YOUR SON HAS HAD A PSYCHOT EPISODE. HE SOMEHOW MANAG TO ESCAPE--
--AND MURDERED ONE OF OUR SECURITY GUARDS.
MR. BOWSKI SAW IT HAPPEN.
Y-YEAH.
GUY WAS OUTTA CONTROL.
OH, GOD!
I NEVER THOUGHT IT WOULD COME TO THIS.
I... I'LL CALL THE AUTHORITIES.
PROBABLY BETTER COMING FROM YOU.
I CONSIDER YOU AND HENRY FAMILY, WARREN.
YOU CAN COUNT ON EGGH INNOVATIONS TO HIM THE BEST LE TEAM MONEY CAN BUY.

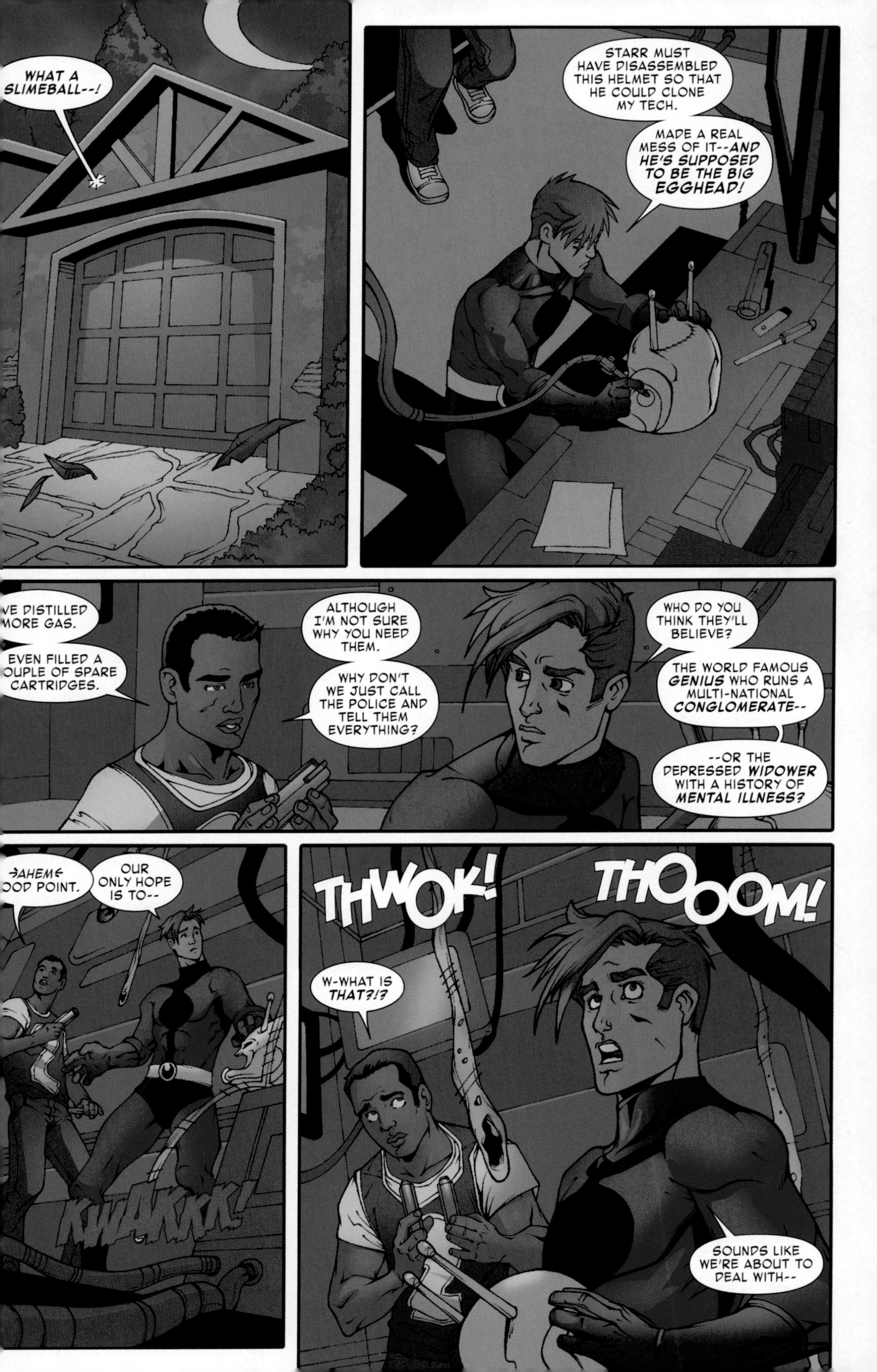
WHAT A SLIMEBALL--!
STARR MUST HAVE DISASSEMBLED THIS HELMET SO THAT HE COULD CLONE MY TECH.
MADE A REAL MESS OF IT--AND HE'S SUPPOSED TO BE THE BIG EGGHEAD!
VE DISTILLED MORE GAS.
EVEN FILLED A OUPLE OF SPARE CARTRIDGES.
ALTHOUGH I'M NOT SURE WHY YOU NEED THEM.
WHY DON'T WE JUST CALL THE POLICE AND TELL THEM EVERYTHING?
WHO DO YOU THINK THEY'LL BELIEVE?
THE WORLD FAMOUS GENIUS WHO RUNS A MULTI-NATIONAL CONGLOMERATE--
--OR THE DEPRESSED WIDOWER WITH A HISTORY OF MENTAL ILLNESS?
→AHEM← OOD POINT.
OUR ONLY HOPE IS TO--
KWAKKK!
THWOK!
THOOOM!
W-WHAT IS THAT?!?
SOUNDS LIKE WE'RE ABOUT TO DEAL WITH--

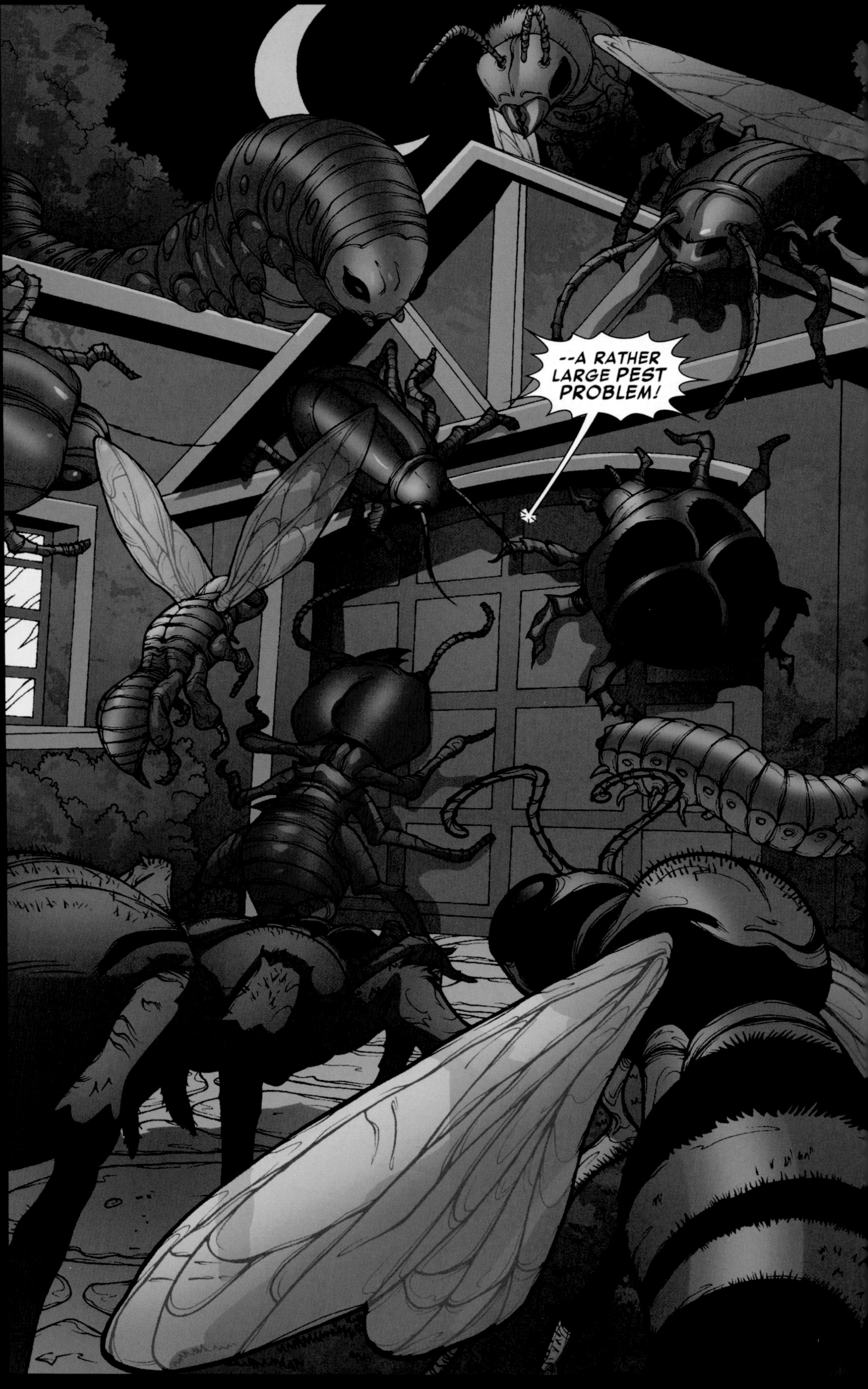
--A RATHER LARGE PEST PROBLEM!

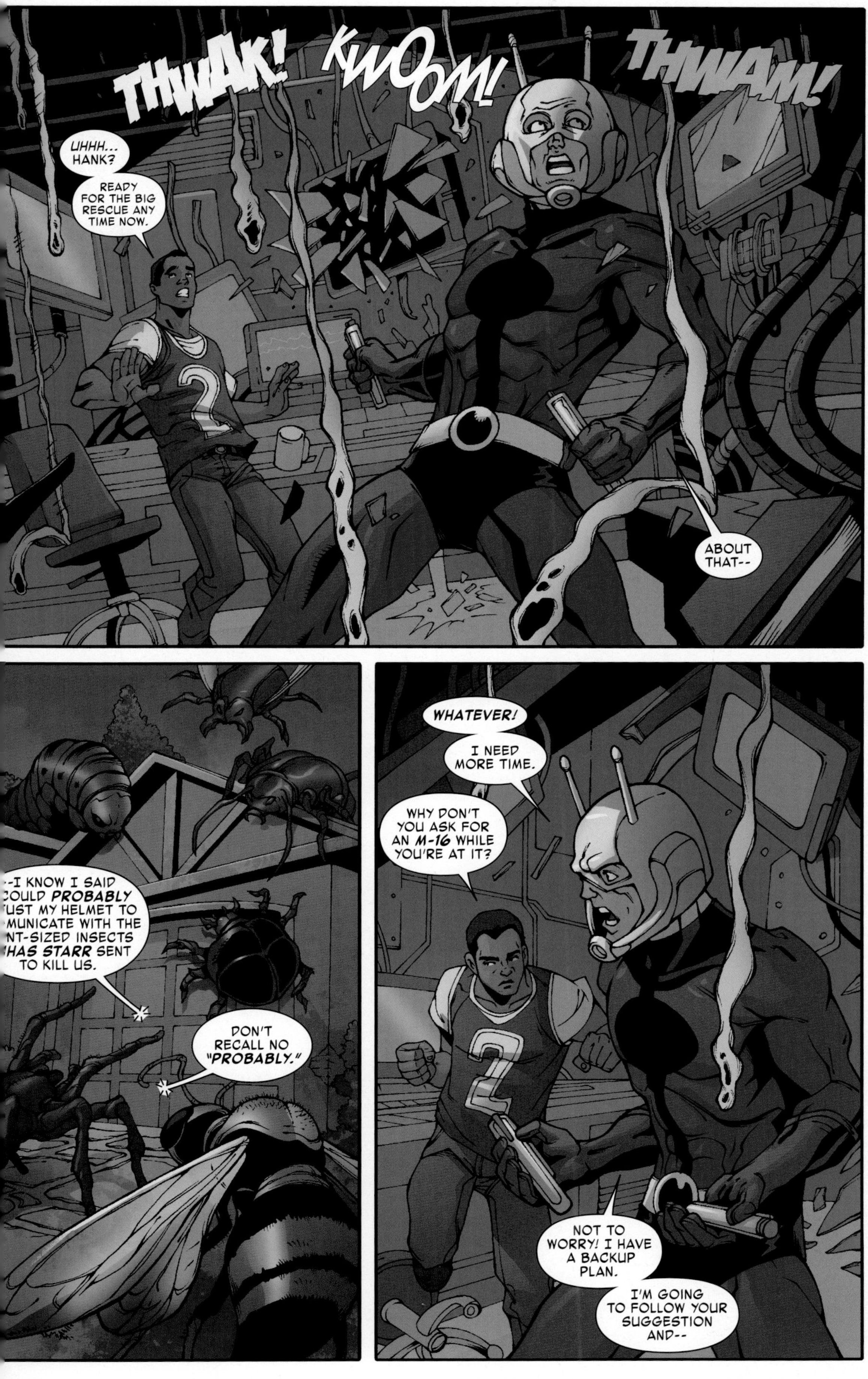
THWAK! KWOOOM! THWAM!
UHHH... HANK?
READY FOR THE BIG RESCUE ANY TIME NOW.
ABOUT THAT--
--I KNOW I SAID COULD PROBABLY UST MY HELMET TO MUNICATE WITH THE NT-SIZED INSECTS HAS STARR SENT TO KILL US.
DON'T RECALL NO "PROBABLY."
WHATEVER!
I NEED MORE TIME.
WHY DON'T YOU ASK FOR AN M-16 WHILE YOU'RE AT IT?
NOT TO WORRY! I HAVE A BACKUP PLAN.
I'M GOING TO FOLLOW YOUR SUGGESTION AND--

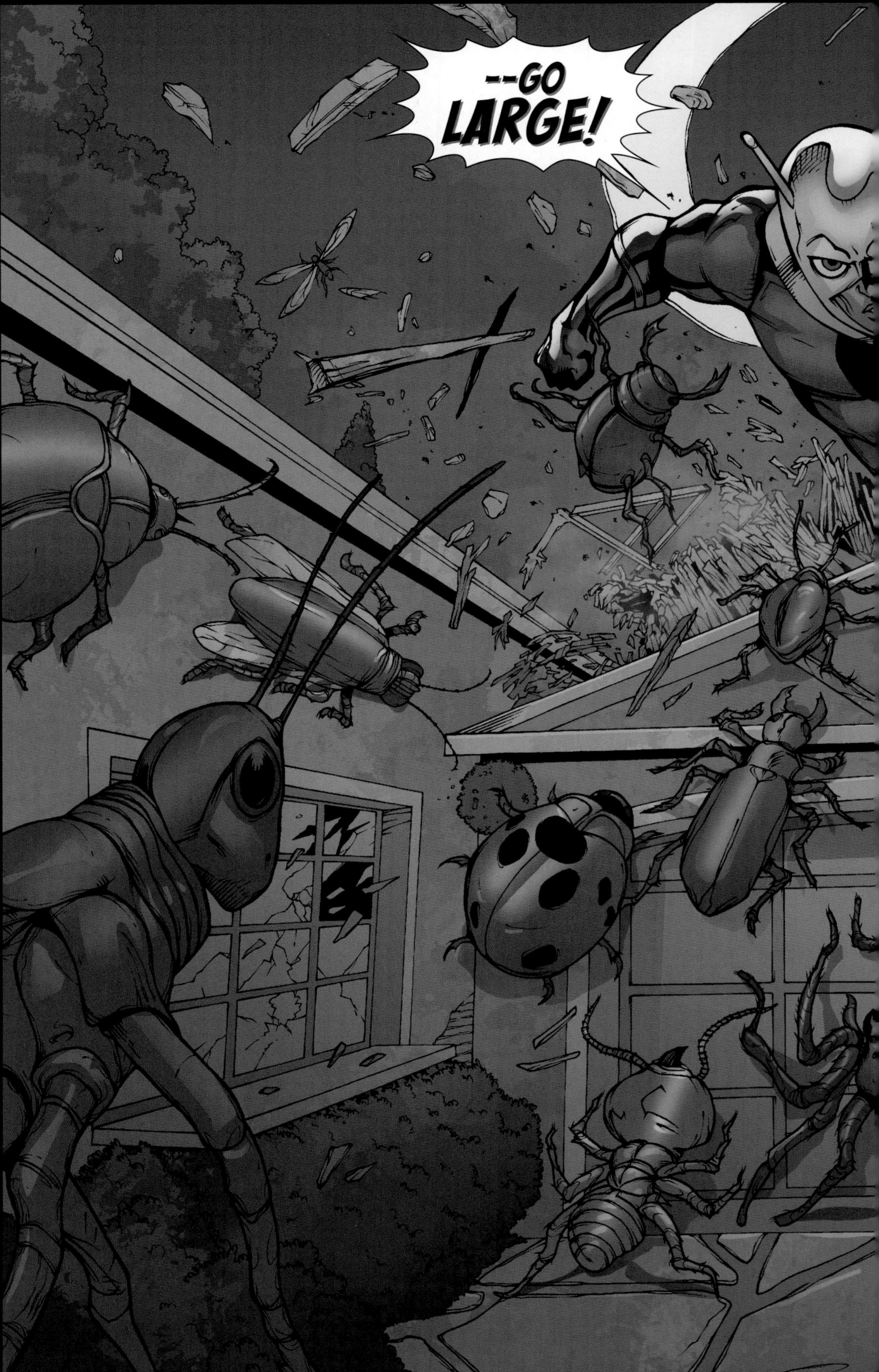
--GO LARGE!

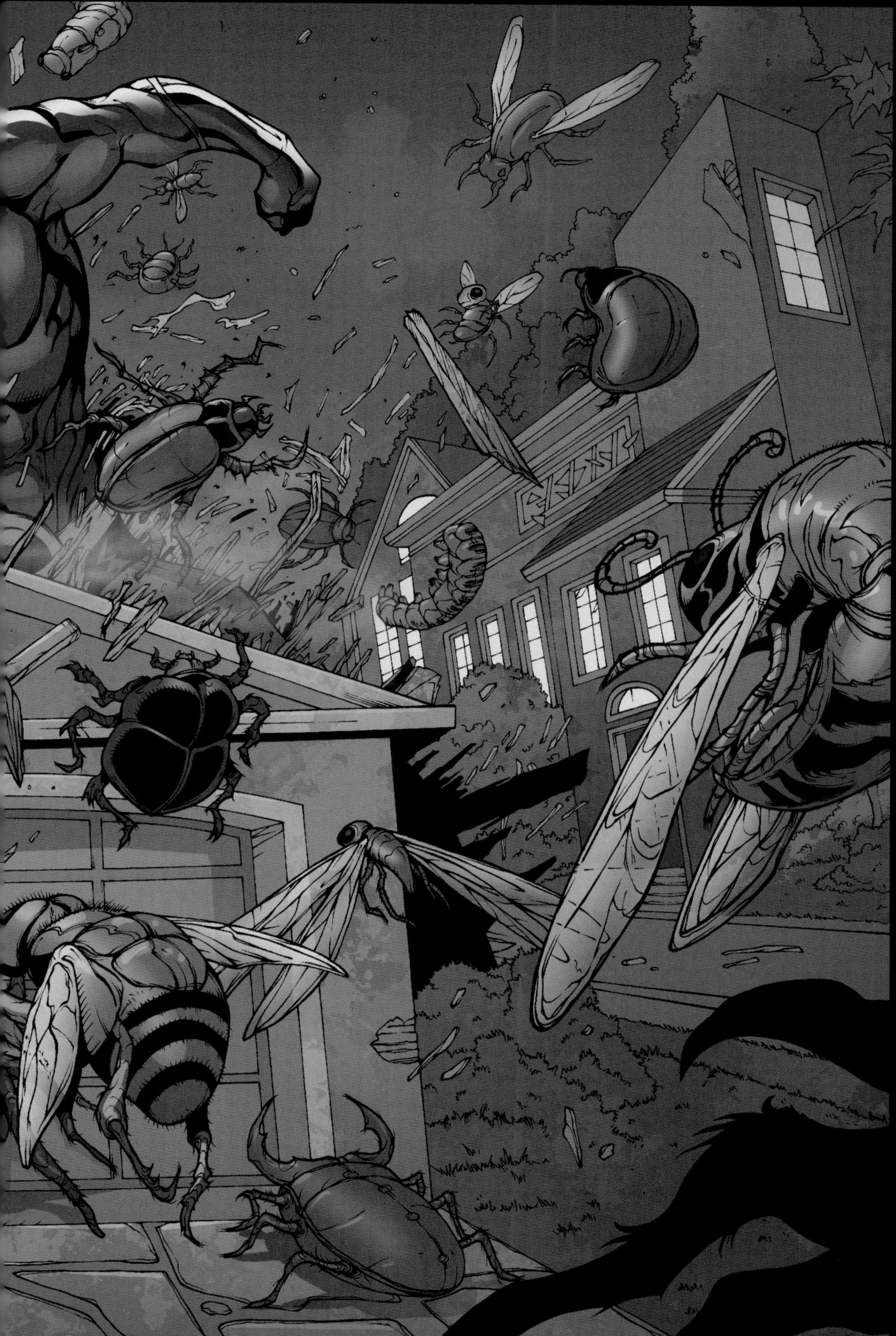

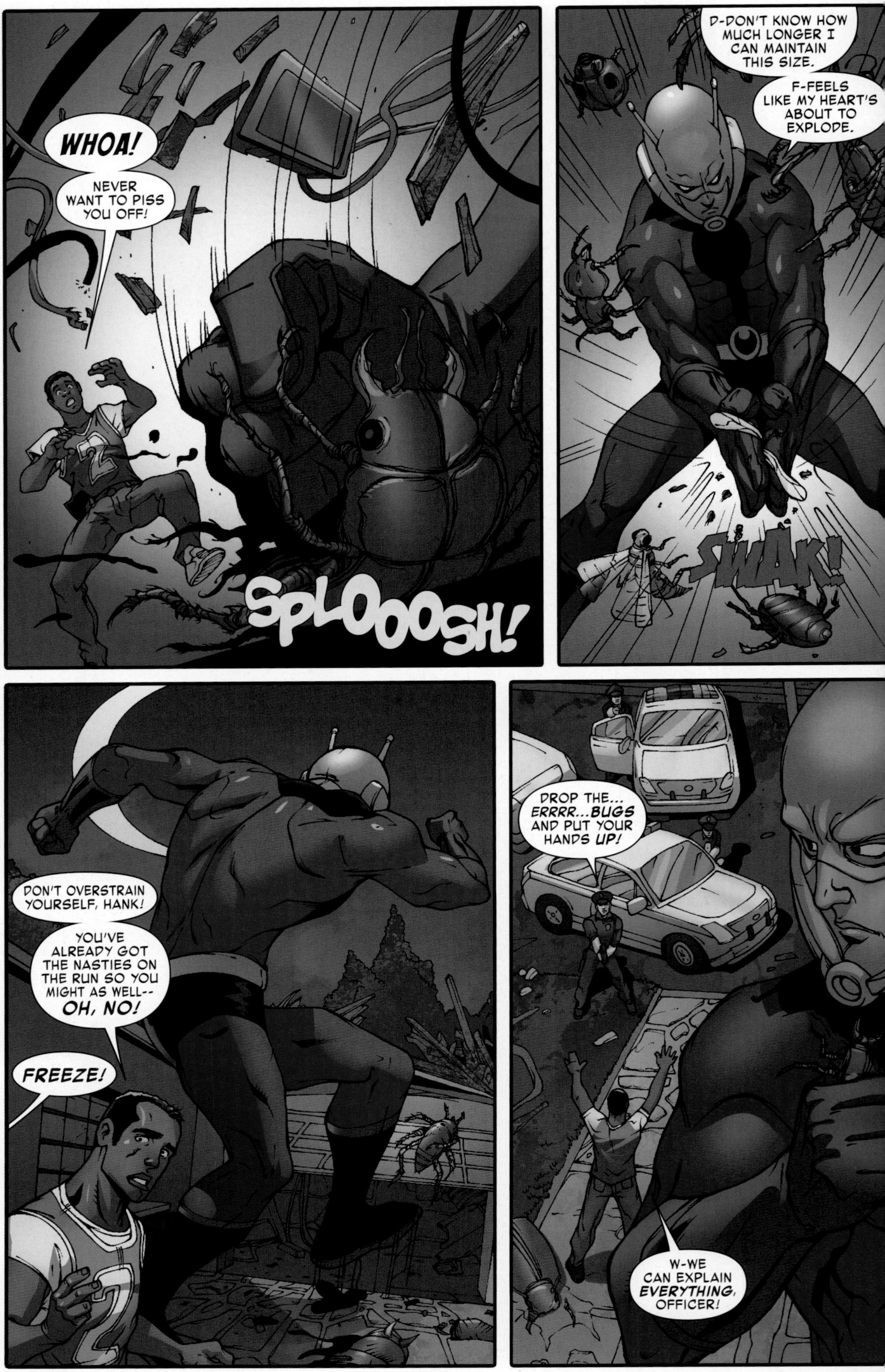

WHOA!
NEVER WANT TO PISS YOU OFF!
SPLOOOOSH!
D-DON'T KNOW HOW MUCH LONGER I CAN MAINTAIN THIS SIZE.
F-FEELS LIKE MY HEART'S ABOUT TO EXPLODE.
SWAK!
DON'T OVERSTRAIN YOURSELF, HANK!
YOU'VE ALREADY GOT THE NASTIES ON THE RUN SO YOU MIGHT AS WELL-- OH, NO!
FREEZE!
DROP THE... ERRRR...BUGS AND PUT YOUR HANDS UP!
W-WE CAN EXPLAIN EVERYTHING, OFFICER!

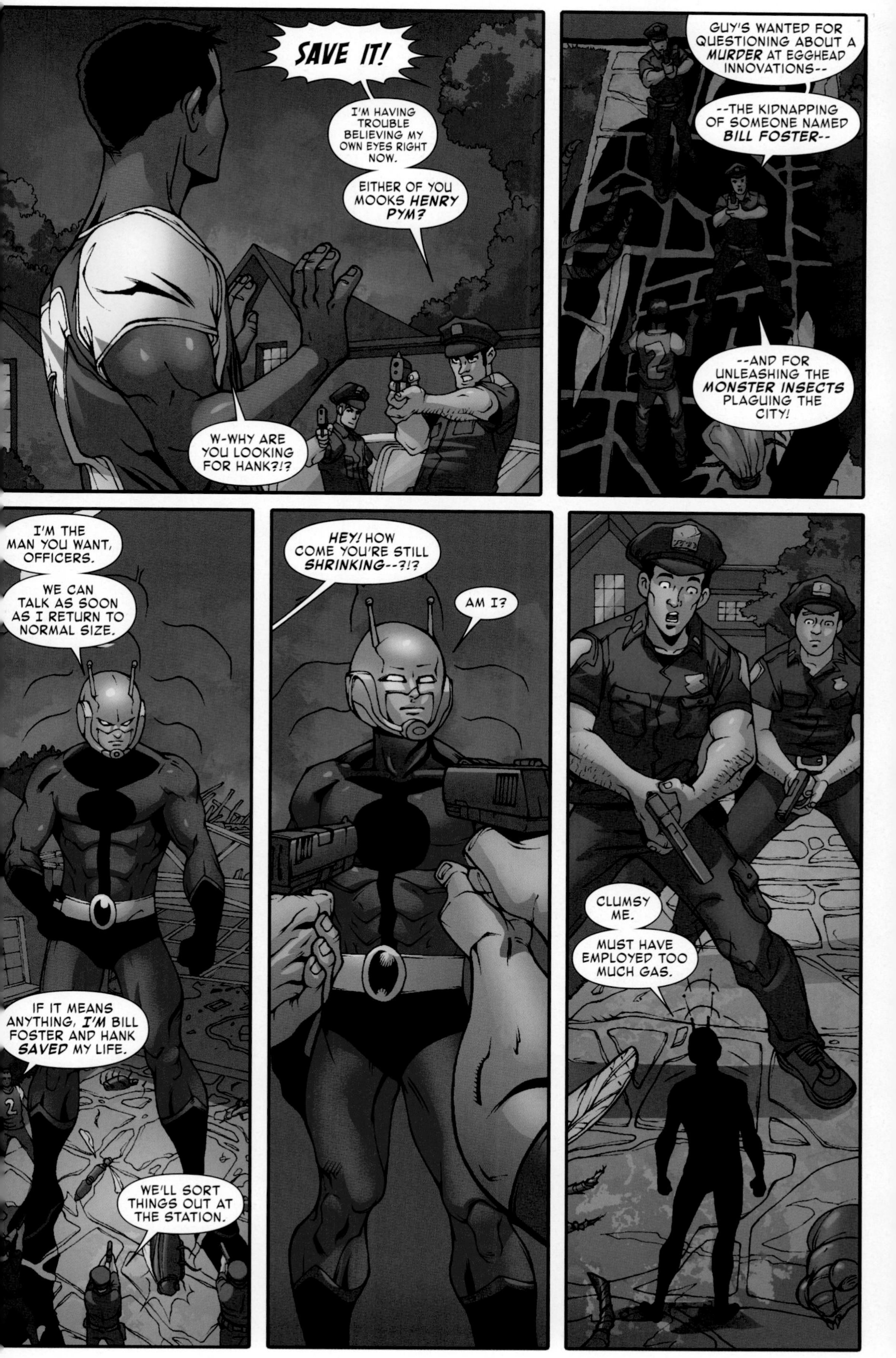
SAVE IT!
I'M HAVING TROUBLE BELIEVING MY OWN EYES RIGHT NOW.
EITHER OF YOU MOOKS HENRY PYM?
W-WHY ARE YOU LOOKING FOR HANK?!?
GUY'S WANTED FOR QUESTIONING ABOUT A MURDER AT EGGHEAD INNOVATIONS--
--THE KIDNAPPING OF SOMEONE NAMED BILL FOSTER--
--AND FOR UNLEASHING THE MONSTER INSECTS PLAGUING THE CITY!
I'M THE MAN YOU WANT, OFFICERS.
WE CAN TALK AS SOON AS I RETURN TO NORMAL SIZE.
IF IT MEANS ANYTHING, I'M BILL FOSTER AND HANK SAVED MY LIFE.
WE'LL SORT THINGS OUT AT THE STATION.
HEY! HOW COME YOU'RE STILL SHRINKING--?!?
AM I?
CLUMSY ME.
MUST HAVE EMPLOYED TOO MUCH GAS.

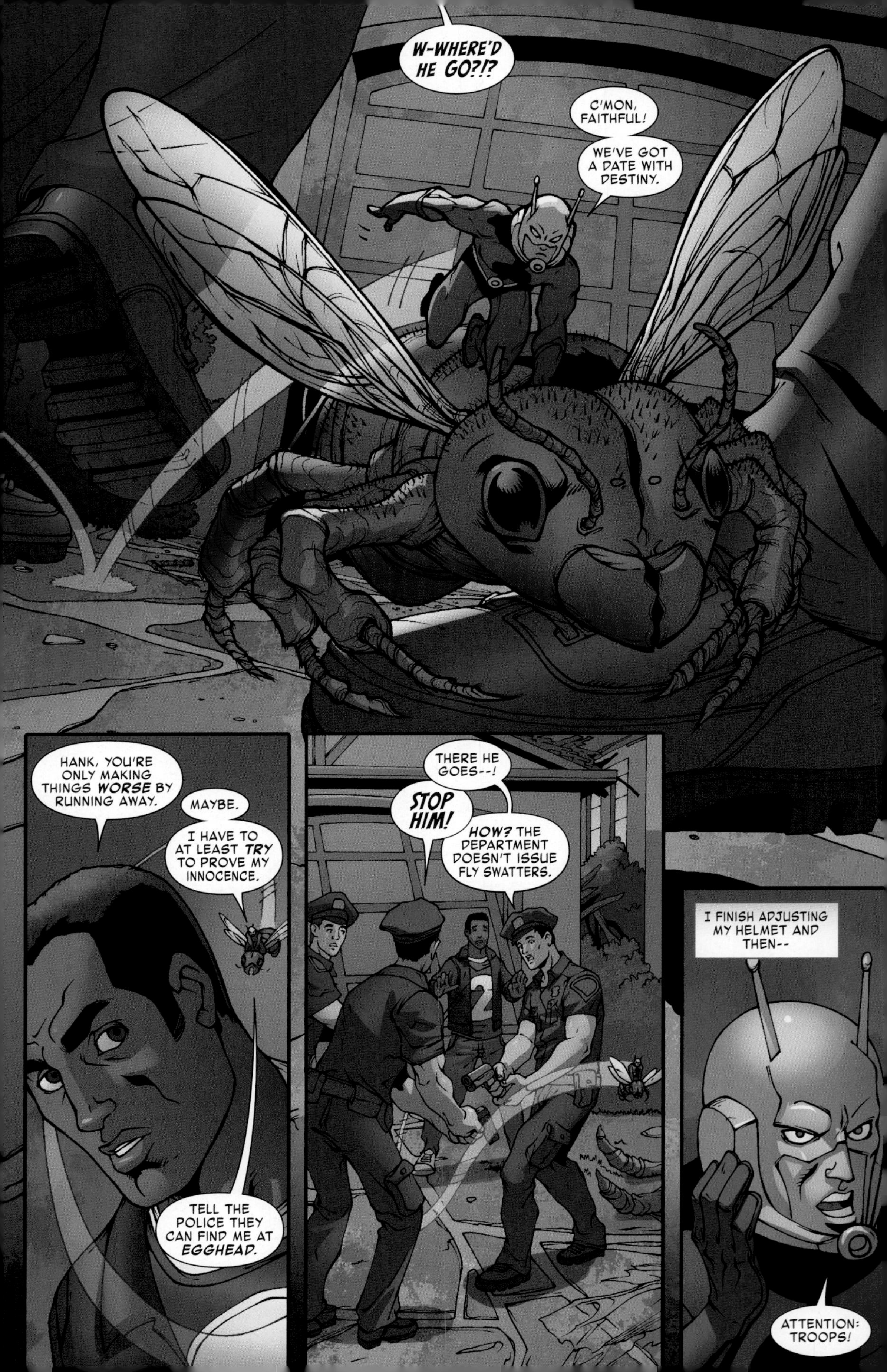
W-WHERE'D HE GO?!?
C'MON, FAITHFUL!
WE'VE GOT A DATE WITH DESTINY.
HANK, YOU'RE ONLY MAKING THINGS WORSE BY RUNNING AWAY.
MAYBE.
I HAVE TO AT LEAST TRY TO PROVE MY INNOCENCE.
TELL THE POLICE THEY CAN FIND ME AT EGGHEAD.
THERE HE GOES--!
STOP HIM!
HOW? THE DEPARTMENT DOESN'T ISSUE FLY SWATTERS.
I FINISH ADJUSTING MY HELMET AND THEN--
ATTENTION: TROOPS!

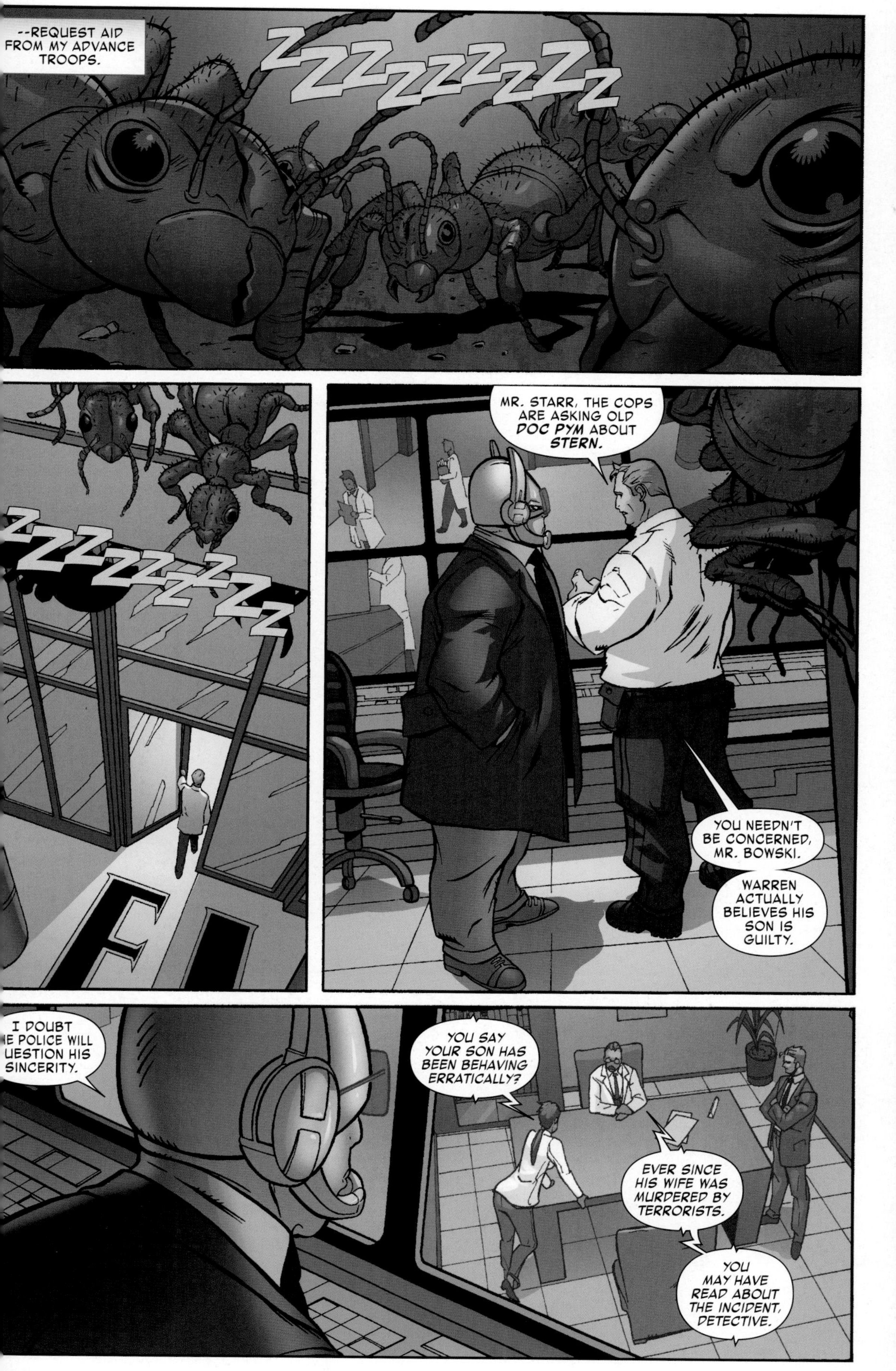
--REQUEST AID FROM MY ADVANCE TROOPS.
ZZZZZZZZZZZ
ZZZZZZZZZZ
MR. STARR, THE COPS ARE ASKING OLD DOC PYM ABOUT STERN.
YOU NEEDN'T BE CONCERNED, MR. BOWSKI.
WARREN ACTUALLY BELIEVES HIS SON IS GUILTY.
I DOUBT E POLICE WILL UESTION HIS SINCERITY.
YOU SAY YOUR SON HAS BEEN BEHAVING ERRATICALLY?
EVER SINCE HIS WIFE WAS MURDERED BY TERRORISTS.
YOU MAY HAVE READ ABOUT THE INCIDENT, DETECTIVE.

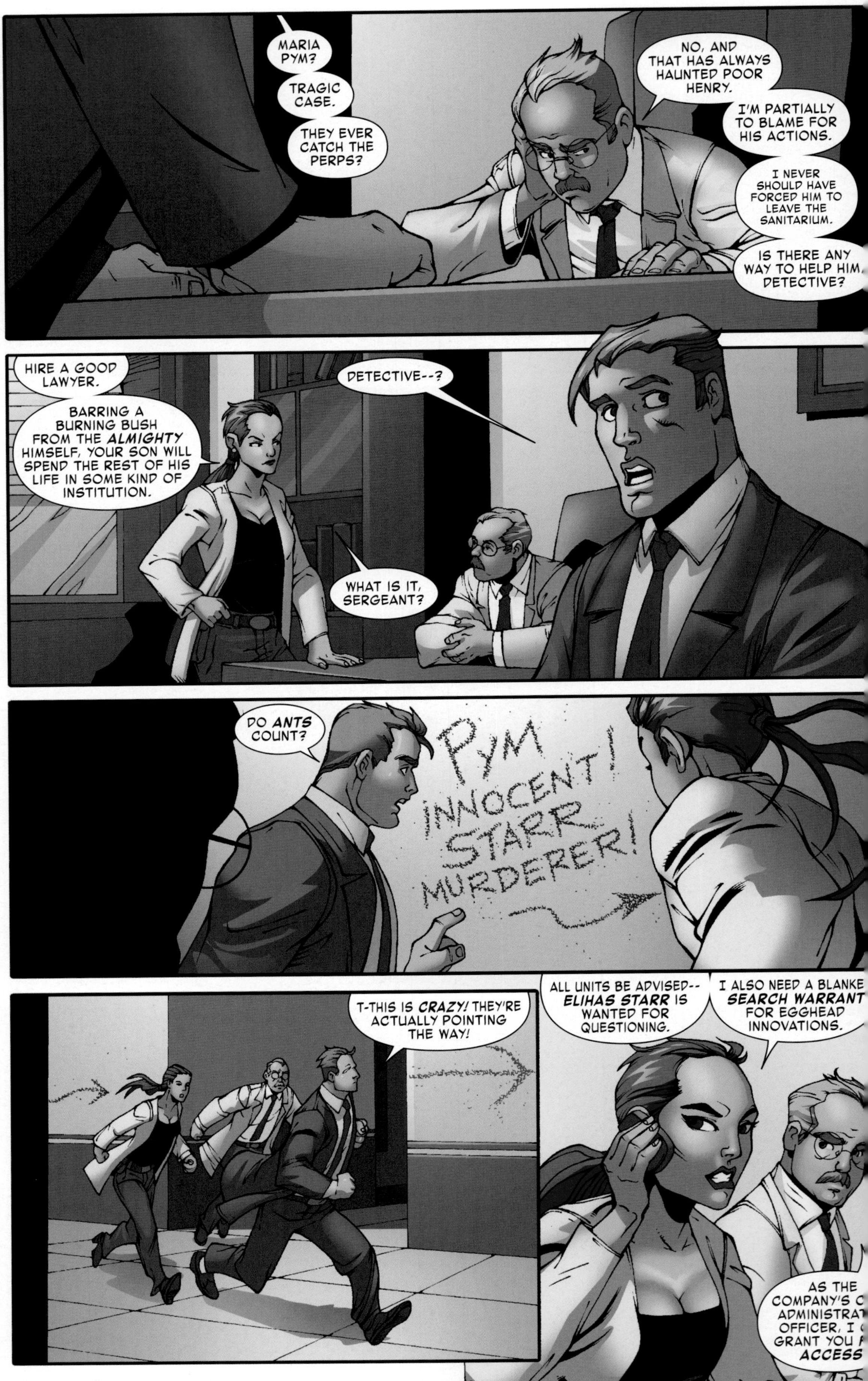
MARIA PYM?
TRAGIC CASE.
THEY EVER CATCH THE PERPS?
NO, AND THAT HAS ALWAYS HAUNTED POOR HENRY.
I'M PARTIALLY TO BLAME FOR HIS ACTIONS.
I NEVER SHOULD HAVE FORCED HIM TO LEAVE THE SANITARIUM.
IS THERE ANY WAY TO HELP HIM, DETECTIVE?
HIRE A GOOD LAWYER.
BARRING A BURNING BUSH FROM THE ALMIGHTY HIMSELF, YOUR SON WILL SPEND THE REST OF HIS LIFE IN SOME KIND OF INSTITUTION.
DETECTIVE--?
WHAT IS IT, SERGEANT?
DO ANTS COUNT?
PYM INNOCENT! STARR MURDERER!
T-THIS IS CRAZY! THEY'RE ACTUALLY POINTING THE WAY!
ALL UNITS BE ADVISED-- ELIHAS STARR IS WANTED FOR QUESTIONING.
I ALSO NEED A BLANKE SEARCH WARRANT FOR EGGHEAD INNOVATIONS.
AS THE COMPANY'S C ADMINISTRAT OFFICER, I GRANT YOU ACCESS

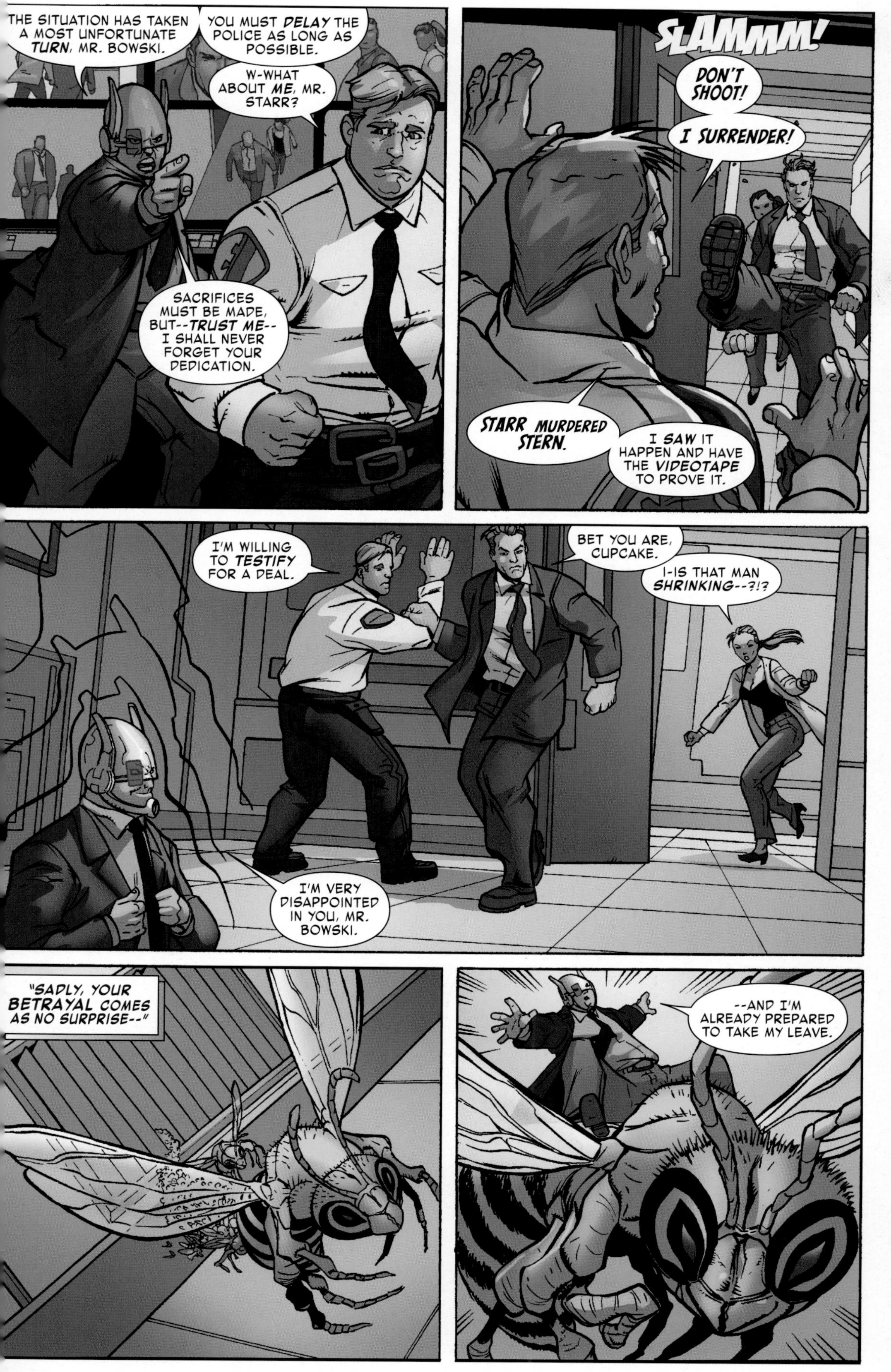
THE SITUATION HAS TAKEN A MOST UNFORTUNATE TURN, MR. BOWSKI.
YOU MUST DELAY THE POLICE AS LONG AS POSSIBLE.
W-WHAT ABOUT ME, MR. STARR?
SACRIFICES MUST BE MADE, BUT--TRUST ME--I SHALL NEVER FORGET YOUR DEDICATION.
SLAMMM!
DON'T SHOOT!
I SURRENDER!
STARR MURDERED STERN.
I SAW IT HAPPEN AND HAVE THE VIDEOTAPE TO PROVE IT.
I'M WILLING TO TESTIFY FOR A DEAL.
BET YOU ARE, CUPCAKE.
I-IS THAT MAN SHRINKING--?!?
I'M VERY DISAPPOINTED IN YOU, MR. BOWSKI.
"SADLY, YOUR BETRAYAL COMES AS NO SURPRISE--"
--AND I'M ALREADY PREPARED TO TAKE MY LEAVE.

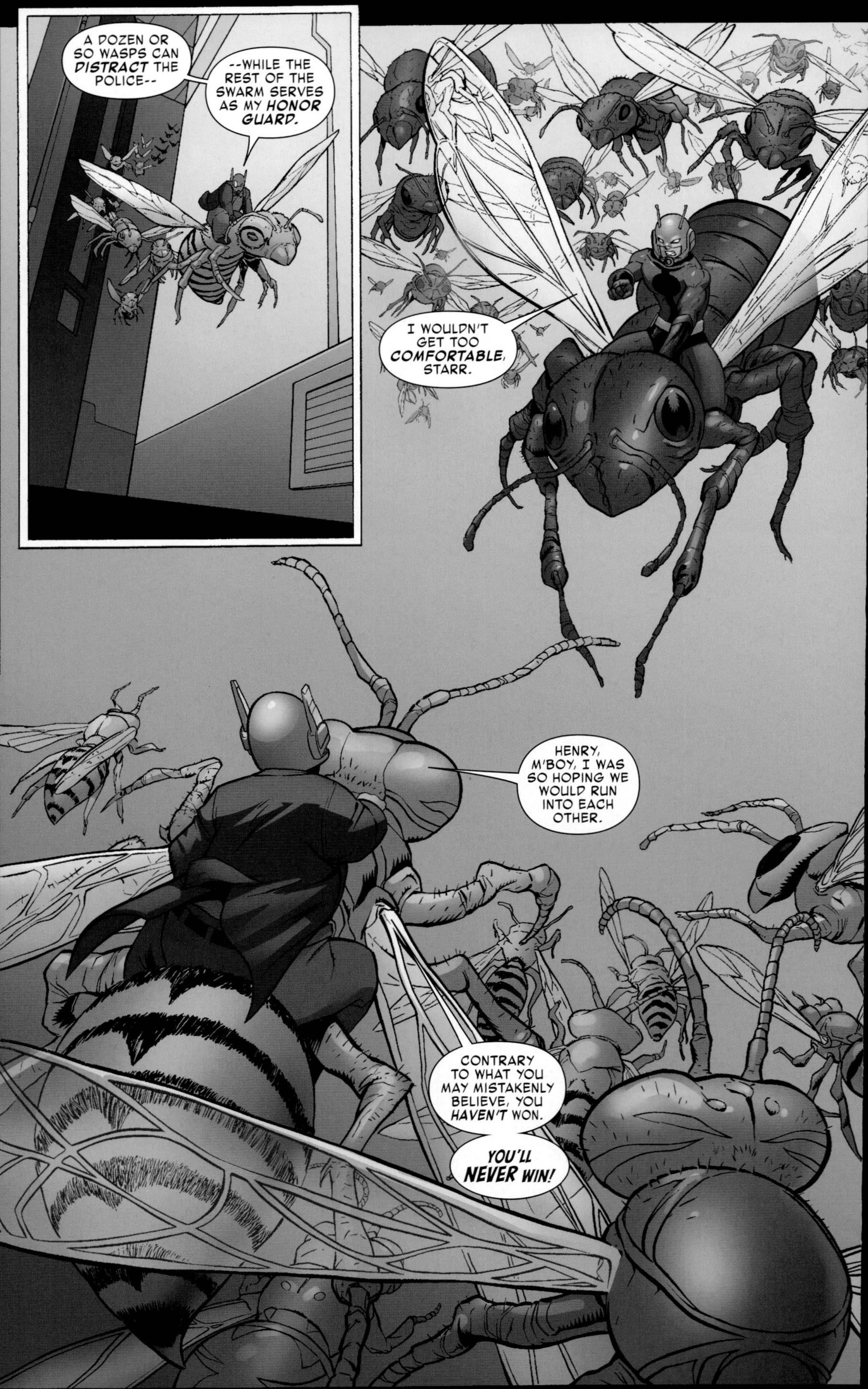
A DOZEN OR SO WASPS CAN DISTRACT THE POLICE--
--WHILE THE REST OF THE SWARM SERVES AS MY HONOR GUARD.
I WOULDN'T GET TOO COMFORTABLE, STARR.
HENRY, M'BOY, I WAS SO HOPING WE WOULD RUN INTO EACH OTHER.
CONTRARY TO WHAT YOU MAY MISTAKENLY BELIEVE, YOU HAVEN'T WON.
YOU'LL NEVER WIN!

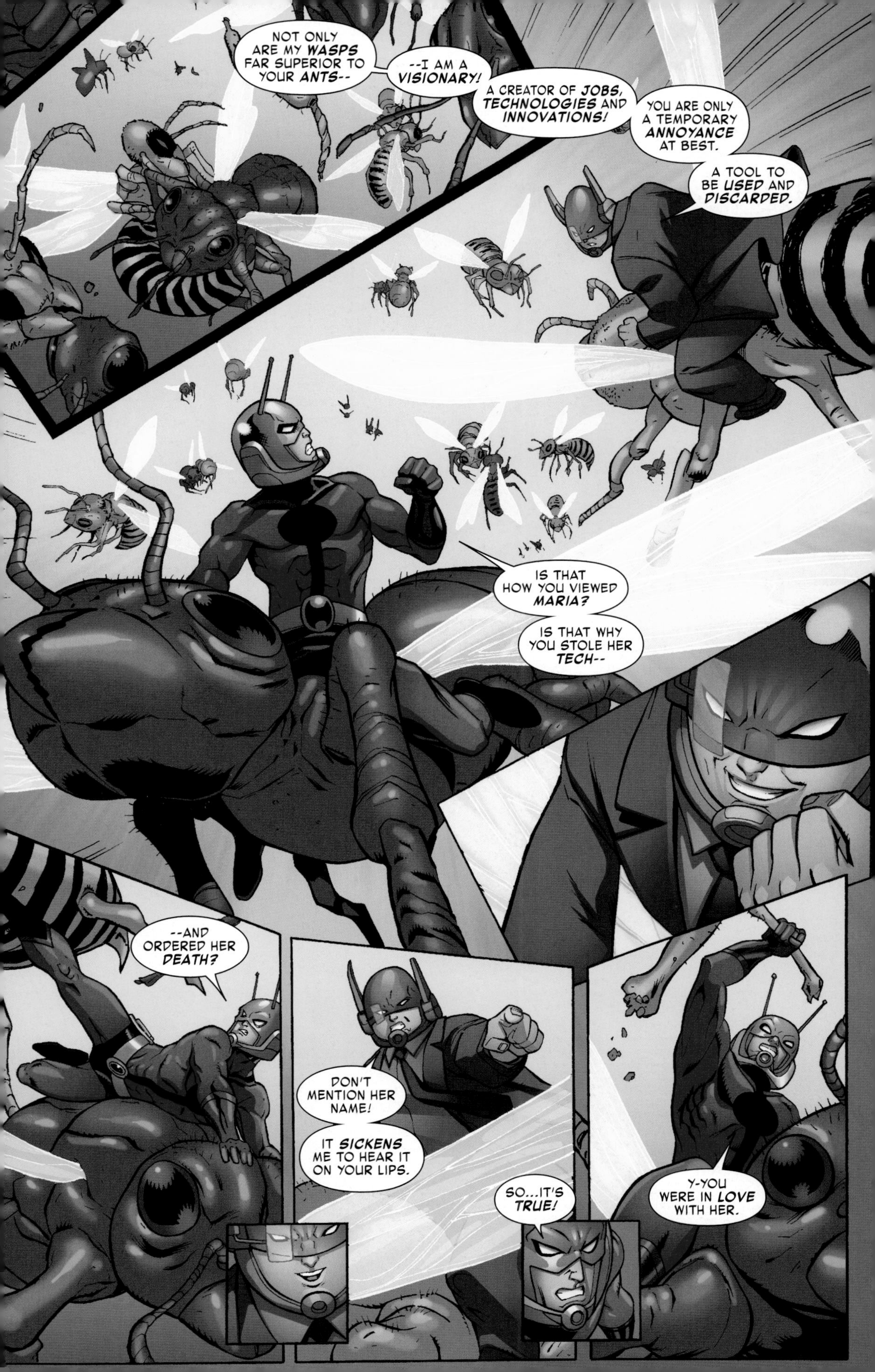
NOT ONLY ARE MY WASPS FAR SUPERIOR TO YOUR ANTS--
--I AM A VISIONARY!
A CREATOR OF JOBS, TECHNOLOGIES AND INNOVATIONS!
YOU ARE ONLY A TEMPORARY ANNOYANCE AT BEST.
A TOOL TO BE USED AND DISCARDED.
IS THAT HOW YOU VIEWED MARIA?
IS THAT WHY YOU STOLE HER TECH--
--AND ORDERED HER DEATH?
DON'T MENTION HER NAME!
IT SICKENS ME TO HEAR IT ON YOUR LIPS.
SO...IT'S TRUE!
Y-YOU WERE IN LOVE WITH HER.

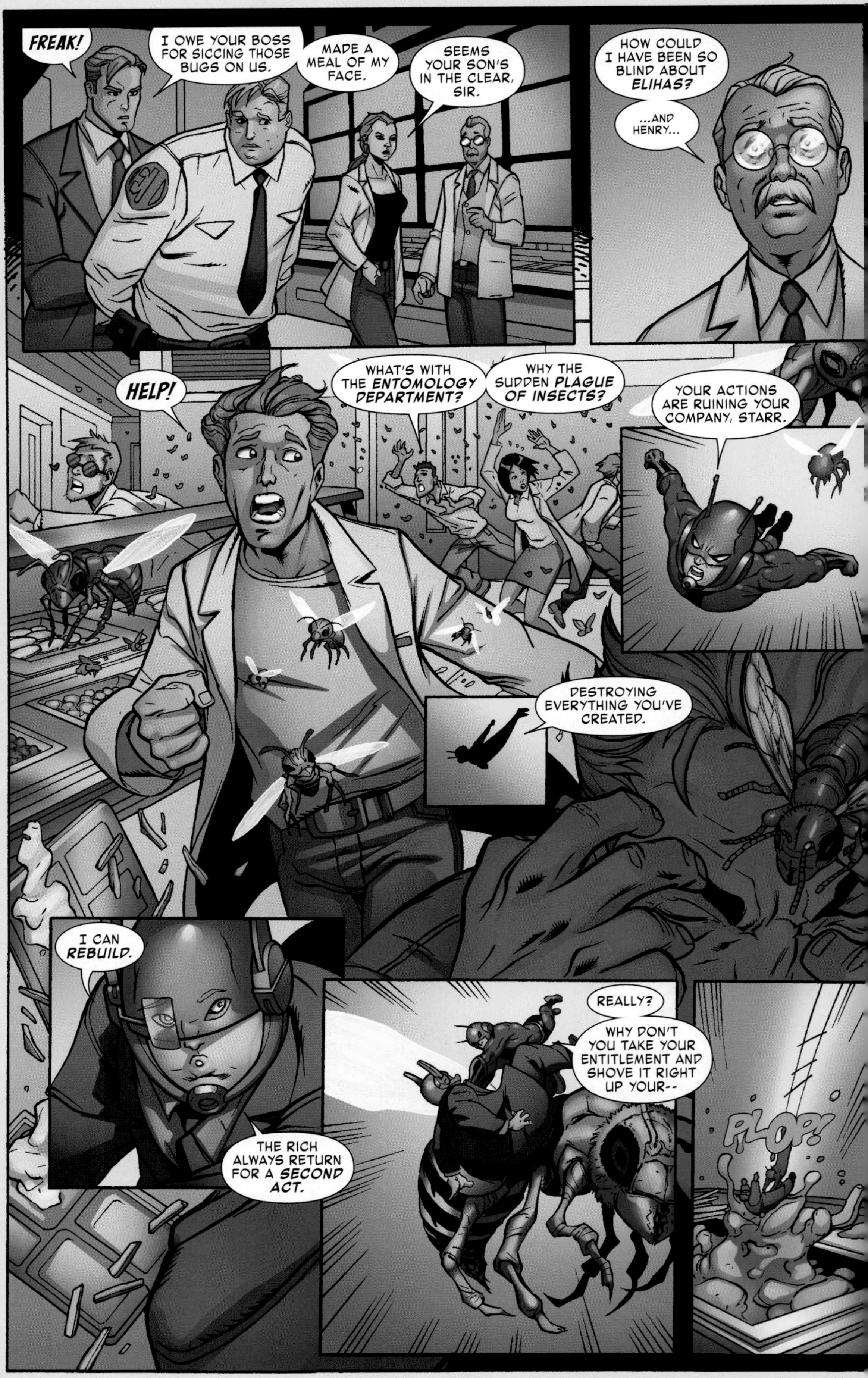
FREAK!
I OWE YOUR BOSS FOR SICCING THOSE BUGS ON US.
MADE A MEAL OF MY FACE.
SEEMS YOUR SON'S IN THE CLEAR, SIR.
HOW COULD I HAVE BEEN SO BLIND ABOUT ELIHAS?
...AND HENRY...
HELP!
WHAT'S WITH THE ENTOMOLOGY DEPARTMENT?
WHY THE SUDDEN PLAGUE OF INSECTS?
YOUR ACTIONS ARE RUINING YOUR COMPANY, STARR.
DESTROYING EVERYTHING YOU'VE CREATED.
I CAN REBUILD.
THE RICH ALWAYS RETURN FOR A SECOND ACT.
REALLY?
WHY DON'T YOU TAKE YOUR ENTITLEMENT AND SHOVE IT RIGHT UP YOUR--
PLOP!

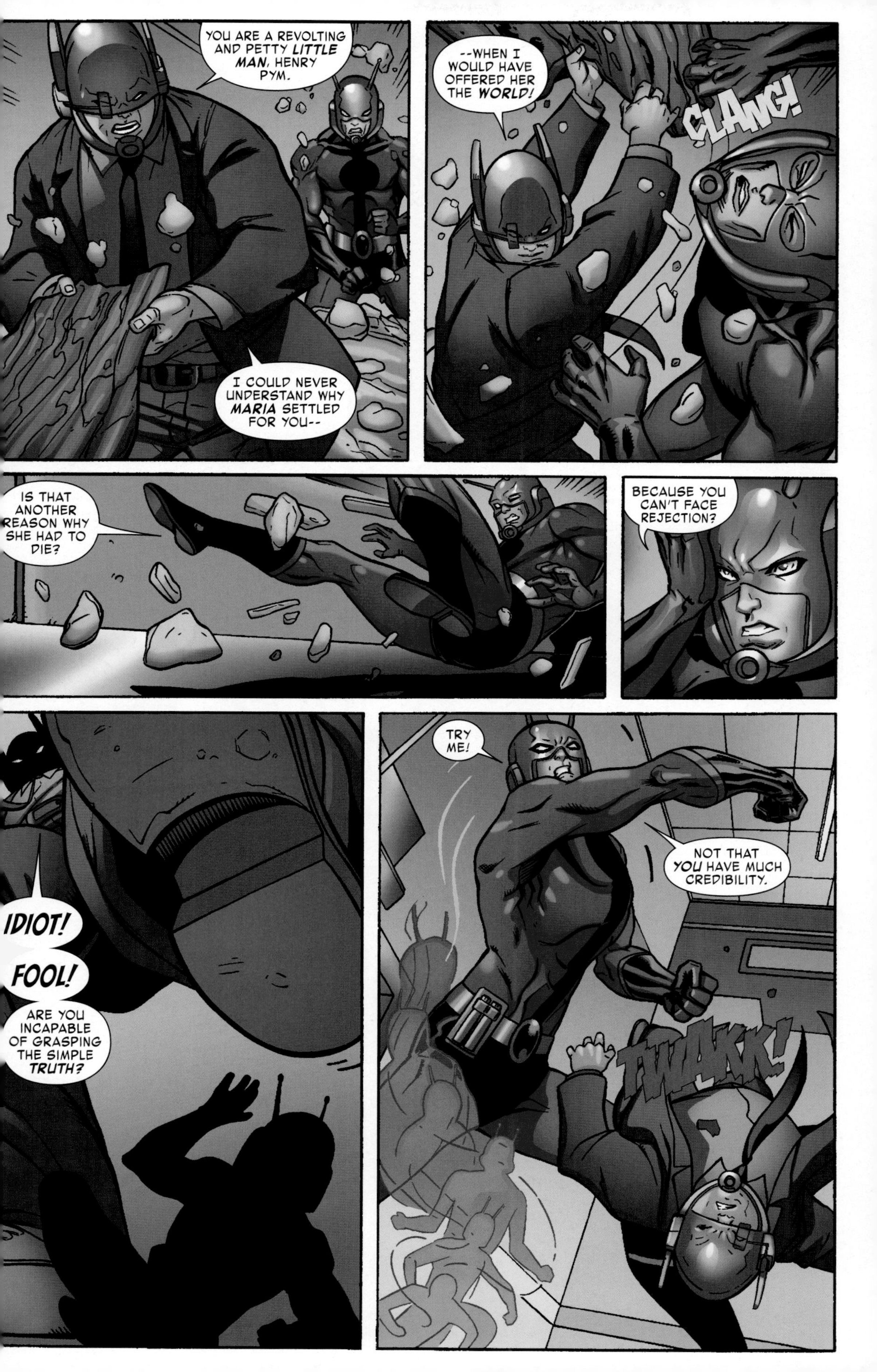

YOU ARE A REVOLTING AND PETTY LITTLE MAN, HENRY PYM.
I COULD NEVER UNDERSTAND WHY MARIA SETTLED FOR YOU--
--WHEN I WOULD HAVE OFFERED HER THE WORLD!
CLANG!
IS THAT ANOTHER REASON WHY SHE HAD TO DIE?
BECAUSE YOU CAN'T FACE REJECTION?
IDIOT!
FOOL!
ARE YOU INCAPABLE OF GRASPING THE SIMPLE TRUTH?
TRY ME!
NOT THAT YOU HAVE MUCH CREDIBILITY.
TWAKK!

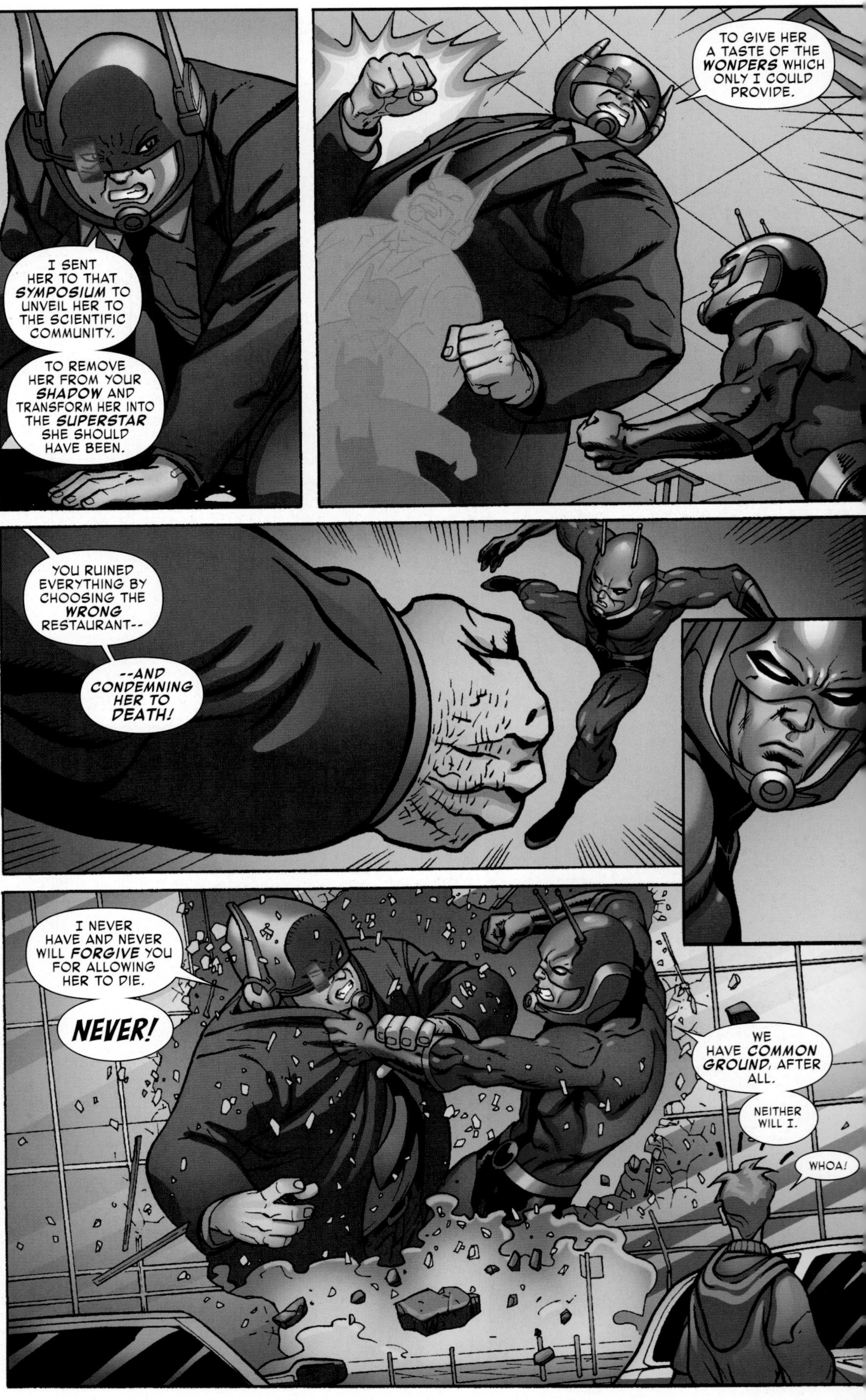

I SENT HER TO THAT SYMPOSIUM TO UNVEIL HER TO THE SCIENTIFIC COMMUNITY.
TO REMOVE HER FROM YOUR SHADOW AND TRANSFORM HER INTO THE SUPERSTAR SHE SHOULD HAVE BEEN.
TO GIVE HER A TASTE OF THE WONDERS WHICH ONLY I COULD PROVIDE.
YOU RUINED EVERYTHING BY CHOOSING THE WRONG RESTAURANT--
--AND CONDEMNING HER TO DEATH!
I NEVER HAVE AND NEVER WILL FORGIVE YOU FOR ALLOWING HER TO DIE.
NEVER!
WE HAVE COMMON GROUND, AFTER ALL.
NEITHER WILL I.
WHOA!

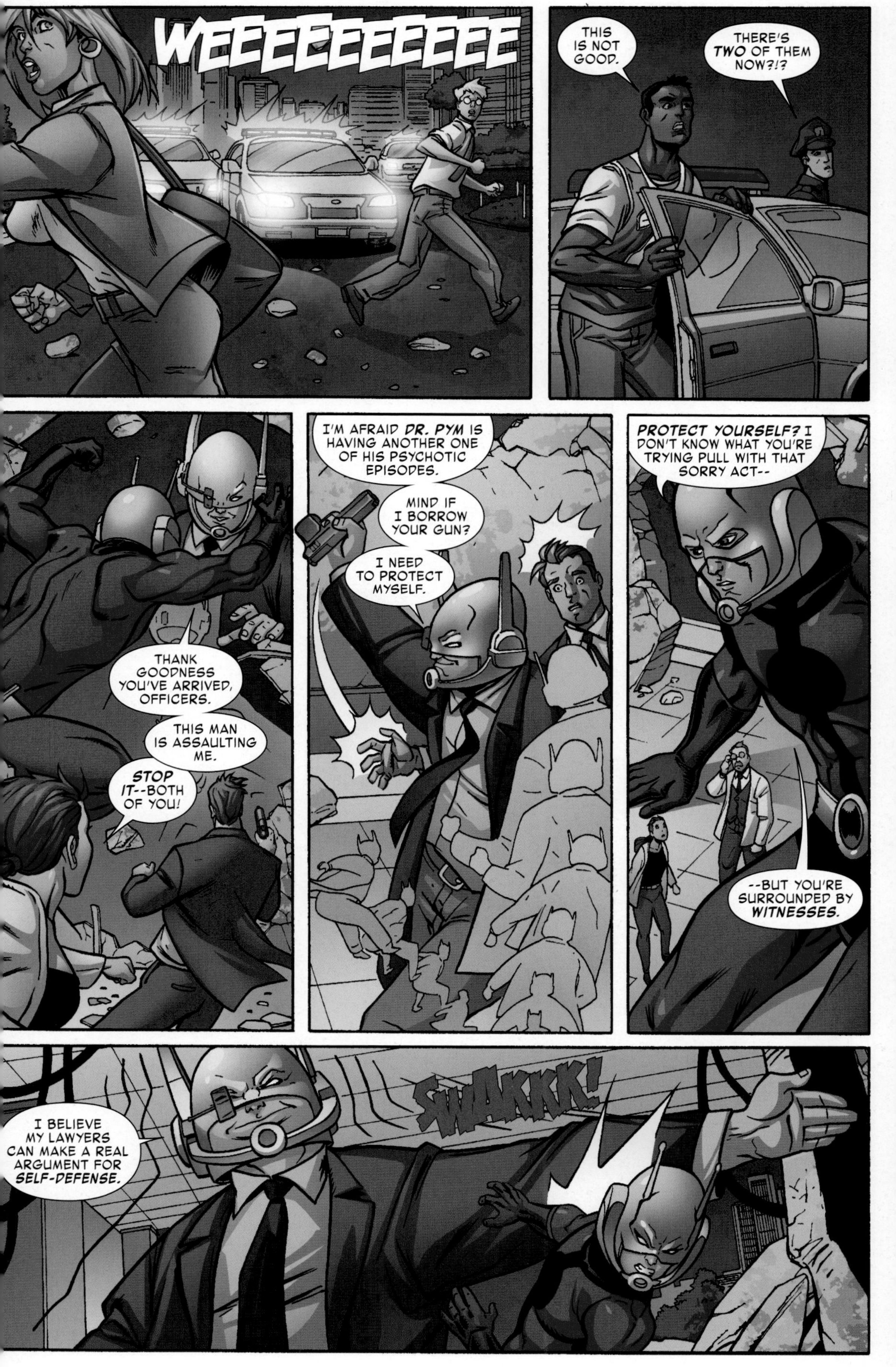

WEEEEEEEEEEE
THIS IS NOT GOOD.
THERE'S TWO OF THEM NOW?!?
THANK GOODNESS YOU'VE ARRIVED, OFFICERS.
THIS MAN IS ASSAULTING ME.
STOP IT--BOTH OF YOU!
I'M AFRAID DR. PYM IS HAVING ANOTHER ONE OF HIS PSYCHOTIC EPISODES.
MIND IF I BORROW YOUR GUN?
I NEED TO PROTECT MYSELF.
PROTECT YOURSELF? I DON'T KNOW WHAT YOU'RE TRYING PULL WITH THAT SORRY ACT--
--BUT YOU'RE SURROUNDED BY WITNESSES.
I BELIEVE MY LAWYERS CAN MAKE A REAL ARGUMENT FOR SELF-DEFENSE.
SWAKKK!

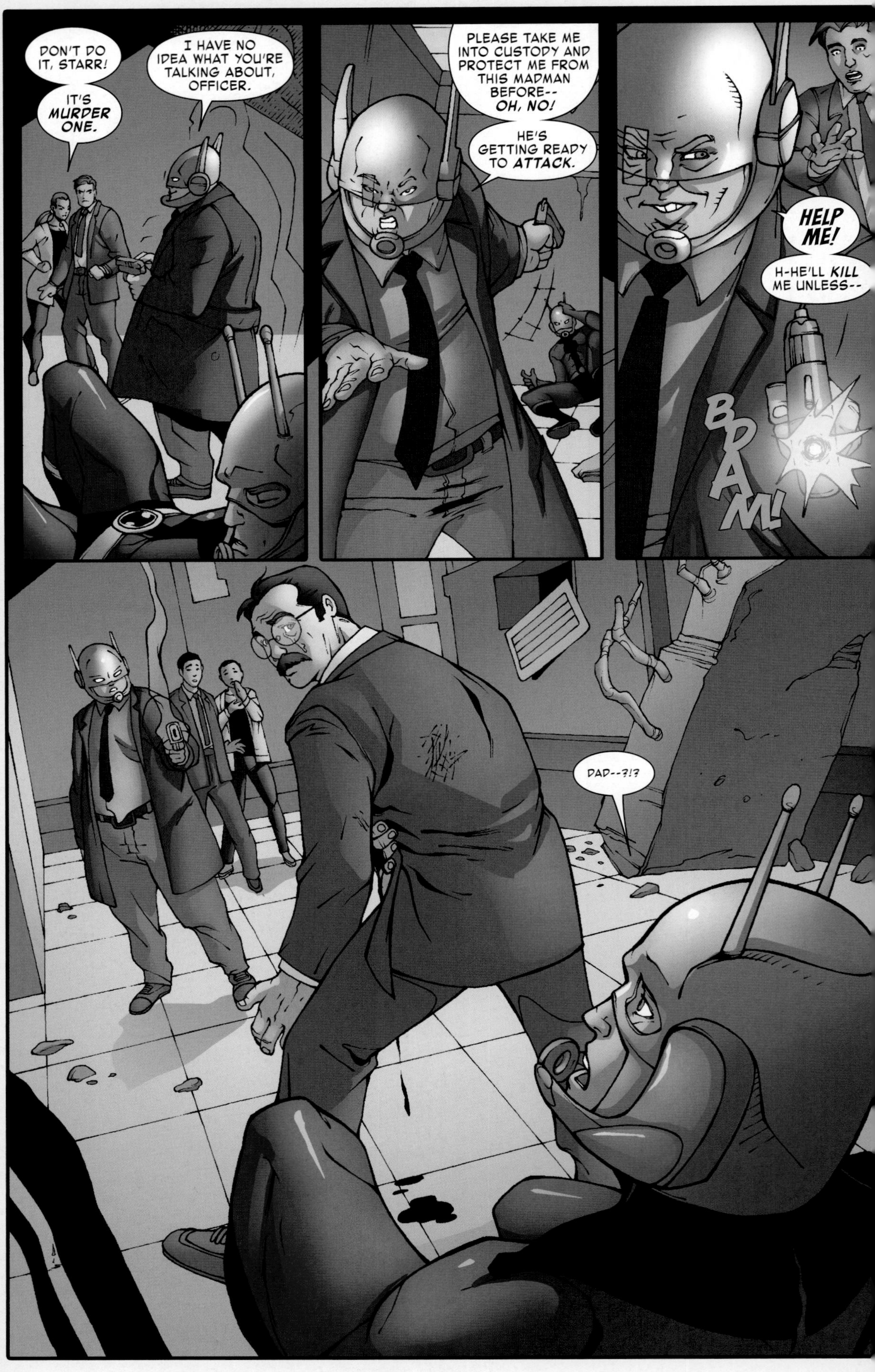
DON'T DO IT, STARR!
IT'S MURDER ONE.
I HAVE NO IDEA WHAT YOU'RE TALKING ABOUT, OFFICER.
PLEASE TAKE ME INTO CUSTODY AND PROTECT ME FROM THIS MADMAN BEFORE-- OH, NO!
HE'S GETTING READY TO ATTACK.
HELP ME!
H-HE'LL KILL ME UNLESS--
BDAM!
DAD--?!?

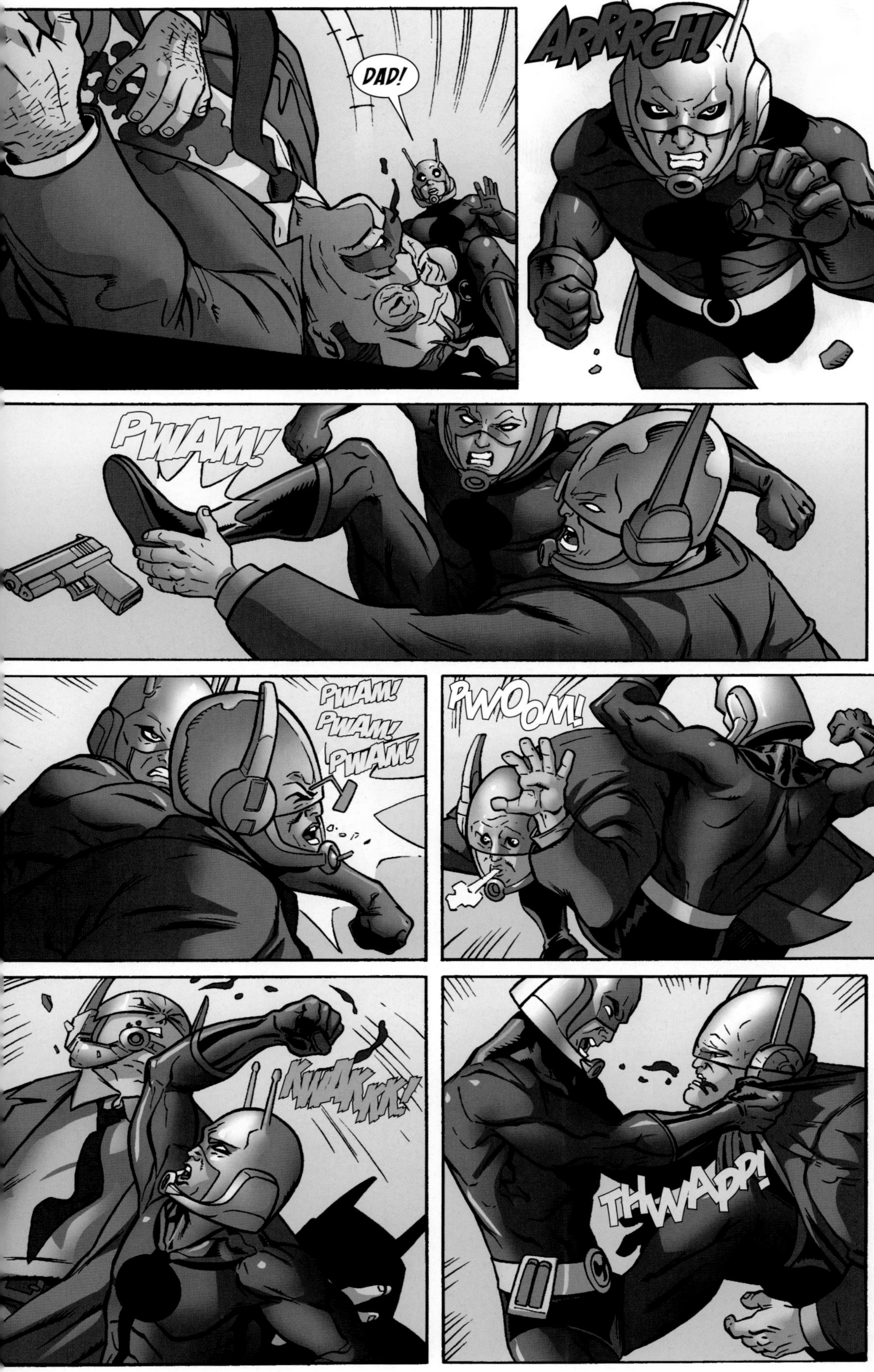
DAD!
ARRRRGH!
PWAM!
PWAM!
PWAM!
PWAM!
PWOOM!
KWAKKK!
THWAPP!

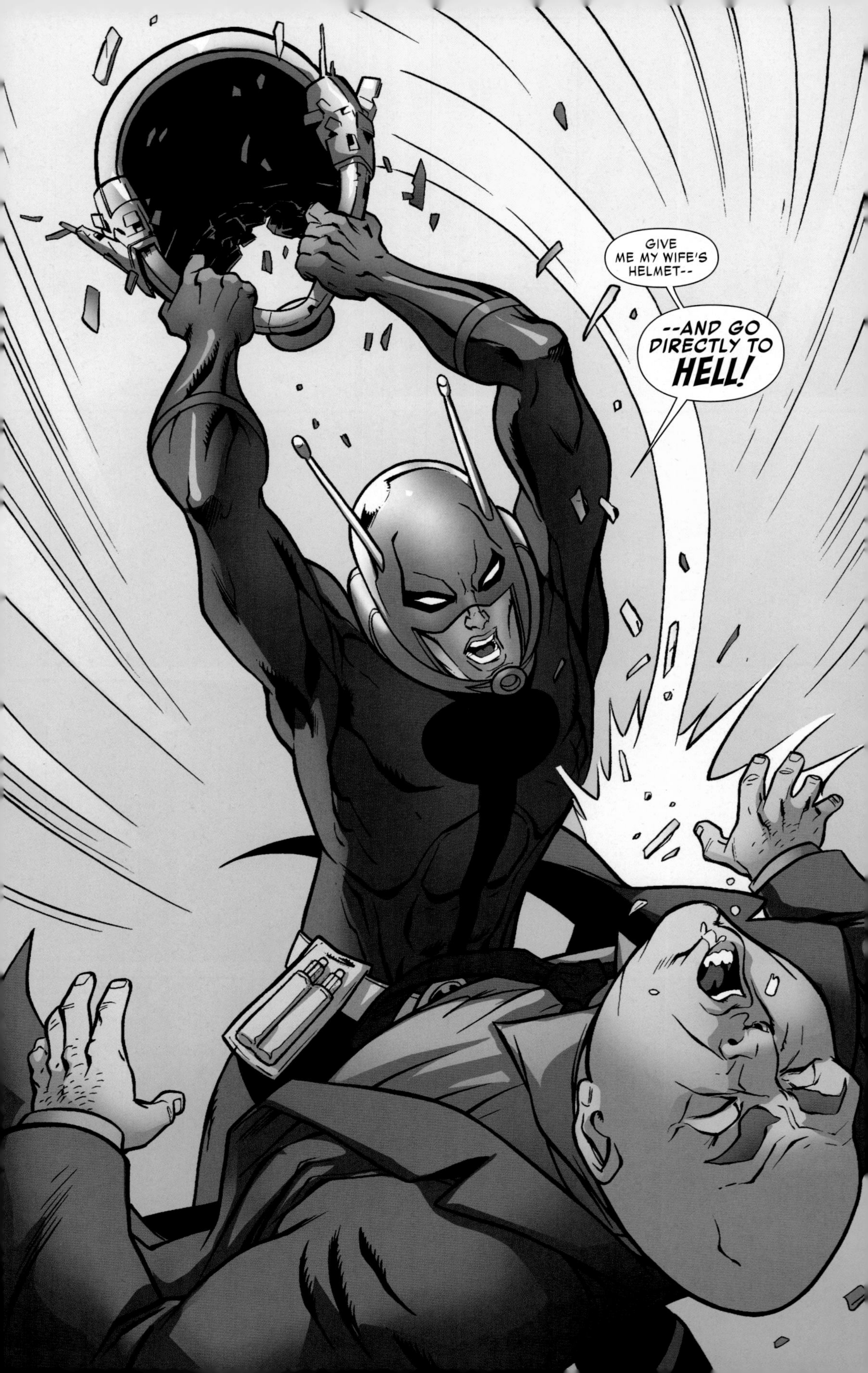
GIVE ME MY WIFE'S HELMET--
--AND GO DIRECTLY TO HELL!

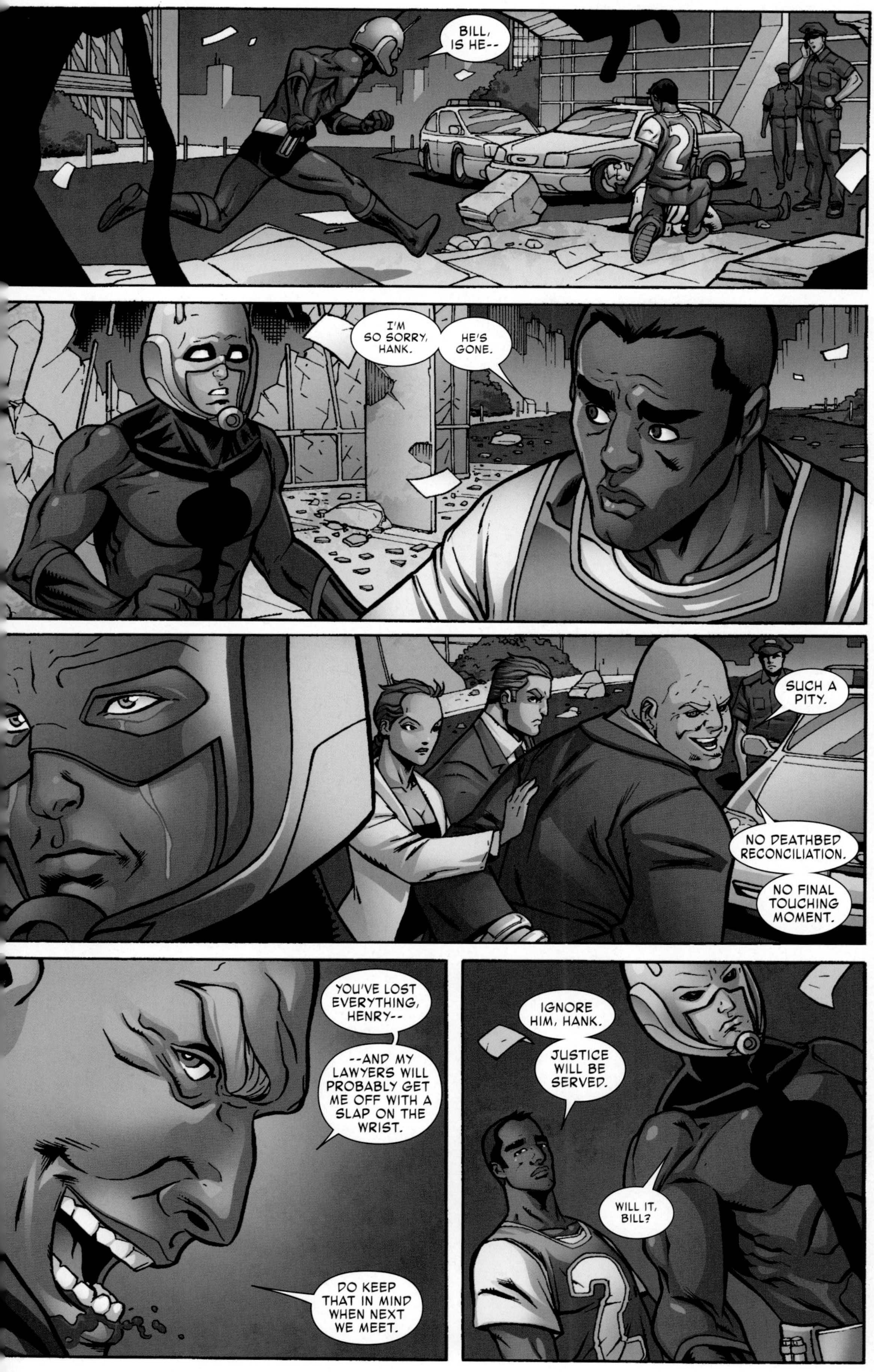
BILL, IS HE--
I'M SO SORRY, HANK.
HE'S GONE.
SUCH A PITY.
NO DEATHBED RECONCILIATION.
NO FINAL TOUCHING MOMENT.
YOU'VE LOST EVERYTHING, HENRY--
--AND MY LAWYERS WILL PROBABLY GET ME OFF WITH A SLAP ON THE WRIST.
DO KEEP THAT IN MIND WHEN NEXT WE MEET.
IGNORE HIM, HANK.
JUSTICE WILL BE SERVED.
WILL IT, BILL?

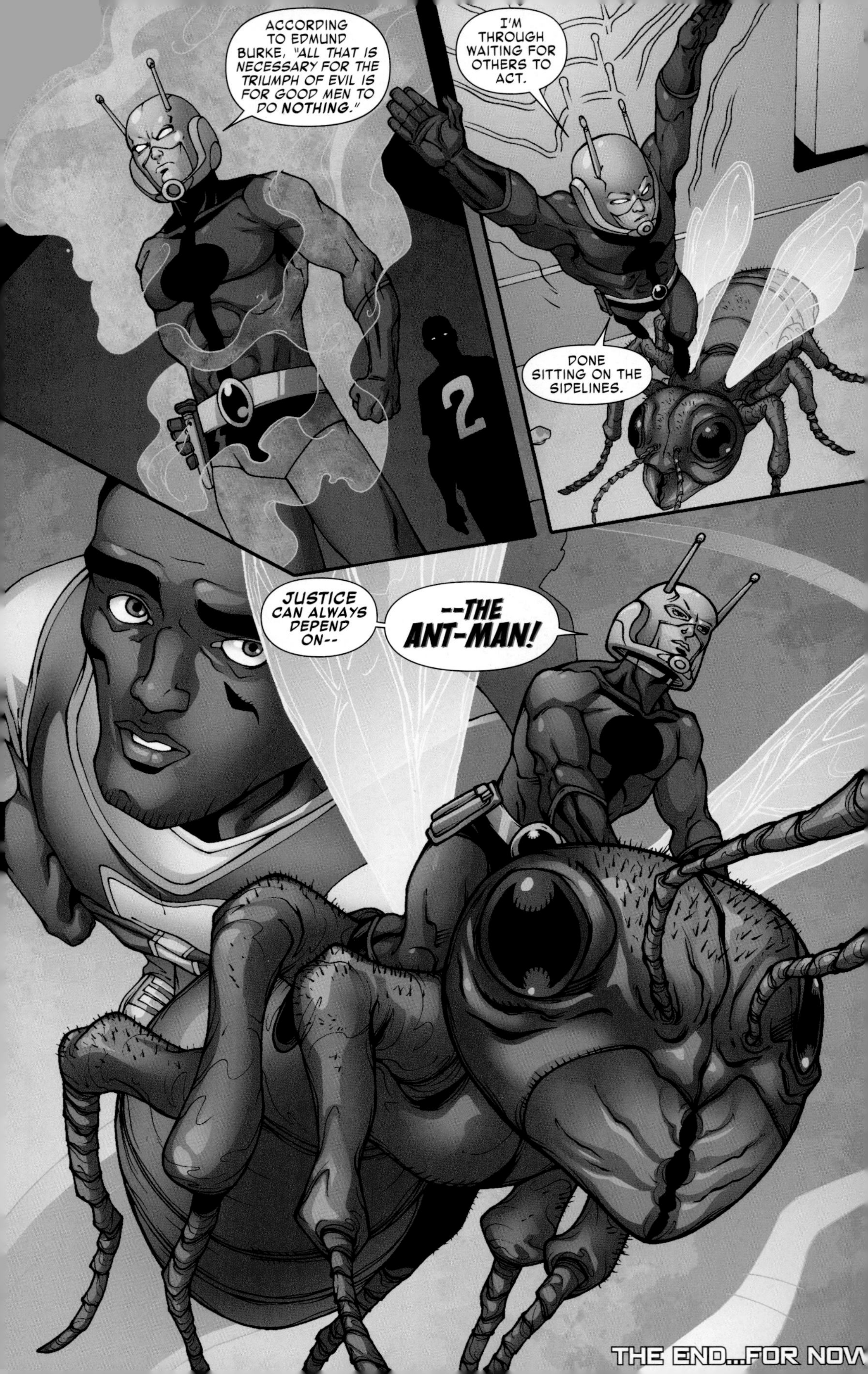
ACCORDING TO EDMUND BURKE, "ALL THAT IS NECESSARY FOR THE TRIUMPH OF EVIL IS FOR GOOD MEN TO DO NOTHING."
I'M THROUGH WAITING FOR OTHERS TO ACT.
DONE SITTING ON THE SIDELINES.
2
JUSTICE CAN ALWAYS DEPEND ON--
--THE ANT-MAN!
THE END...FOR NOW

WHERE ARE THEY NOW? *AVENGERS ACADEMY (2010) #1* DETERMINED TO KEEP THE TRADITION ALIVE, FOUNDING AVENGER HANK PYM LEADS A CORE TEAM OF VETERAN HEROES IN CREATING A PLACE WHERE THE NEXT GENERATION OF EARTH'S MIGHTIEST CAN BE TRAINED BY THE GREATEST OF THOSE WHO PRECEDED THEM.

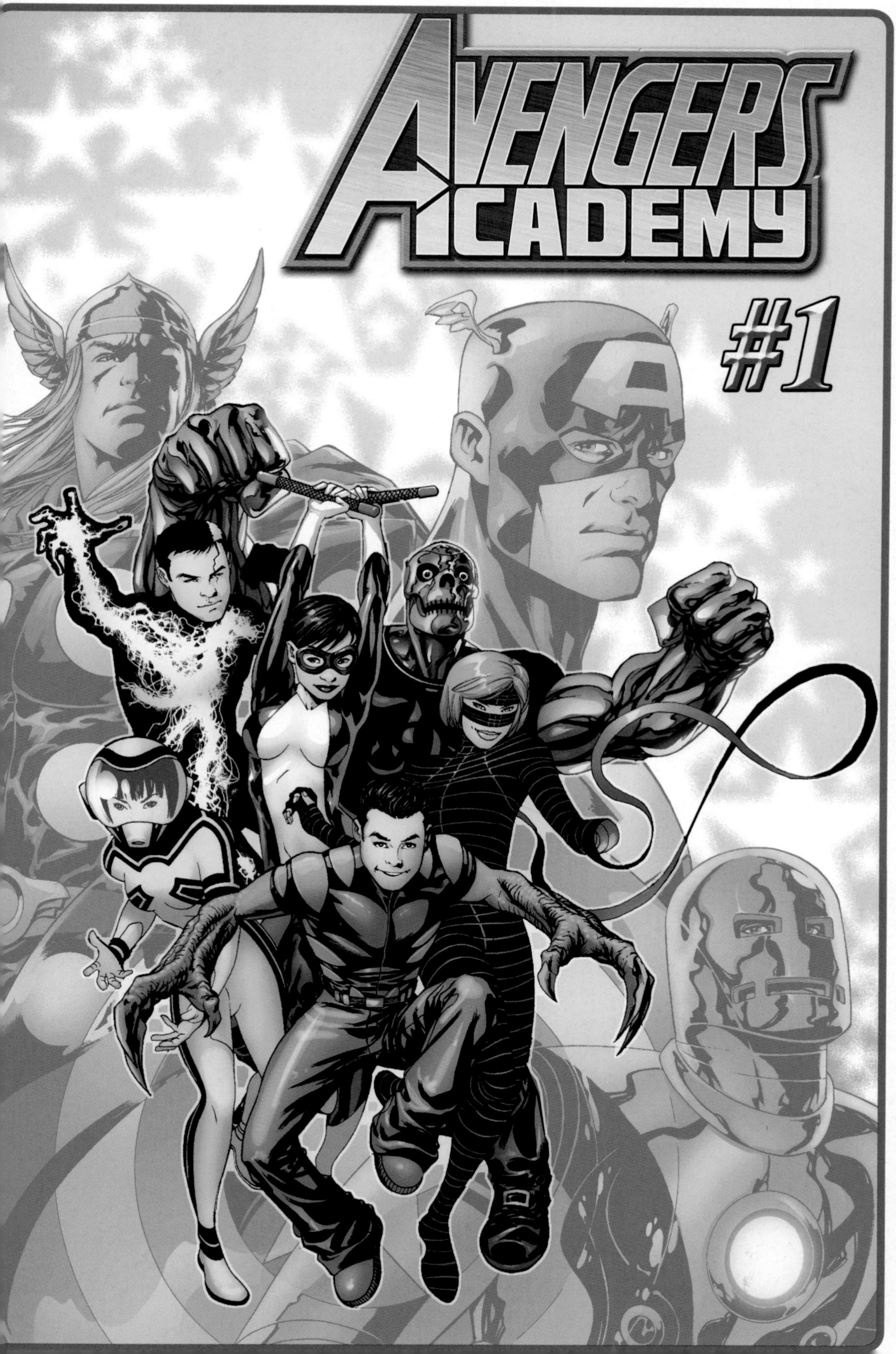
AVENGERS
ACADEMY
#1

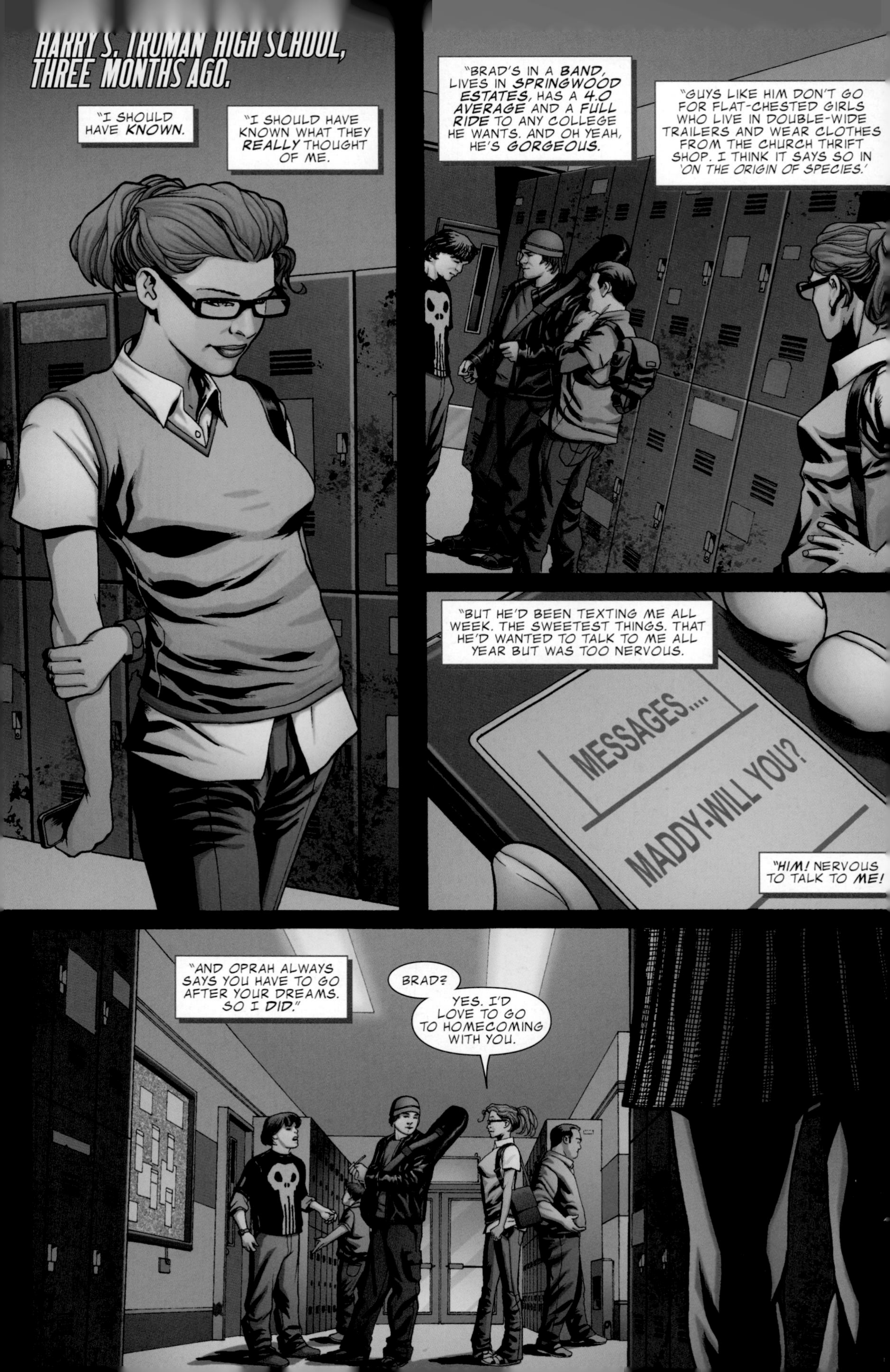

HARRY S. TRUMAN HIGH SCHOOL, THREE MONTHS AGO.
"I SHOULD HAVE **KNOWN**.
"I SHOULD HAVE KNOWN WHAT THEY **REALLY** THOUGHT OF ME.
"BRAD'S IN A **BAND**, LIVES IN **SPRINGWOOD ESTATES**, HAS A **4.0 AVERAGE** AND A **FULL RIDE** TO ANY COLLEGE HE WANTS. AND OH YEAH, HE'S **GORGEOUS**.
"GUYS LIKE HIM DON'T GO FOR FLAT-CHESTED GIRLS WHO LIVE IN DOUBLE-WIDE TRAILERS AND WEAR CLOTHES FROM THE CHURCH THRIFT SHOP. I THINK IT SAYS SO IN *'ON THE ORIGIN OF SPECIES.'*
"BUT HE'D BEEN TEXTING ME ALL WEEK. THE SWEETEST THINGS. THAT HE'D WANTED TO TALK TO ME ALL YEAR BUT WAS TOO NERVOUS.
MESSAGES....
MADDY-WILL YOU?
"**HIM!** NERVOUS TO TALK TO **ME!**
"AND OPRAH ALWAYS SAYS YOU HAVE TO GO AFTER YOUR DREAMS. SO I **DID**."
BRAD?
YES. I'D LOVE TO GO TO HOMECOMING WITH YOU.

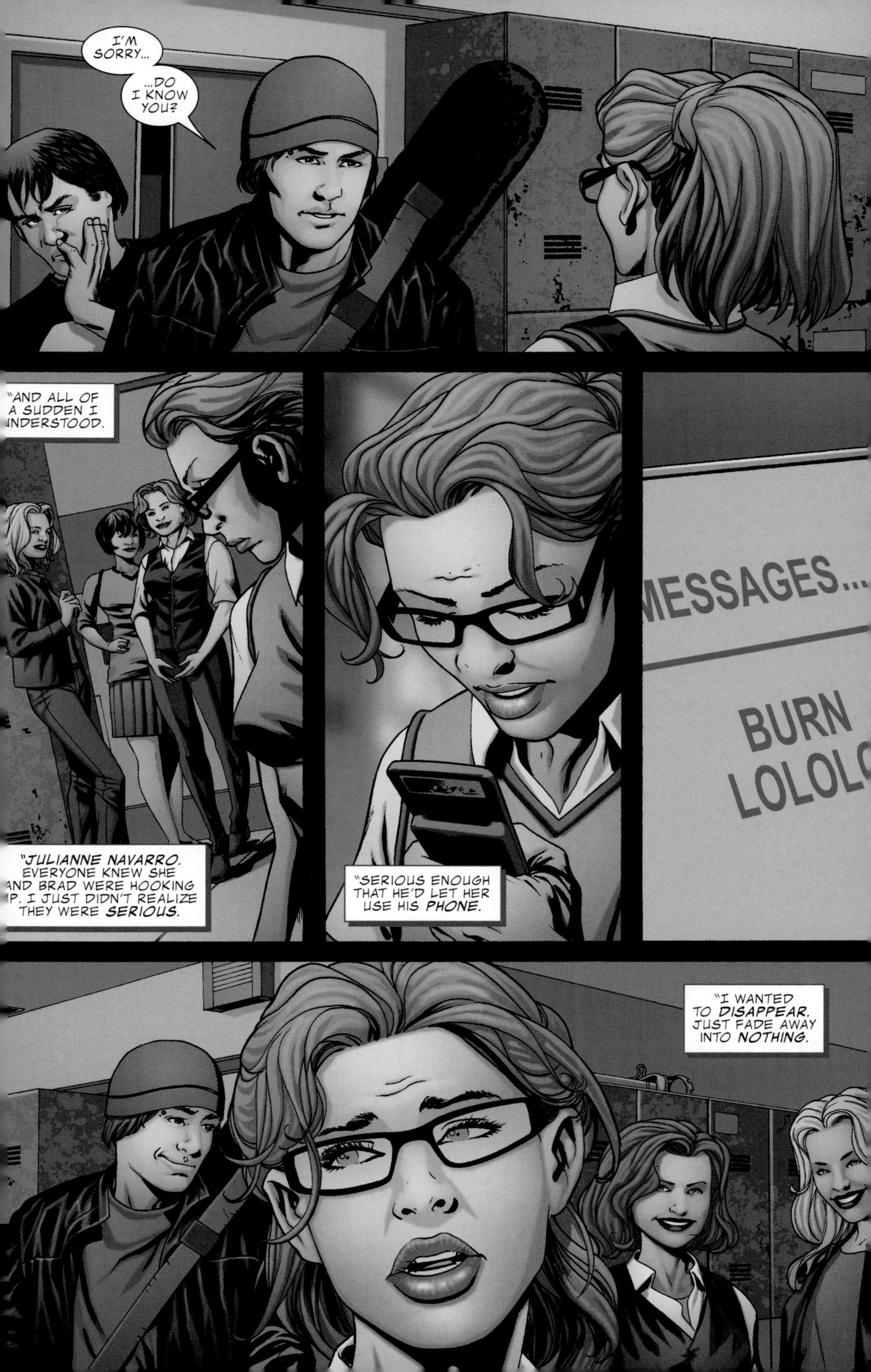
I'M SORRY...
...DO I KNOW YOU?
"AND ALL OF A SUDDEN I UNDERSTOOD.
"JULIANNE NAVARRO. EVERYONE KNEW SHE AND BRAD WERE HOOKING UP. I JUST DIDN'T REALIZE THEY WERE SERIOUS.
"SERIOUS ENOUGH THAT HE'D LET HER USE HIS PHONE.
MESSAGES...
BURN
LOLOLO
"I WANTED TO DISAPPEAR. JUST FADE AWAY INTO NOTHING.

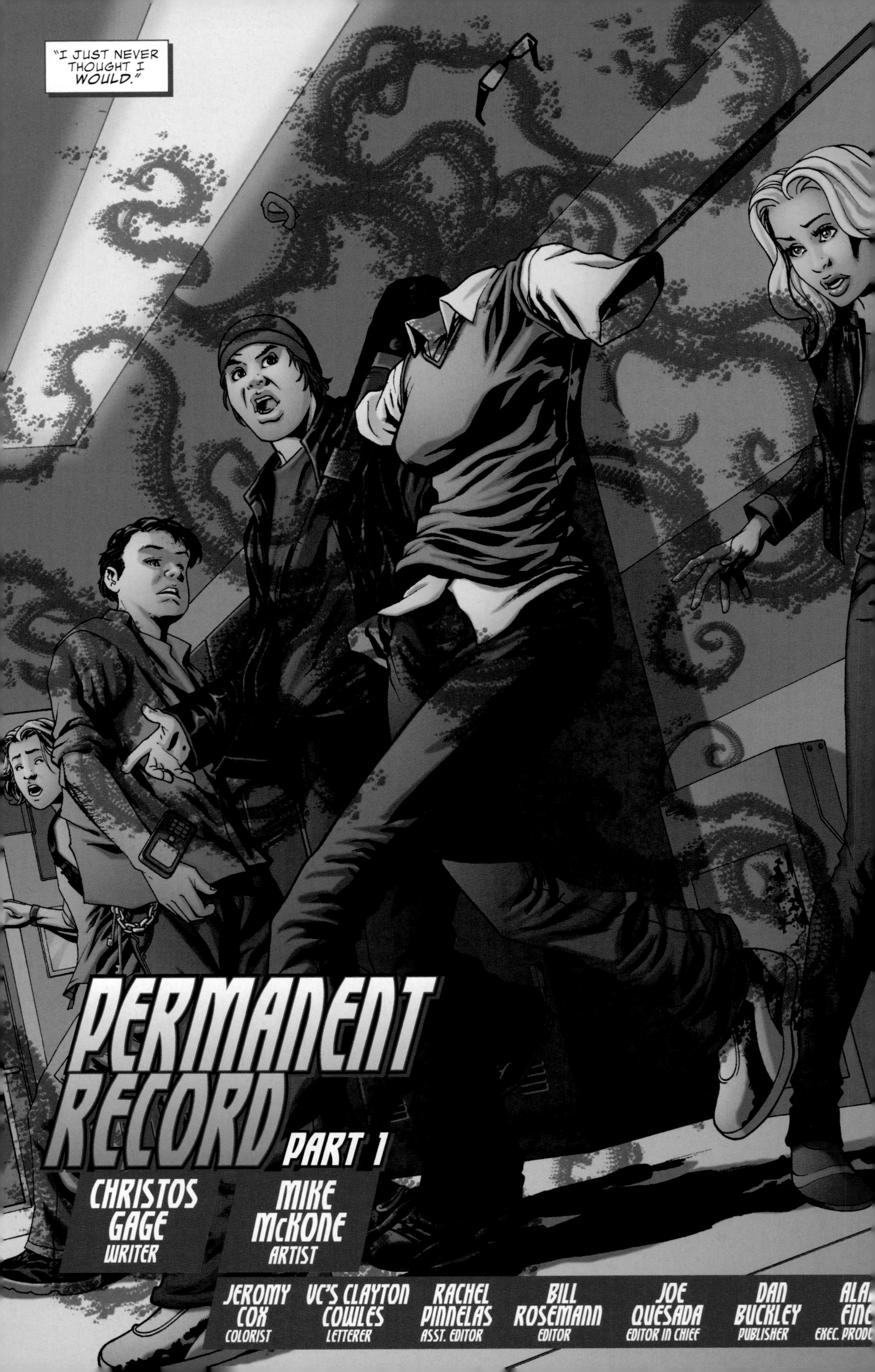
"I JUST NEVER THOUGHT I WOULD."
PERMANENT RECORD PART 1
CHRISTOS GAGE WRITER
MIKE McKONE ARTIST
JEROMY COX COLORIST
VC'S CLAYTON COWLES LETTERER
RACHEL PINNELAS ASST. EDITOR
BILL ROSEMANN EDITOR
JOE QUESADA EDITOR IN CHIEF
DAN BUCKLEY PUBLISHER

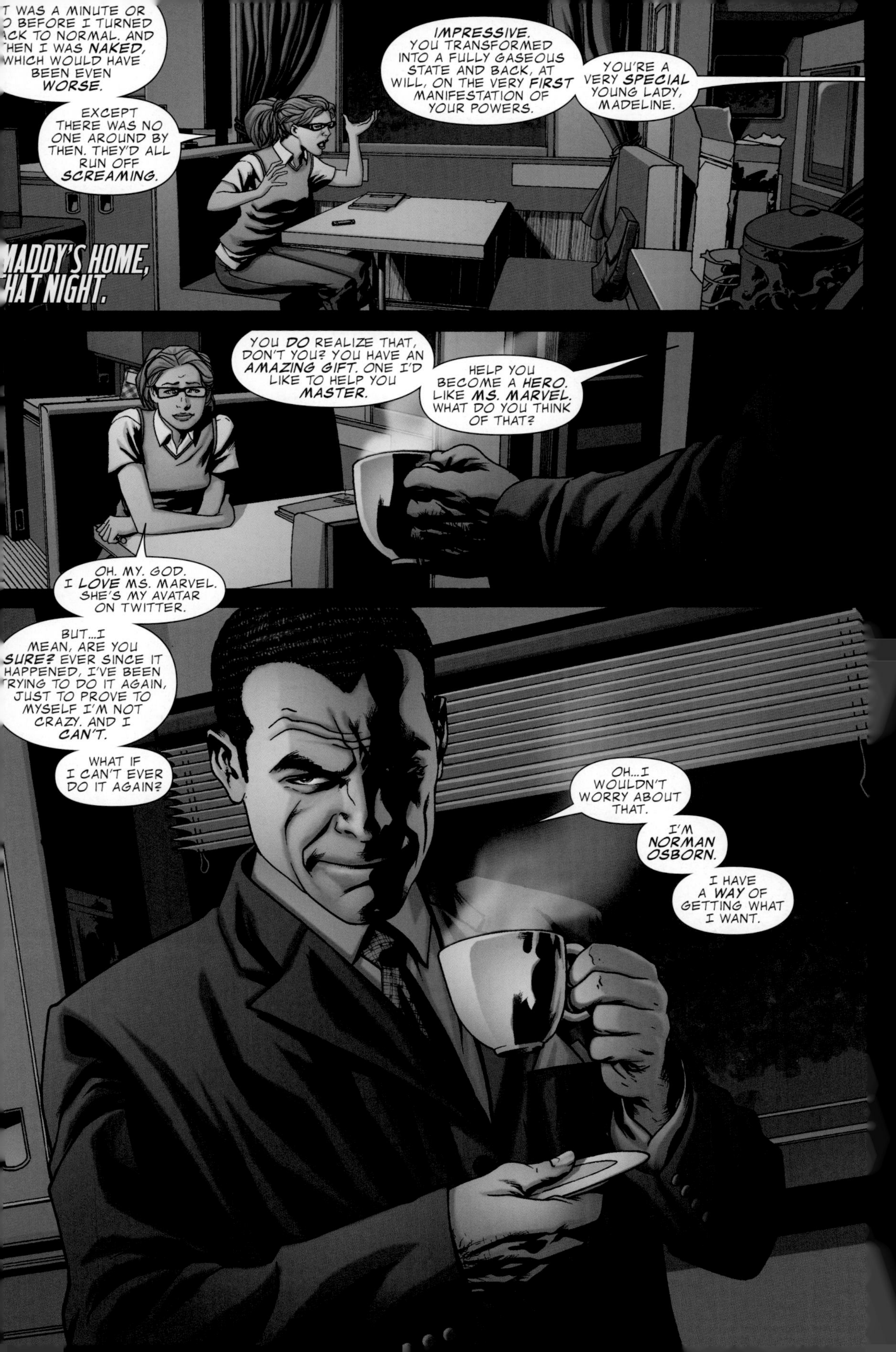

T WAS A MINUTE OR
O BEFORE I TURNED
ACK TO NORMAL. AND
THEN I WAS NAKED,
WHICH WOULD HAVE
BEEN EVEN
WORSE.
EXCEPT THERE WAS NO ONE AROUND BY THEN. THEY'D ALL RUN OFF SCREAMING.
MADDY'S HOME,
HAT NIGHT.
IMPRESSIVE. YOU TRANSFORMED INTO A FULLY GASEOUS STATE AND BACK, AT WILL, ON THE VERY FIRST MANIFESTATION OF YOUR POWERS.
YOU'RE A VERY SPECIAL YOUNG LADY, MADELINE.
YOU DO REALIZE THAT, DON'T YOU? YOU HAVE AN AMAZING GIFT. ONE I'D LIKE TO HELP YOU MASTER.
HELP YOU BECOME A HERO. LIKE MS. MARVEL. WHAT DO YOU THINK OF THAT?
OH. MY. GOD. I LOVE MS. MARVEL. SHE'S MY AVATAR ON TWITTER.
BUT...I MEAN, ARE YOU SURE? EVER SINCE IT HAPPENED, I'VE BEEN
RYING TO DO IT AGAIN, JUST TO PROVE TO MYSELF I'M NOT CRAZY. AND I CAN'T.
WHAT IF I CAN'T EVER DO IT AGAIN?
OH...I WOULDN'T WORRY ABOUT THAT.
I'M NORMAN OSBORN.
I HAVE A WAY OF GETTING WHAT I WANT.

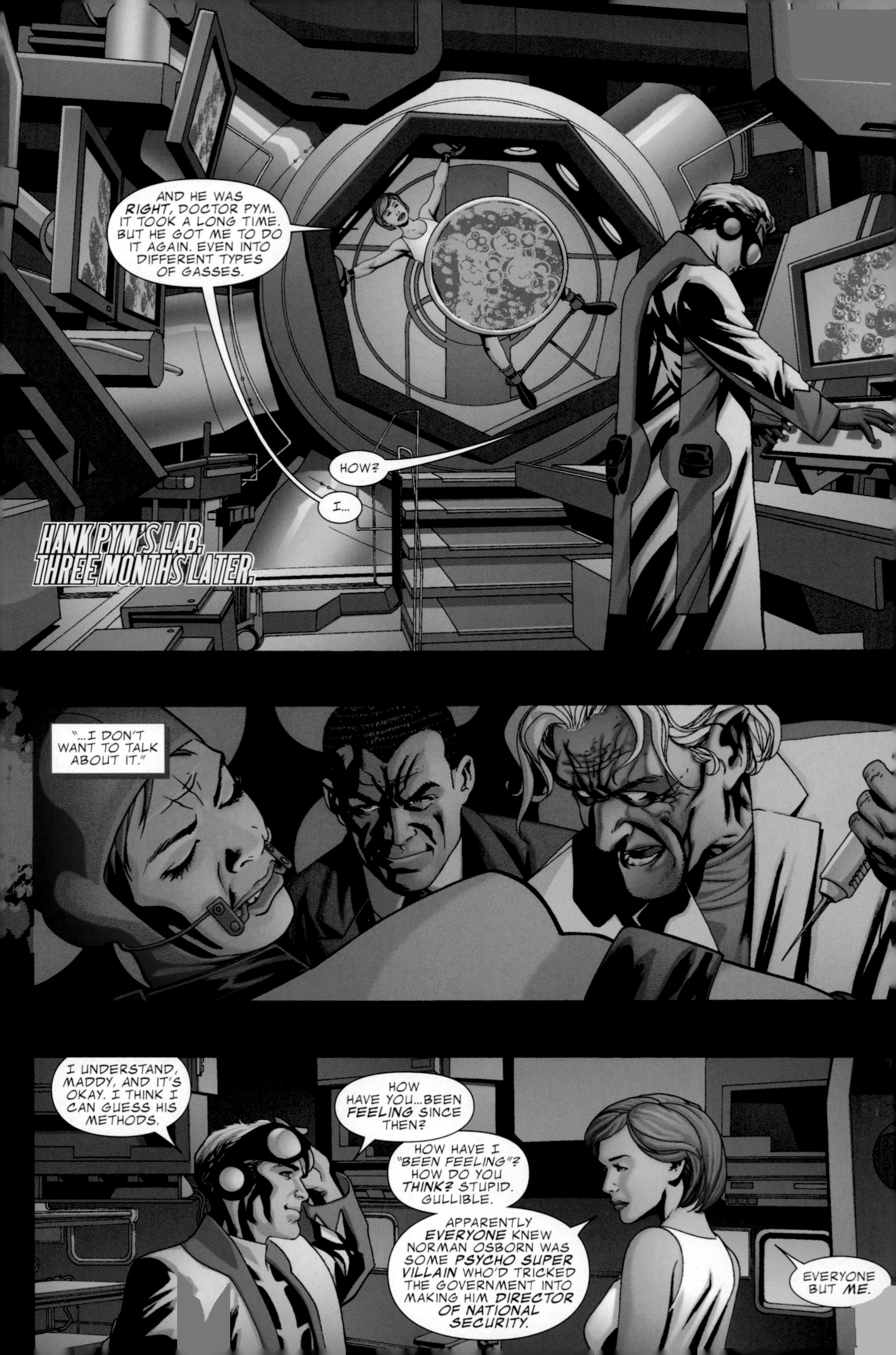
HANK PYM'S LAB. THREE MONTHS LATER.
AND HE WAS RIGHT, DOCTOR PYM. IT TOOK A LONG TIME. BUT HE GOT ME TO DO IT AGAIN. EVEN INTO DIFFERENT TYPES OF GASSES.
HOW?
I...
"...I DON'T WANT TO TALK ABOUT IT."
I UNDERSTAND, MADDY, AND IT'S OKAY. I THINK I CAN GUESS HIS METHODS.
HOW HAVE YOU...BEEN FEELING SINCE THEN?
HOW HAVE I "BEEN FEELING"? HOW DO YOU THINK? STUPID. GULLIBLE.
APPARENTLY EVERYONE KNEW NORMAN OSBORN WAS SOME PSYCHO SUPER VILLAIN WHO'D TRICKED THE GOVERNMENT INTO MAKING HIM DIRECTOR OF NATIONAL SECURITY.
EVERYONE BUT ME.

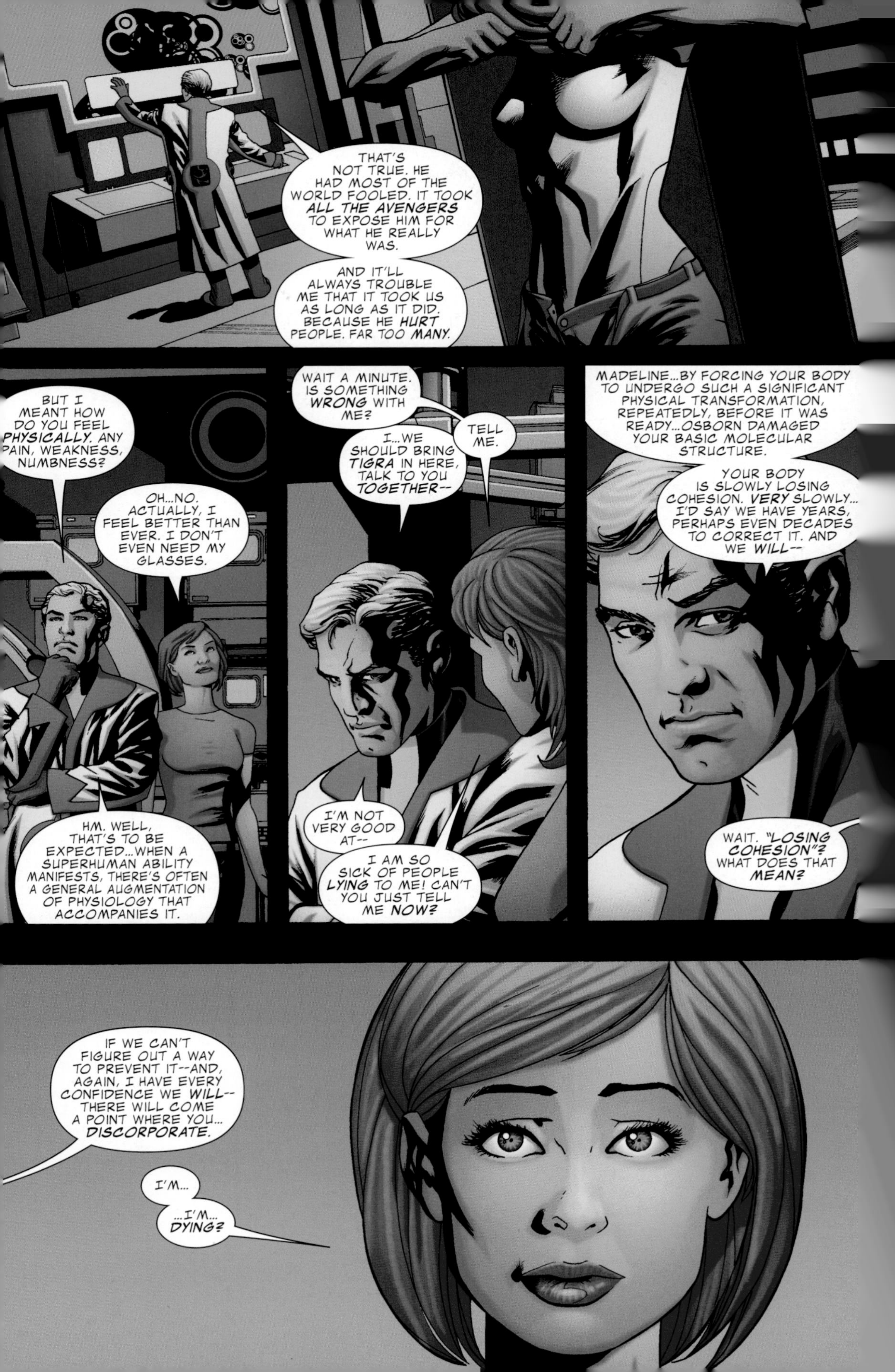

THAT'S NOT TRUE. HE HAD MOST OF THE WORLD FOOLED. IT TOOK ALL THE AVENGERS TO EXPOSE HIM FOR WHAT HE REALLY WAS.
AND IT'LL ALWAYS TROUBLE ME THAT IT TOOK US AS LONG AS IT DID. BECAUSE HE HURT PEOPLE. FAR TOO MANY.
BUT I MEANT HOW DO YOU FEEL PHYSICALLY. ANY PAIN, WEAKNESS, NUMBNESS?
OH...NO. ACTUALLY, I FEEL BETTER THAN EVER. I DON'T EVEN NEED MY GLASSES.
HM. WELL, THAT'S TO BE EXPECTED...WHEN A SUPERHUMAN ABILITY MANIFESTS, THERE'S OFTEN A GENERAL AUGMENTATION OF PHYSIOLOGY THAT ACCOMPANIES IT.
WAIT A MINUTE. IS SOMETHING WRONG WITH ME?
TELL ME.
I...WE SHOULD BRING TIGRA IN HERE, TALK TO YOU TOGETHER--
I'M NOT VERY GOOD AT--
I AM SO SICK OF PEOPLE LYING TO ME! CAN'T YOU JUST TELL ME NOW?
MADELINE...BY FORCING YOUR BODY TO UNDERGO SUCH A SIGNIFICANT PHYSICAL TRANSFORMATION, REPEATEDLY, BEFORE IT WAS READY...OSBORN DAMAGED YOUR BASIC MOLECULAR STRUCTURE.
YOUR BODY IS SLOWLY LOSING COHESION. VERY SLOWLY... I'D SAY WE HAVE YEARS, PERHAPS EVEN DECADES TO CORRECT IT. AND WE WILL--
WAIT. "LOSING COHESION"? WHAT DOES THAT MEAN?
IF WE CAN'T FIGURE OUT A WAY TO PREVENT IT--AND, AGAIN, I HAVE EVERY CONFIDENCE WE WILL--THERE WILL COME A POINT WHERE YOU... DISCORPORATE.
I'M...
...I'M... DYING?

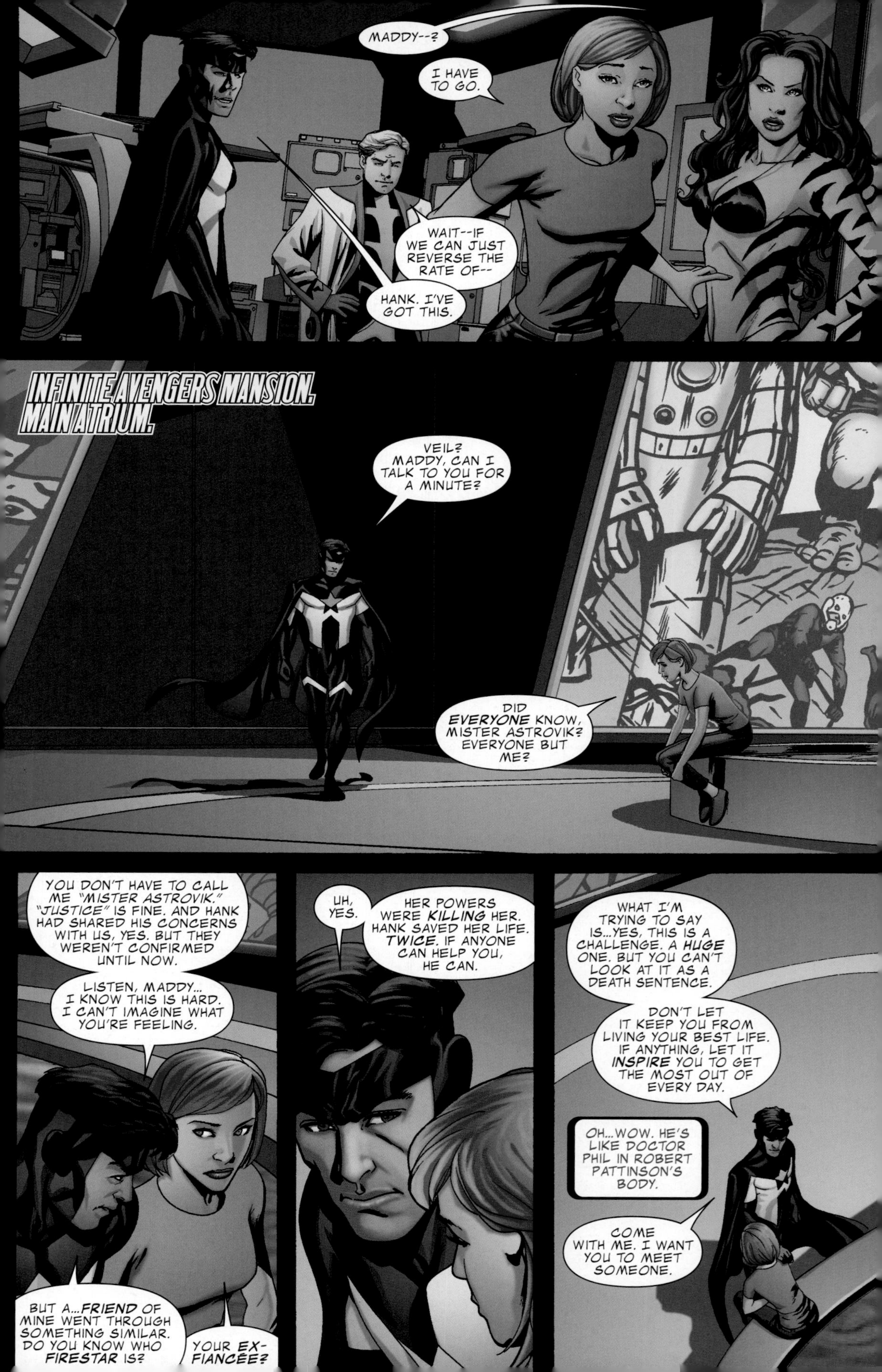
MADDY--?
I HAVE TO GO.
WAIT--IF WE CAN JUST REVERSE THE RATE OF--
HANK. I'VE GOT THIS.
INFINITE AVENGERS MANSION. MAIN ATRIUM.
VEIL? MADDY, CAN I TALK TO YOU FOR A MINUTE?
DID EVERYONE KNOW, MISTER ASTROVIK? EVERYONE BUT ME?
YOU DON'T HAVE TO CALL ME "MISTER ASTROVIK." "JUSTICE" IS FINE. AND HANK HAD SHARED HIS CONCERNS WITH US, YES. BUT THEY WEREN'T CONFIRMED UNTIL NOW.
LISTEN, MADDY... I KNOW THIS IS HARD. I CAN'T IMAGINE WHAT YOU'RE FEELING.
BUT A...FRIEND OF MINE WENT THROUGH SOMETHING SIMILAR. DO YOU KNOW WHO FIRESTAR IS?
YOUR EX-FIANCÉE?
UH, YES.
HER POWERS WERE KILLING HER. HANK SAVED HER LIFE. TWICE. IF ANYONE CAN HELP YOU, HE CAN.
WHAT I'M TRYING TO SAY IS...YES, THIS IS A CHALLENGE. A HUGE ONE. BUT YOU CAN'T LOOK AT IT AS A DEATH SENTENCE.
DON'T LET IT KEEP YOU FROM LIVING YOUR BEST LIFE. IF ANYTHING, LET IT INSPIRE YOU TO GET THE MOST OUT OF EVERY DAY.
OH...WOW. HE'S LIKE DOCTOR PHIL IN ROBERT PATTINSON'S BODY.
COME WITH ME. I WANT YOU TO MEET SOMEONE.

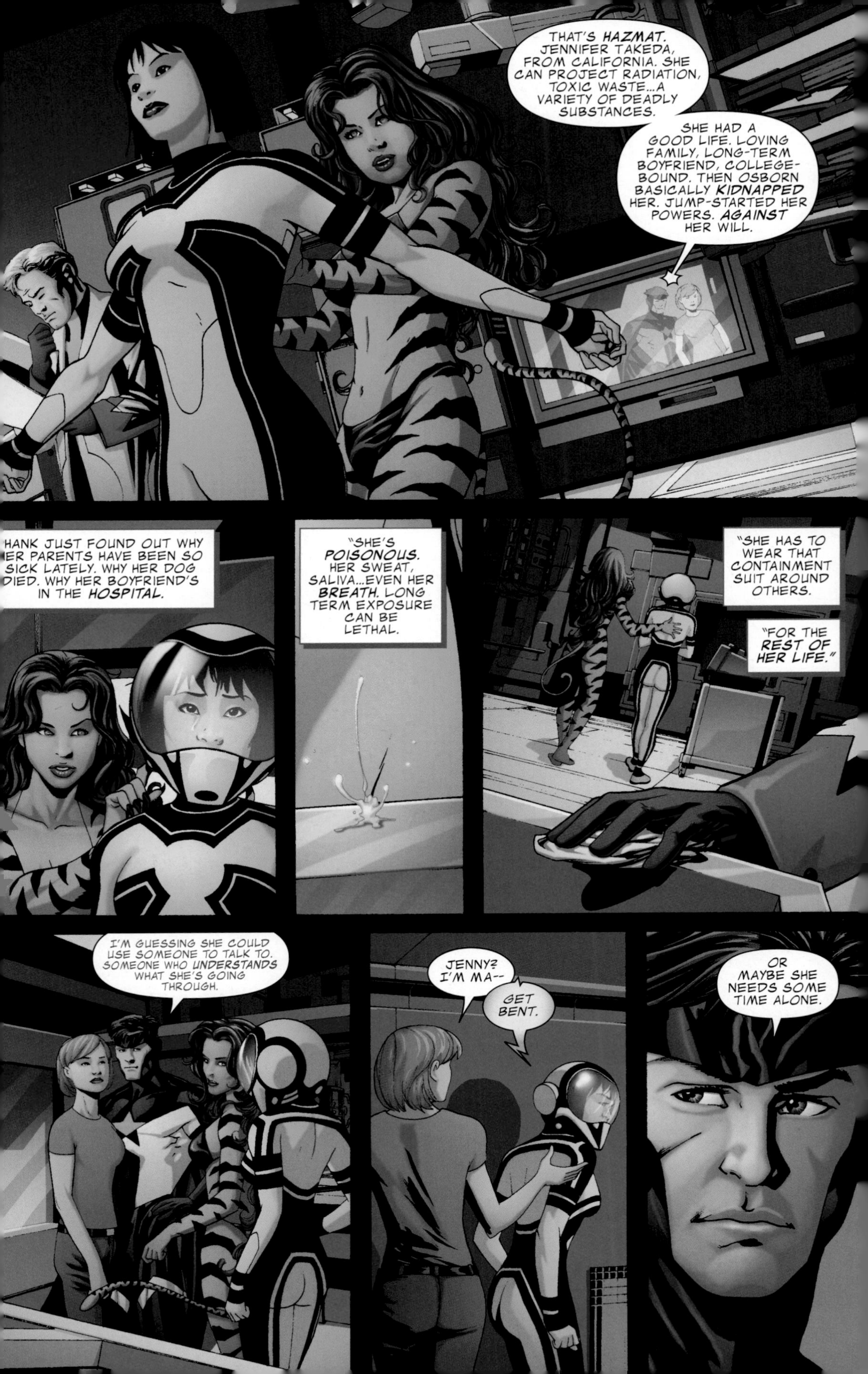
THAT'S HAZMAT. JENNIFER TAKEDA, FROM CALIFORNIA. SHE CAN PROJECT RADIATION, TOXIC WASTE...A VARIETY OF DEADLY SUBSTANCES.
SHE HAD A GOOD LIFE. LOVING FAMILY, LONG-TERM BOYFRIEND, COLLEGE-BOUND. THEN OSBORN BASICALLY KIDNAPPED HER. JUMP-STARTED HER POWERS. AGAINST HER WILL.
HANK JUST FOUND OUT WHY ER PARENTS HAVE BEEN SO SICK LATELY. WHY HER DOG DIED. WHY HER BOYFRIEND'S IN THE HOSPITAL.
"SHE'S POISONOUS. HER SWEAT, SALIVA...EVEN HER BREATH. LONG TERM EXPOSURE CAN BE LETHAL.
"SHE HAS TO WEAR THAT CONTAINMENT SUIT AROUND OTHERS.
"FOR THE REST OF HER LIFE."
I'M GUESSING SHE COULD USE SOMEONE TO TALK TO. SOMEONE WHO UNDERSTANDS WHAT SHE'S GOING THROUGH.
JENNY? I'M MA--
GET BENT.
OR MAYBE SHE NEEDS SOME TIME ALONE.

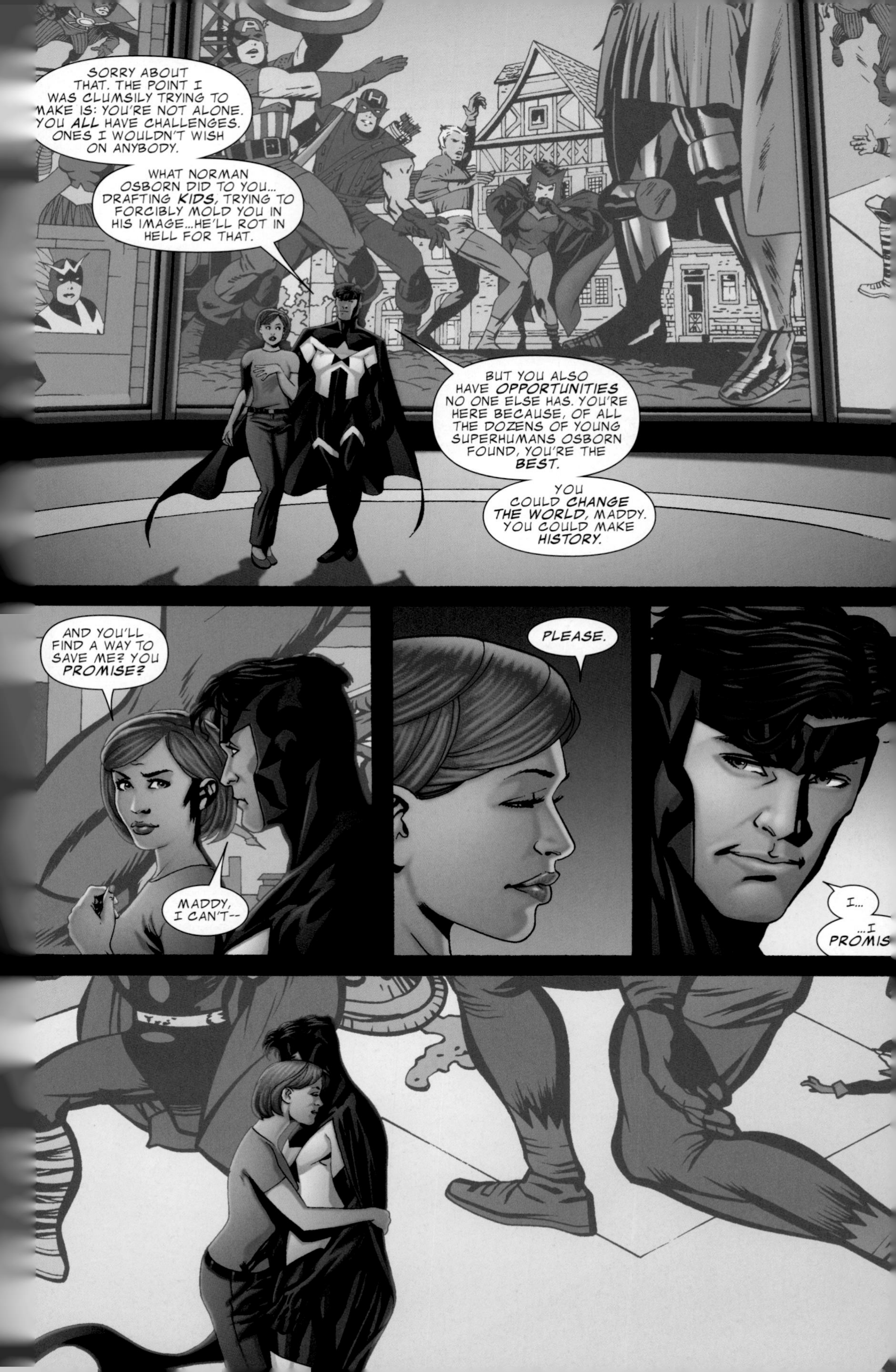

SORRY ABOUT THAT. THE POINT I WAS CLUMSILY TRYING TO MAKE IS: YOU'RE NOT ALONE. YOU ALL HAVE CHALLENGES. ONES I WOULDN'T WISH ON ANYBODY.
WHAT NORMAN OSBORN DID TO YOU... DRAFTING KIDS, TRYING TO FORCIBLY MOLD YOU IN HIS IMAGE...HE'LL ROT IN HELL FOR THAT.
BUT YOU ALSO HAVE OPPORTUNITIES NO ONE ELSE HAS. YOU'RE HERE BECAUSE, OF ALL THE DOZENS OF YOUNG SUPERHUMANS OSBORN FOUND, YOU'RE THE BEST.
YOU COULD CHANGE THE WORLD, MADDY. YOU COULD MAKE HISTORY.
AND YOU'LL FIND A WAY TO SAVE ME? YOU PROMISE?
MADDY, I CAN'T--
PLEASE.
I...
...I PROMIS

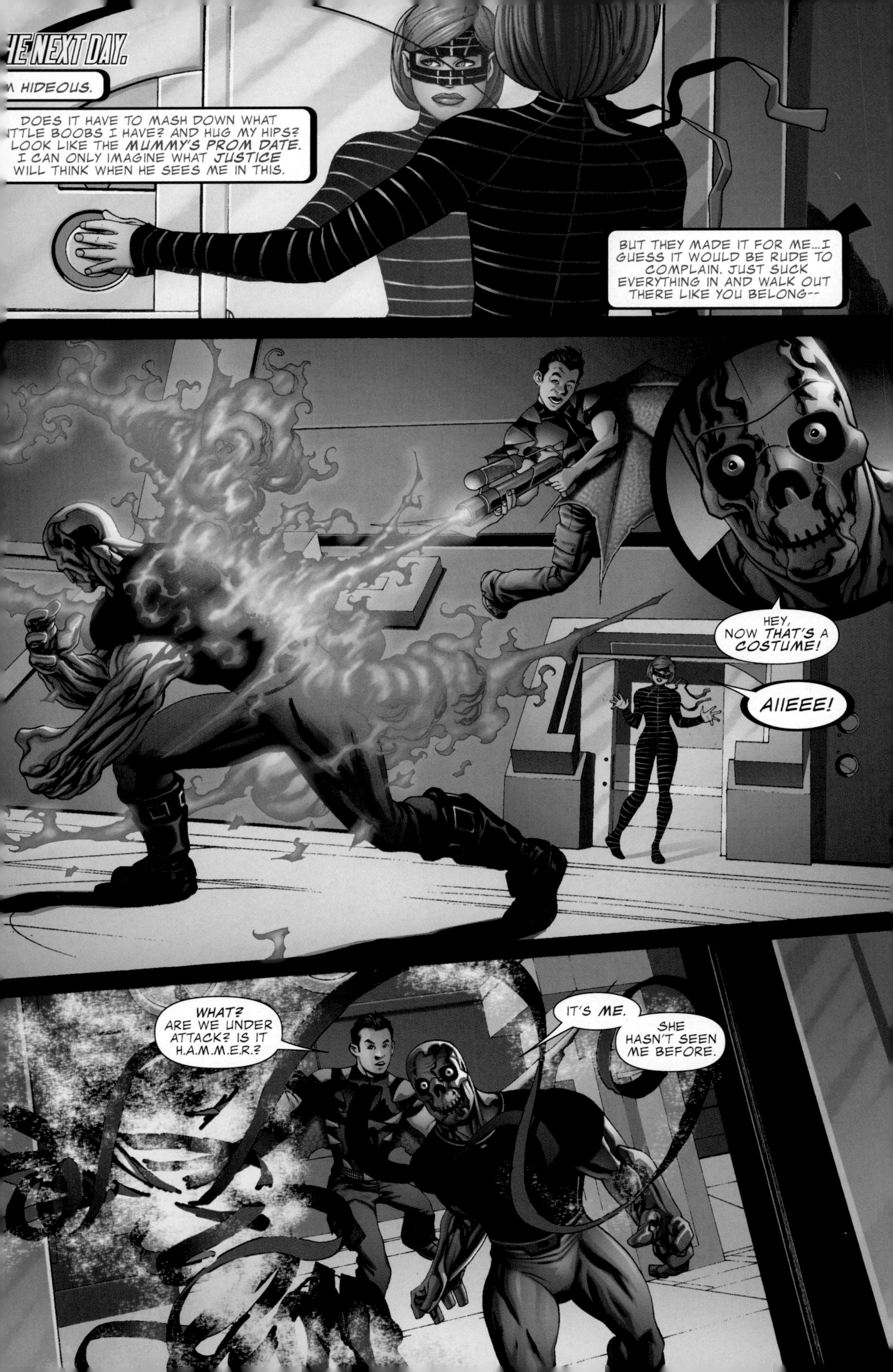

HE NEXT DAY.
M HIDEOUS.
DOES IT HAVE TO MASH DOWN WHAT ITTLE BOOBS I HAVE? AND HUG MY HIPS? LOOK LIKE THE MUMMY'S PROM DATE. I CAN ONLY IMAGINE WHAT JUSTICE WILL THINK WHEN HE SEES ME IN THIS.
BUT THEY MADE IT FOR ME...I GUESS IT WOULD BE RUDE TO COMPLAIN. JUST SUCK EVERYTHING IN AND WALK OUT THERE LIKE YOU BELONG--
HEY, NOW THAT'S A COSTUME!
AIIEEE!
WHAT? ARE WE UNDER ATTACK? IS IT H.A.M.M.E.R.?
IT'S ME.
SHE HASN'T SEEN ME BEFORE.

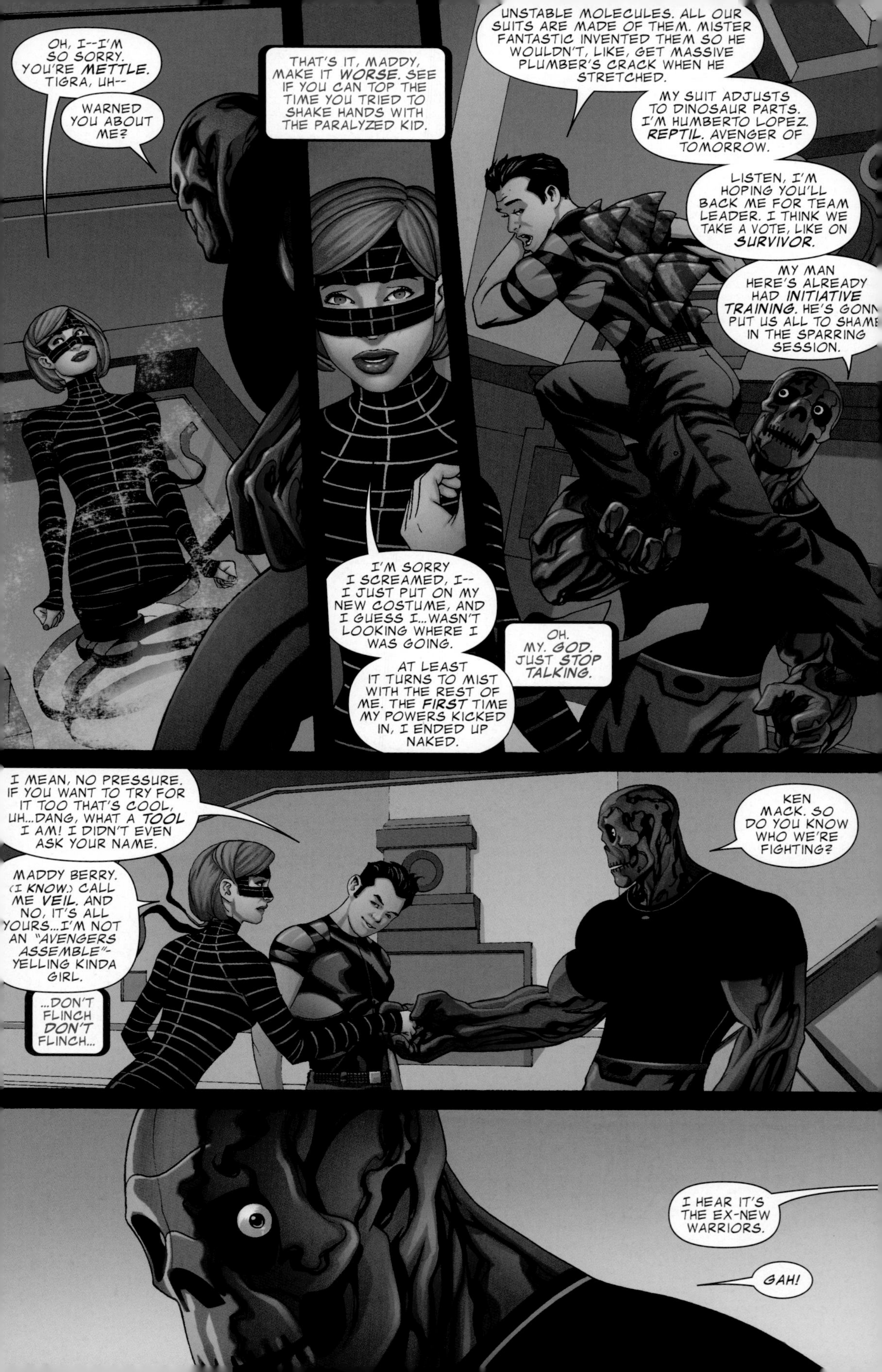
OH, I--I'M SO SORRY. YOU'RE METTLE. TIGRA, UH--
WARNED YOU ABOUT ME?
THAT'S IT, MADDY, MAKE IT WORSE. SEE IF YOU CAN TOP THE TIME YOU TRIED TO SHAKE HANDS WITH THE PARALYZED KID.
UNSTABLE MOLECULES. ALL OUR SUITS ARE MADE OF THEM. MISTER FANTASTIC INVENTED THEM SO HE WOULDN'T, LIKE, GET MASSIVE PLUMBER'S CRACK WHEN HE STRETCHED.
MY SUIT ADJUSTS TO DINOSAUR PARTS. I'M HUMBERTO LOPEZ. REPTIL. AVENGER OF TOMORROW.
LISTEN, I'M HOPING YOU'LL BACK ME FOR TEAM LEADER. I THINK WE TAKE A VOTE, LIKE ON SURVIVOR.
MY MAN HERE'S ALREADY HAD INITIATIVE TRAINING. HE'S GONN PUT US ALL TO SHAME IN THE SPARRING SESSION.
I'M SORRY I SCREAMED, I-- I JUST PUT ON MY NEW COSTUME, AND I GUESS I...WASN'T LOOKING WHERE I WAS GOING.
AT LEAST IT TURNS TO MIST WITH THE REST OF ME. THE FIRST TIME MY POWERS KICKED IN, I ENDED UP NAKED.
OH. MY. GOD. JUST STOP TALKING.
I MEAN, NO PRESSURE. IF YOU WANT TO TRY FOR IT TOO THAT'S COOL, UH...DANG, WHAT A TOOL I AM! I DIDN'T EVEN ASK YOUR NAME.
MADDY BERRY. (I KNOW.) CALL ME VEIL. AND NO, IT'S ALL YOURS...I'M NOT AN "AVENGERS ASSEMBLE"-YELLING KINDA GIRL.
...DON'T FLINCH DON'T FLINCH...
KEN MACK. SO DO YOU KNOW WHO WE'RE FIGHTING?
I HEAR IT'S THE EX-NEW WARRIORS.
GAH!

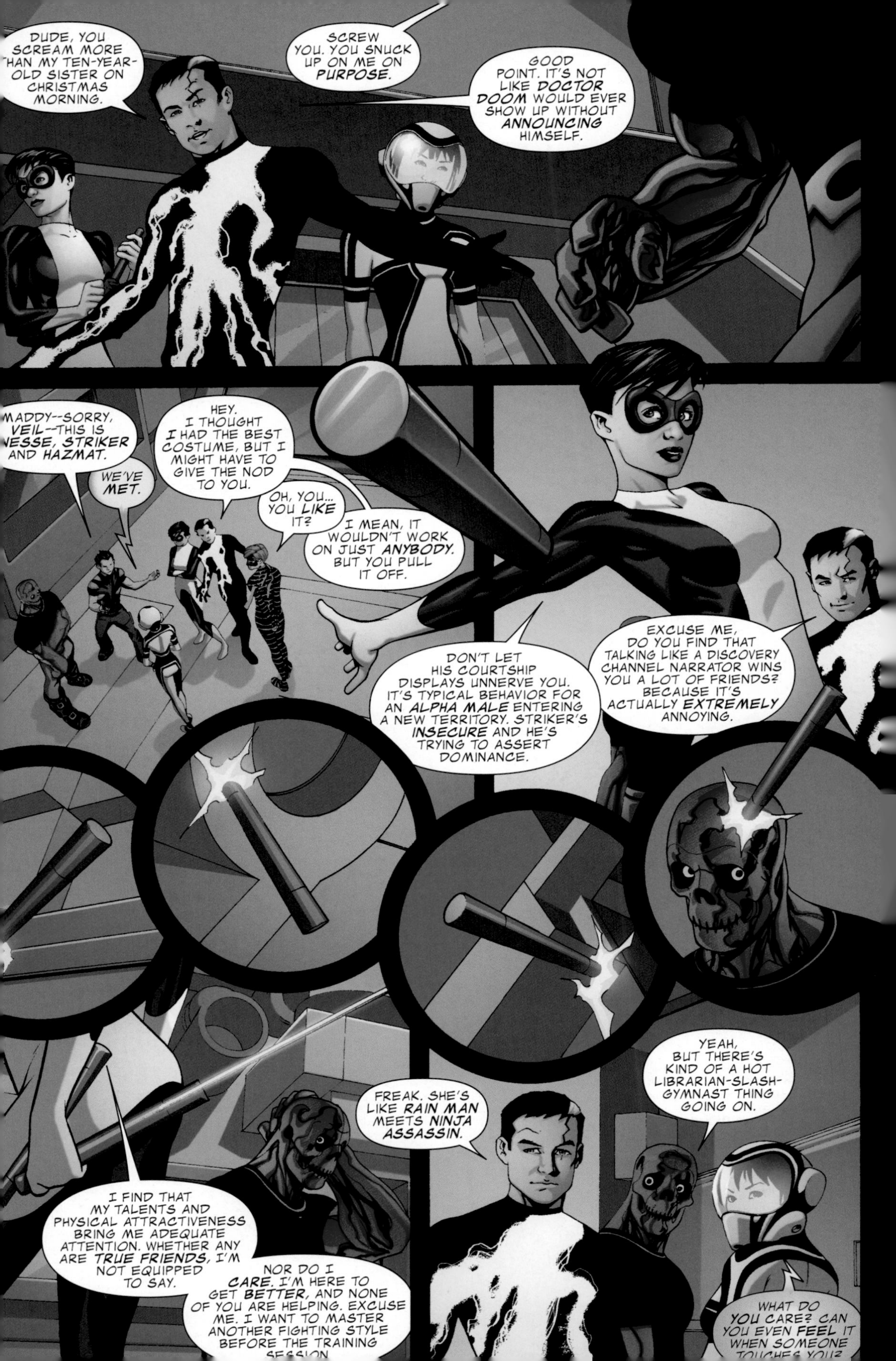
DUDE, YOU SCREAM MORE THAN MY TEN-YEAR-OLD SISTER ON CHRISTMAS MORNING.
SCREW YOU. YOU SNUCK UP ON ME ON PURPOSE.
GOOD POINT. IT'S NOT LIKE DOCTOR DOOM WOULD EVER SHOW UP WITHOUT ANNOUNCING HIMSELF.
MADDY--SORRY, VEIL--THIS IS NESSE, STRIKER AND HAZMAT.
WE'VE MET.
HEY. I THOUGHT I HAD THE BEST COSTUME, BUT I MIGHT HAVE TO GIVE THE NOD TO YOU.
OH, YOU... YOU LIKE IT?
I MEAN, IT WOULDN'T WORK ON JUST ANYBODY. BUT YOU PULL IT OFF.
DON'T LET HIS COURTSHIP DISPLAYS UNNERVE YOU. IT'S TYPICAL BEHAVIOR FOR AN ALPHA MALE ENTERING A NEW TERRITORY. STRIKER'S INSECURE AND HE'S TRYING TO ASSERT DOMINANCE.
EXCUSE ME, DO YOU FIND THAT TALKING LIKE A DISCOVERY CHANNEL NARRATOR WINS YOU A LOT OF FRIENDS? BECAUSE IT'S ACTUALLY EXTREMELY ANNOYING.
I FIND THAT MY TALENTS AND PHYSICAL ATTRACTIVENESS BRING ME ADEQUATE ATTENTION. WHETHER ANY ARE TRUE FRIENDS, I'M NOT EQUIPPED TO SAY.
NOR DO I CARE. I'M HERE TO GET BETTER, AND NONE OF YOU ARE HELPING. EXCUSE ME. I WANT TO MASTER ANOTHER FIGHTING STYLE BEFORE THE TRAINING
FREAK. SHE'S LIKE RAIN MAN MEETS NINJA ASSASSIN.
YEAH, BUT THERE'S KIND OF A HOT LIBRARIAN-SLASH-GYMNAST THING GOING ON.
WHAT DO YOU CARE? CAN YOU EVEN FEEL IT WHEN SOMEONE

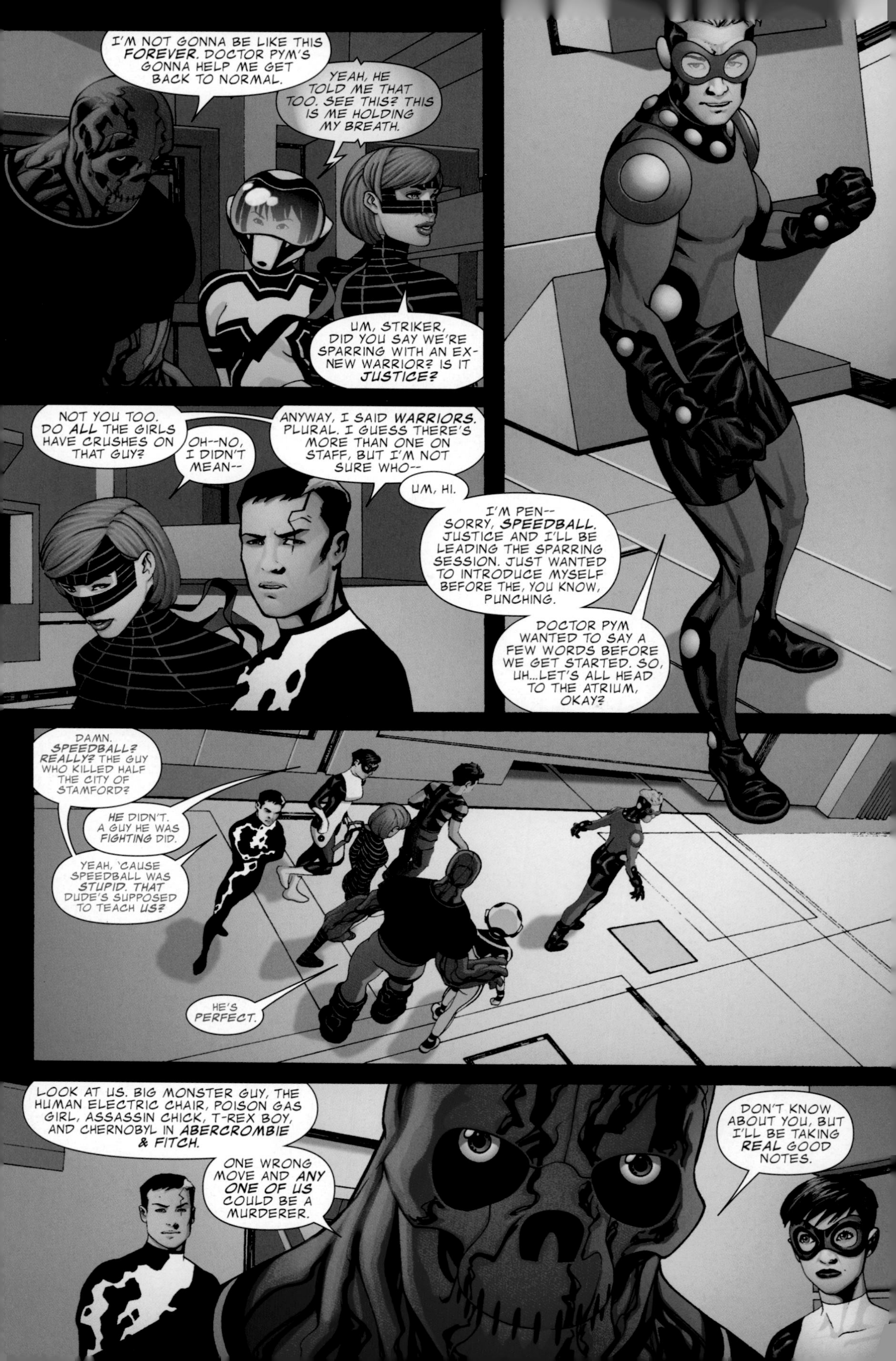
I'M NOT GONNA BE LIKE THIS FOREVER. DOCTOR PYM'S GONNA HELP ME GET BACK TO NORMAL.
YEAH, HE TOLD ME THAT TOO. SEE THIS? THIS IS ME HOLDING MY BREATH.
UM, STRIKER, DID YOU SAY WE'RE SPARRING WITH AN EX-NEW WARRIOR? IS IT JUSTICE?
NOT YOU TOO. DO ALL THE GIRLS HAVE CRUSHES ON THAT GUY?
OH--NO, I DIDN'T MEAN--
ANYWAY, I SAID WARRIORS. PLURAL. I GUESS THERE'S MORE THAN ONE ON STAFF, BUT I'M NOT SURE WHO--
UM, HI.
I'M PEN-- SORRY, SPEEDBALL. JUSTICE AND I'LL BE LEADING THE SPARRING SESSION. JUST WANTED TO INTRODUCE MYSELF BEFORE THE, YOU KNOW, PUNCHING.
DOCTOR PYM WANTED TO SAY A FEW WORDS BEFORE WE GET STARTED. SO, UH...LET'S ALL HEAD TO THE ATRIUM, OKAY?
DAMN. SPEEDBALL? REALLY? THE GUY WHO KILLED HALF THE CITY OF STAMFORD?
HE DIDN'T. A GUY HE WAS FIGHTING DID.
YEAH, 'CAUSE SPEEDBALL WAS STUPID. THAT DUDE'S SUPPOSED TO TEACH US?
HE'S PERFECT.
LOOK AT US. BIG MONSTER GUY, THE HUMAN ELECTRIC CHAIR, POISON GAS GIRL, ASSASSIN CHICK, T-REX BOY, AND CHERNOBYL IN ABERCROMBIE & FITCH.
ONE WRONG MOVE AND ANY ONE OF US COULD BE A MURDERER.
DON'T KNOW ABOUT YOU, BUT I'LL BE TAKING REAL GOOD NOTES.

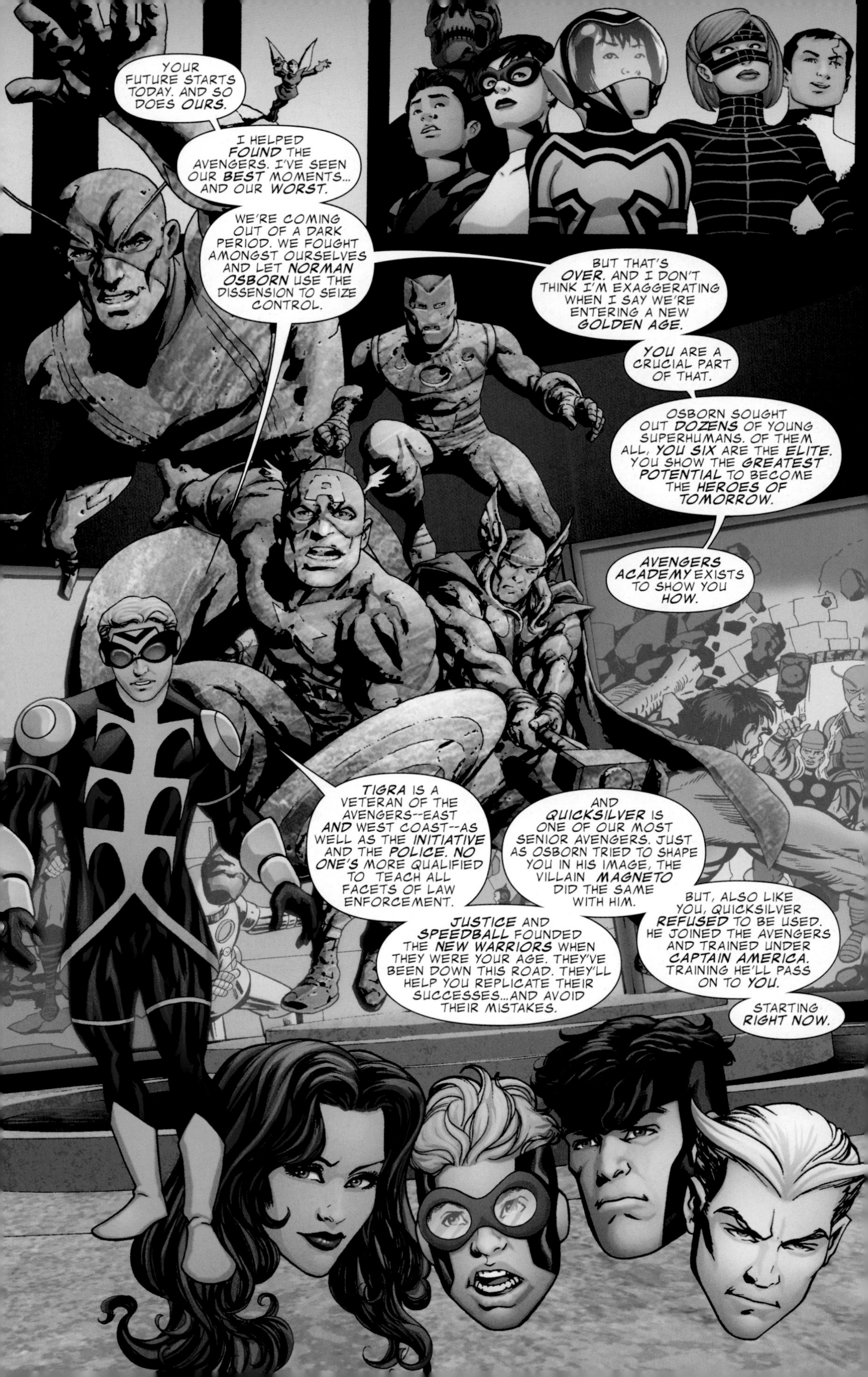
YOUR FUTURE STARTS TODAY. AND SO DOES OURS.
I HELPED FOUND THE AVENGERS. I'VE SEEN OUR BEST MOMENTS... AND OUR WORST.
WE'RE COMING OUT OF A DARK PERIOD. WE FOUGHT AMONGST OURSELVES AND LET NORMAN OSBORN USE THE DISSENSION TO SEIZE CONTROL.
BUT THAT'S OVER. AND I DON'T THINK I'M EXAGGERATING WHEN I SAY WE'RE ENTERING A NEW GOLDEN AGE.
YOU ARE A CRUCIAL PART OF THAT.
OSBORN SOUGHT OUT DOZENS OF YOUNG SUPERHUMANS. OF THEM ALL, YOU SIX ARE THE ELITE. YOU SHOW THE GREATEST POTENTIAL TO BECOME THE HEROES OF TOMORROW.
AVENGERS ACADEMY EXISTS TO SHOW YOU HOW.
TIGRA IS A VETERAN OF THE AVENGERS--EAST AND WEST COAST--AS WELL AS THE INITIATIVE AND THE POLICE. NO ONE'S MORE QUALIFIED TO TEACH ALL FACETS OF LAW ENFORCEMENT.
JUSTICE AND SPEEDBALL FOUNDED THE NEW WARRIORS WHEN THEY WERE YOUR AGE. THEY'VE BEEN DOWN THIS ROAD. THEY'LL HELP YOU REPLICATE THEIR SUCCESSES...AND AVOID THEIR MISTAKES.
AND QUICKSILVER IS ONE OF OUR MOST SENIOR AVENGERS. JUST AS OSBORN TRIED TO SHAPE YOU IN HIS IMAGE, THE VILLAIN MAGNETO DID THE SAME WITH HIM.
BUT, ALSO LIKE YOU, QUICKSILVER REFUSED TO BE USED. HE JOINED THE AVENGERS AND TRAINED UNDER CAPTAIN AMERICA. TRAINING HE'LL PASS ON TO YOU.
STARTING RIGHT NOW.

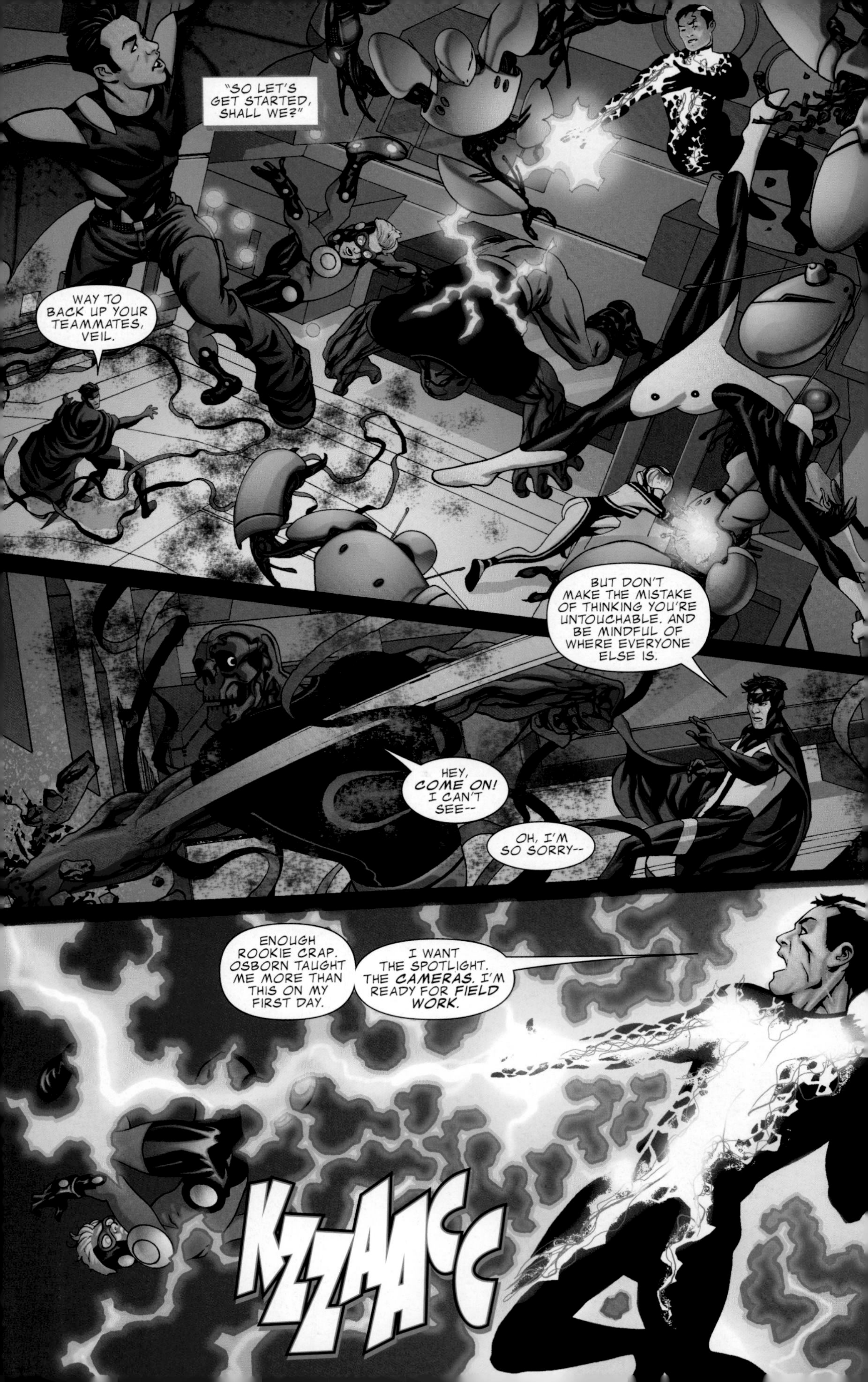
"SO LET'S GET STARTED, SHALL WE?"
WAY TO BACK UP YOUR TEAMMATES, VEIL.
BUT DON'T MAKE THE MISTAKE OF THINKING YOU'RE UNTOUCHABLE. AND BE MINDFUL OF WHERE EVERYONE ELSE IS.
HEY, COME ON! I CAN'T SEE--
OH, I'M SO SORRY--
ENOUGH ROOKIE CRAP. OSBORN TAUGHT ME MORE THAN THIS ON MY FIRST DAY.
I WANT THE SPOTLIGHT. THE CAMERAS. I'M READY FOR FIELD WORK.
KZZAACC

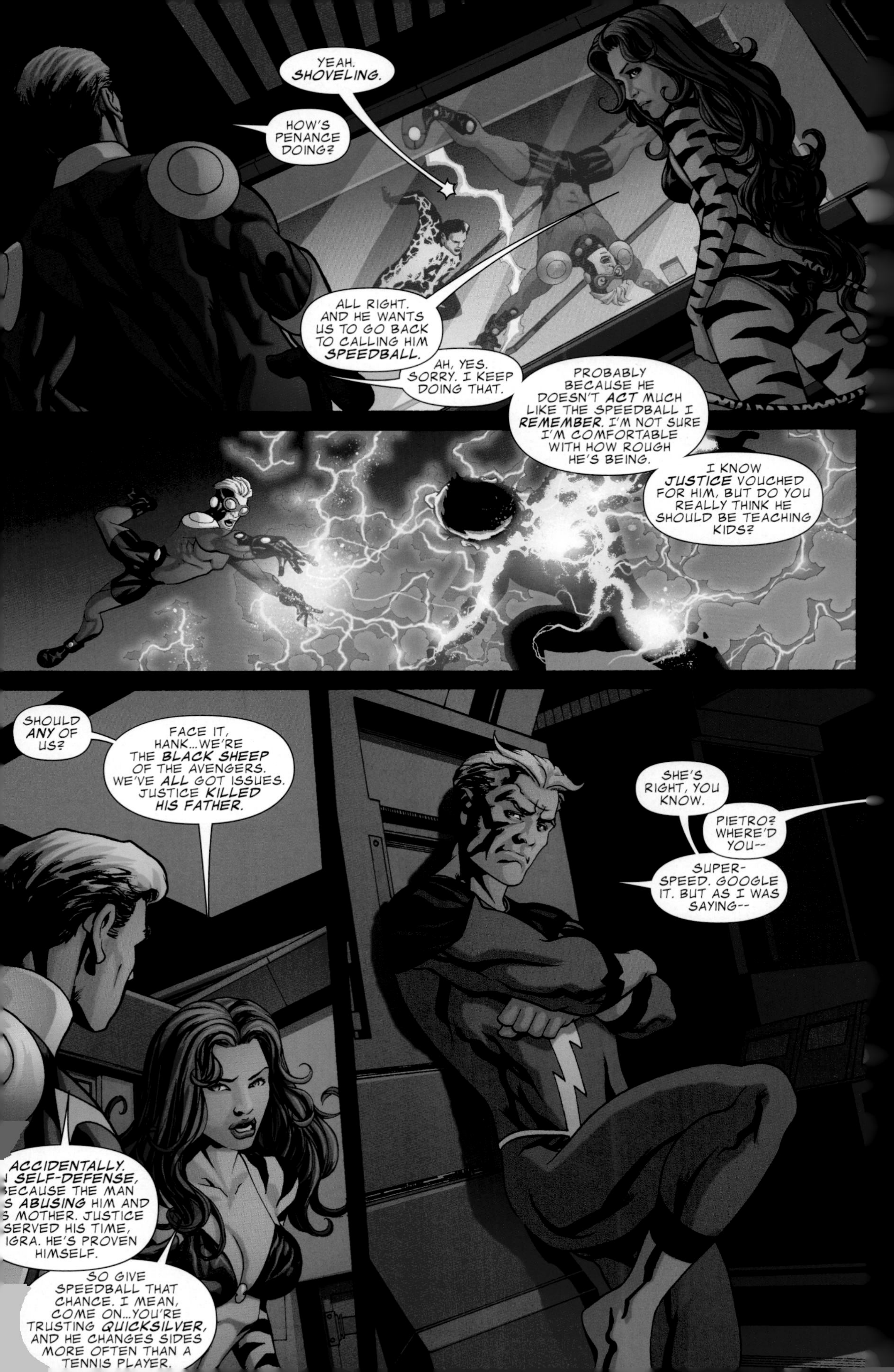
HOW'S PENANCE DOING?
YEAH. SHOVELING.
ALL RIGHT. AND HE WANTS US TO GO BACK TO CALLING HIM SPEEDBALL.
AH, YES. SORRY. I KEEP DOING THAT.
PROBABLY BECAUSE HE DOESN'T ACT MUCH LIKE THE SPEEDBALL I REMEMBER. I'M NOT SURE I'M COMFORTABLE WITH HOW ROUGH HE'S BEING.
I KNOW JUSTICE VOUCHED FOR HIM, BUT DO YOU REALLY THINK HE SHOULD BE TEACHING KIDS?
SHOULD ANY OF US?
FACE IT, HANK...WE'RE THE BLACK SHEEP OF THE AVENGERS. WE'VE ALL GOT ISSUES. JUSTICE KILLED HIS FATHER.
SHE'S RIGHT, YOU KNOW.
PIETRO? WHERE'D YOU--
SUPER-SPEED. GOOGLE IT. BUT AS I WAS SAYING--
ACCIDENTALLY. SELF-DEFENSE, ECAUSE THE MAN ABUSING HIM AND MOTHER. JUSTICE SERVED HIS TIME, IGRA. HE'S PROVEN HIMSELF.
SO GIVE SPEEDBALL THAT CHANCE. I MEAN, COME ON...YOU'RE TRUSTING QUICKSILVER, AND HE CHANGES SIDES MORE OFTEN THAN A TENNIS PLAYER.

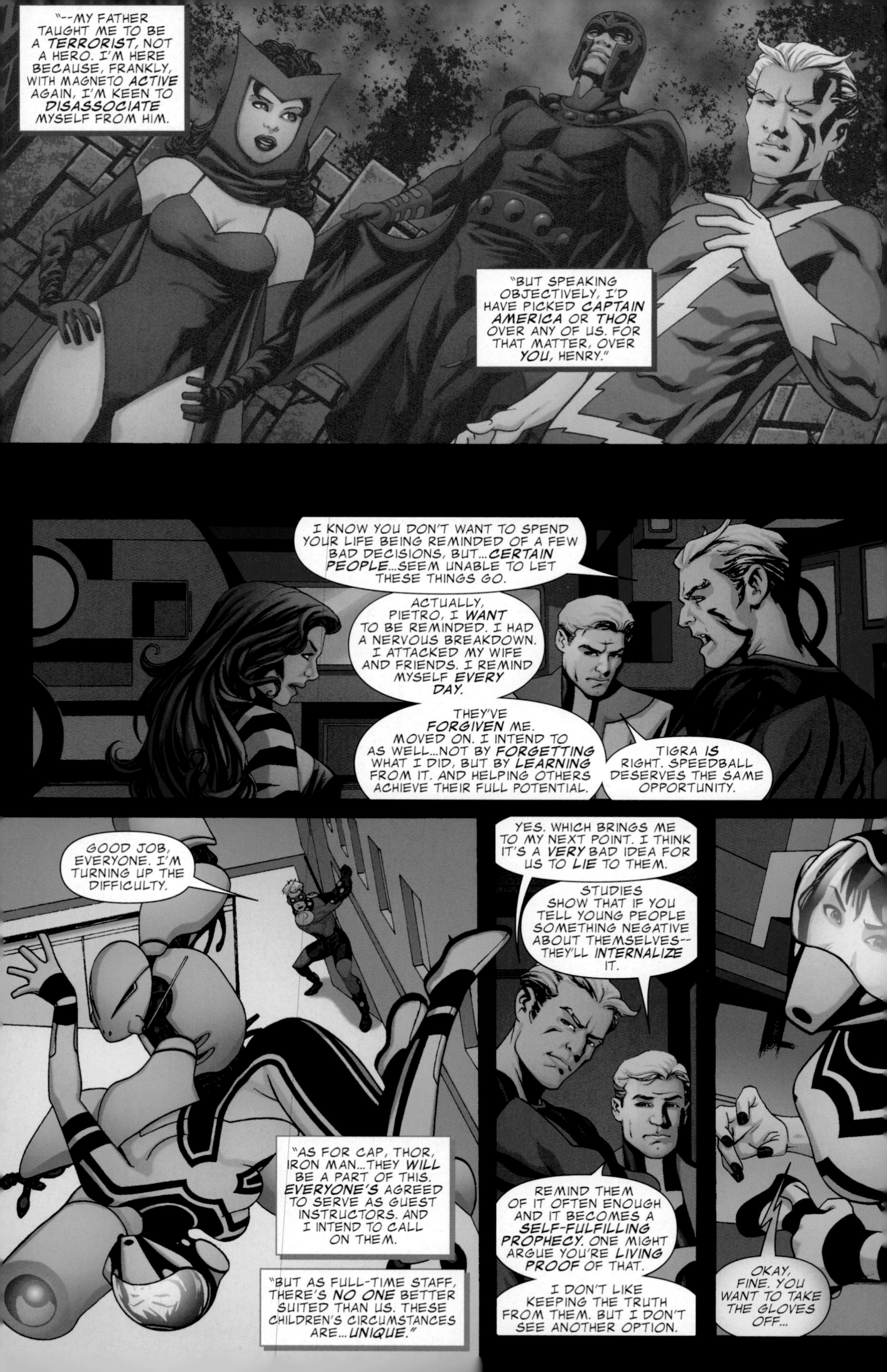
"--MY FATHER TAUGHT ME TO BE A TERRORIST, NOT A HERO. I'M HERE BECAUSE, FRANKLY, WITH MAGNETO ACTIVE AGAIN, I'M KEEN TO DISASSOCIATE MYSELF FROM HIM.
"BUT SPEAKING OBJECTIVELY, I'D HAVE PICKED CAPTAIN AMERICA OR THOR OVER ANY OF US. FOR THAT MATTER, OVER YOU, HENRY."
I KNOW YOU DON'T WANT TO SPEND YOUR LIFE BEING REMINDED OF A FEW BAD DECISIONS, BUT...CERTAIN PEOPLE...SEEM UNABLE TO LET THESE THINGS GO.
ACTUALLY, PIETRO, I WANT TO BE REMINDED. I HAD A NERVOUS BREAKDOWN. I ATTACKED MY WIFE AND FRIENDS. I REMIND MYSELF EVERY DAY.
THEY'VE FORGIVEN ME. MOVED ON. I INTEND TO AS WELL...NOT BY FORGETTING WHAT I DID, BUT BY LEARNING FROM IT. AND HELPING LEARNING OTHERS ACHIEVE THEIR FULL POTENTIAL.
TIGRA IS RIGHT. SPEEDBALL DESERVES THE SAME OPPORTUNITY.
GOOD JOB, EVERYONE. I'M TURNING UP THE DIFFICULTY.
"AS FOR CAP, THOR, IRON MAN...THEY WILL BE A PART OF THIS. EVERYONE'S AGREED TO SERVE AS GUEST INSTRUCTORS. AND I INTEND TO CALL ON THEM.
"BUT AS FULL-TIME STAFF, THERE'S NO ONE BETTER SUITED THAN US. THESE CHILDREN'S CIRCUMSTANCES ARE...UNIQUE."
YES. WHICH BRINGS ME TO MY NEXT POINT. I THINK IT'S A VERY BAD IDEA FOR US TO LIE TO THEM.
STUDIES SHOW THAT IF YOU TELL YOUNG PEOPLE SOMETHING NEGATIVE ABOUT THEMSELVES-- THEY'LL INTERNALIZE IT.
REMIND THEM OF IT OFTEN ENOUGH AND IT BECOMES A SELF-FULFILLING PROPHECY. ONE MIGHT ARGUE YOU'RE LIVING PROOF OF THAT.
I DON'T LIKE KEEPING THE TRUTH FROM THEM. BUT I DON'T SEE ANOTHER OPTION.
OKAY, FINE. YOU WANT TO TAKE THE GLOVES OFF...

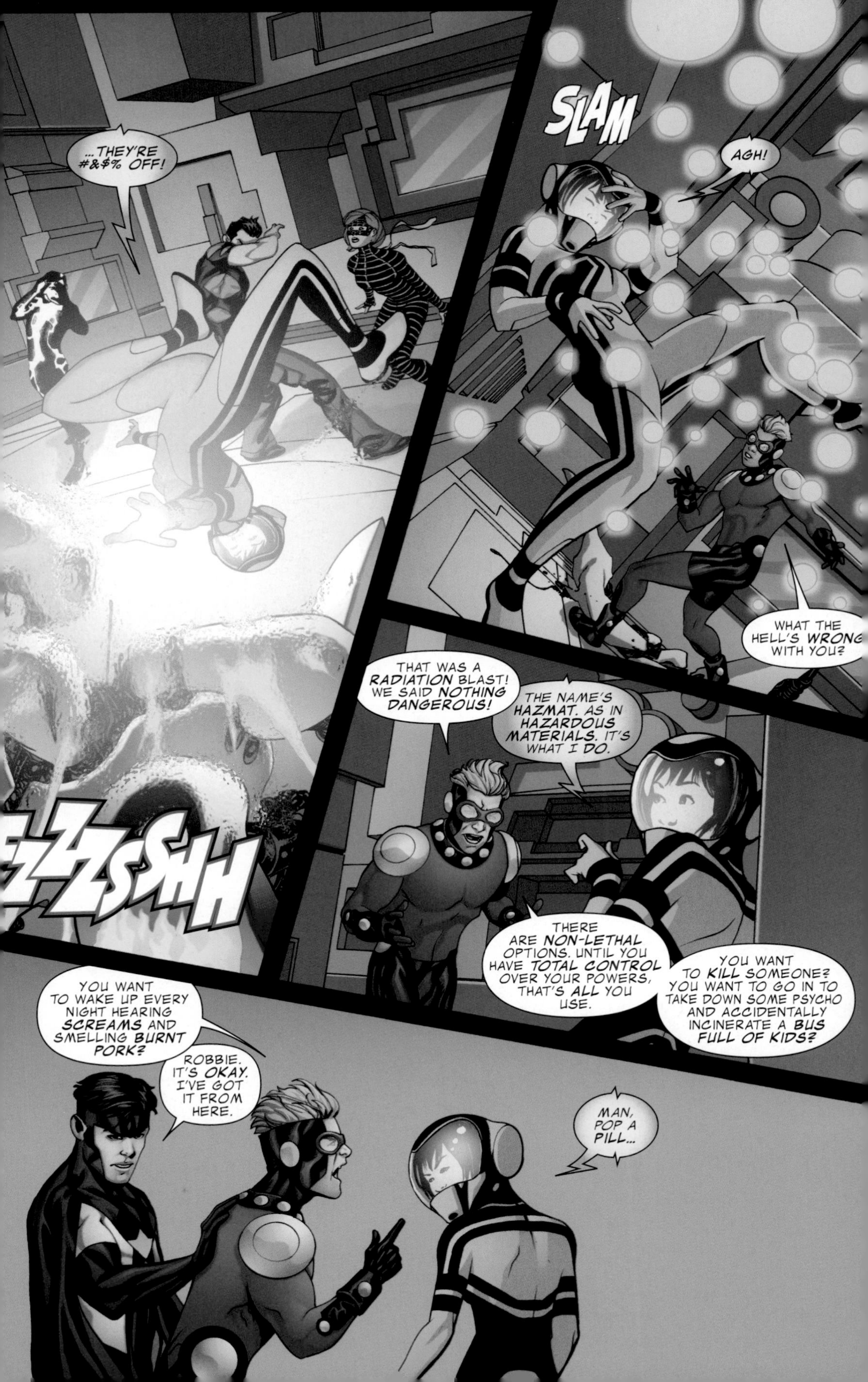
...THEY'RE #&$% OFF!
SLAM
AGH!
FZZZSHH
WHAT THE HELL'S WRONG WITH YOU?
THAT WAS A RADIATION BLAST! WE SAID NOTHING DANGEROUS!
THE NAME'S HAZMAT, AS IN HAZARDOUS MATERIALS. IT'S WHAT I DO.
THERE ARE NON-LETHAL OPTIONS. UNTIL YOU HAVE TOTAL CONTROL OVER YOUR POWERS, THAT'S ALL YOU USE.
YOU WANT TO KILL SOMEONE? YOU WANT TO GO IN TO TAKE DOWN SOME PSYCHO AND ACCIDENTALLY INCINERATE A BUS FULL OF KIDS?
YOU WANT TO WAKE UP EVERY NIGHT HEARING SCREAMS AND SMELLING BURNT PORK?
ROBBIE. IT'S OKAY. I'VE GOT IT FROM HERE.
MAN, POP A PILL...

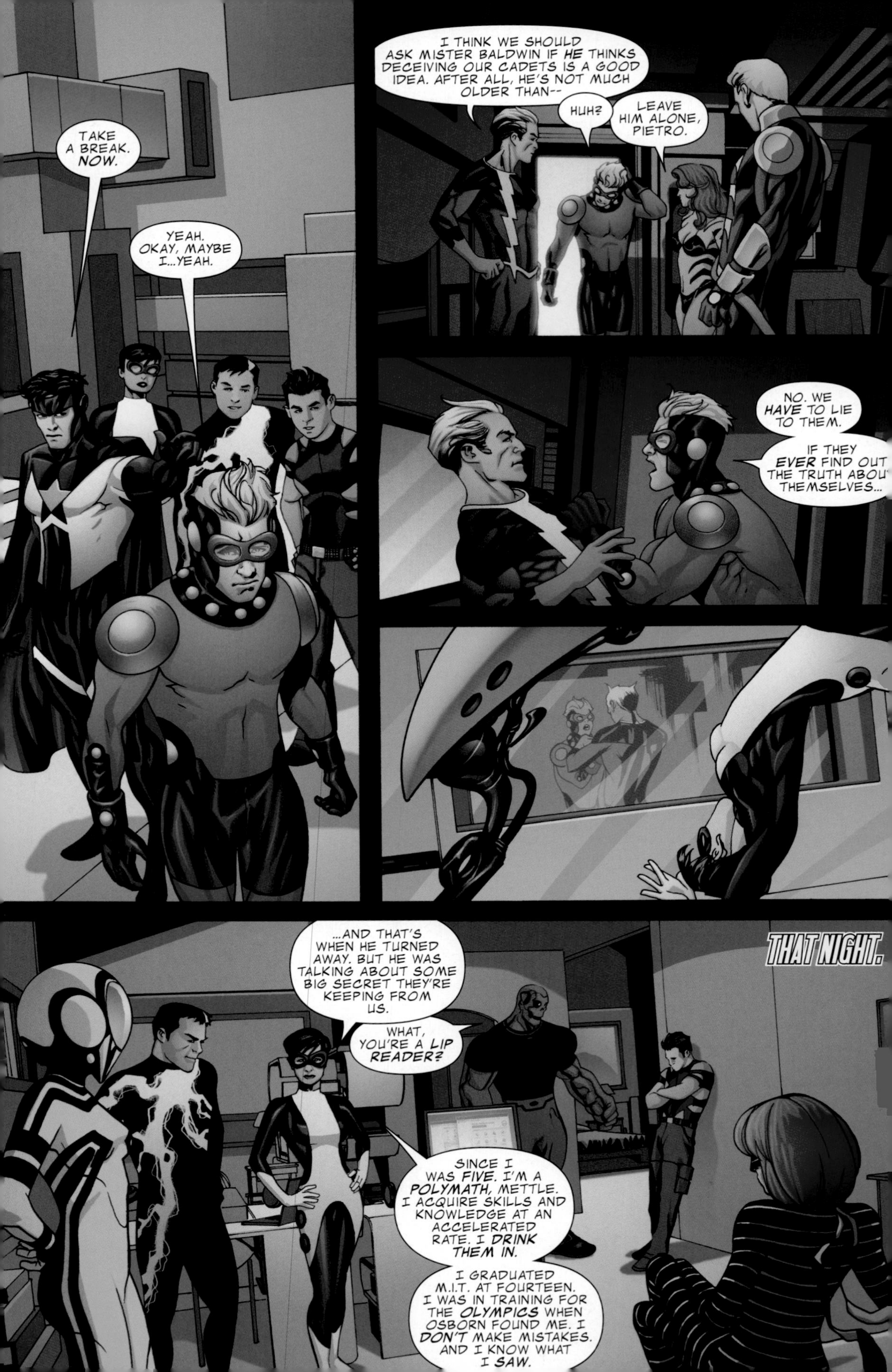
TAKE A BREAK. NOW.
YEAH. OKAY, MAYBE I...YEAH.
I THINK WE SHOULD ASK MISTER BALDWIN IF HE THINKS DECEIVING OUR CADETS IS A GOOD IDEA. AFTER ALL, HE'S NOT MUCH OLDER THAN--
HUH?
LEAVE HIM ALONE, PIETRO.
NO. WE HAVE TO LIE TO THEM.
IF THEY EVER FIND OUT THE TRUTH ABOUT THEMSELVES...
THAT NIGHT.
...AND THAT'S WHEN HE TURNED AWAY. BUT HE WAS TALKING ABOUT SOME BIG SECRET THEY'RE KEEPING FROM US.
WHAT, YOU'RE A LIP READER?
SINCE I WAS FIVE. I'M A POLYMATH, METTLE. I ACQUIRE SKILLS AND KNOWLEDGE AT AN ACCELERATED RATE. I DRINK THEM IN.
I GRADUATED M.I.T. AT FOURTEEN. I WAS IN TRAINING FOR THE OLYMPICS WHEN OSBORN FOUND ME. I DON'T MAKE MISTAKES. AND I KNOW WHAT I SAW.

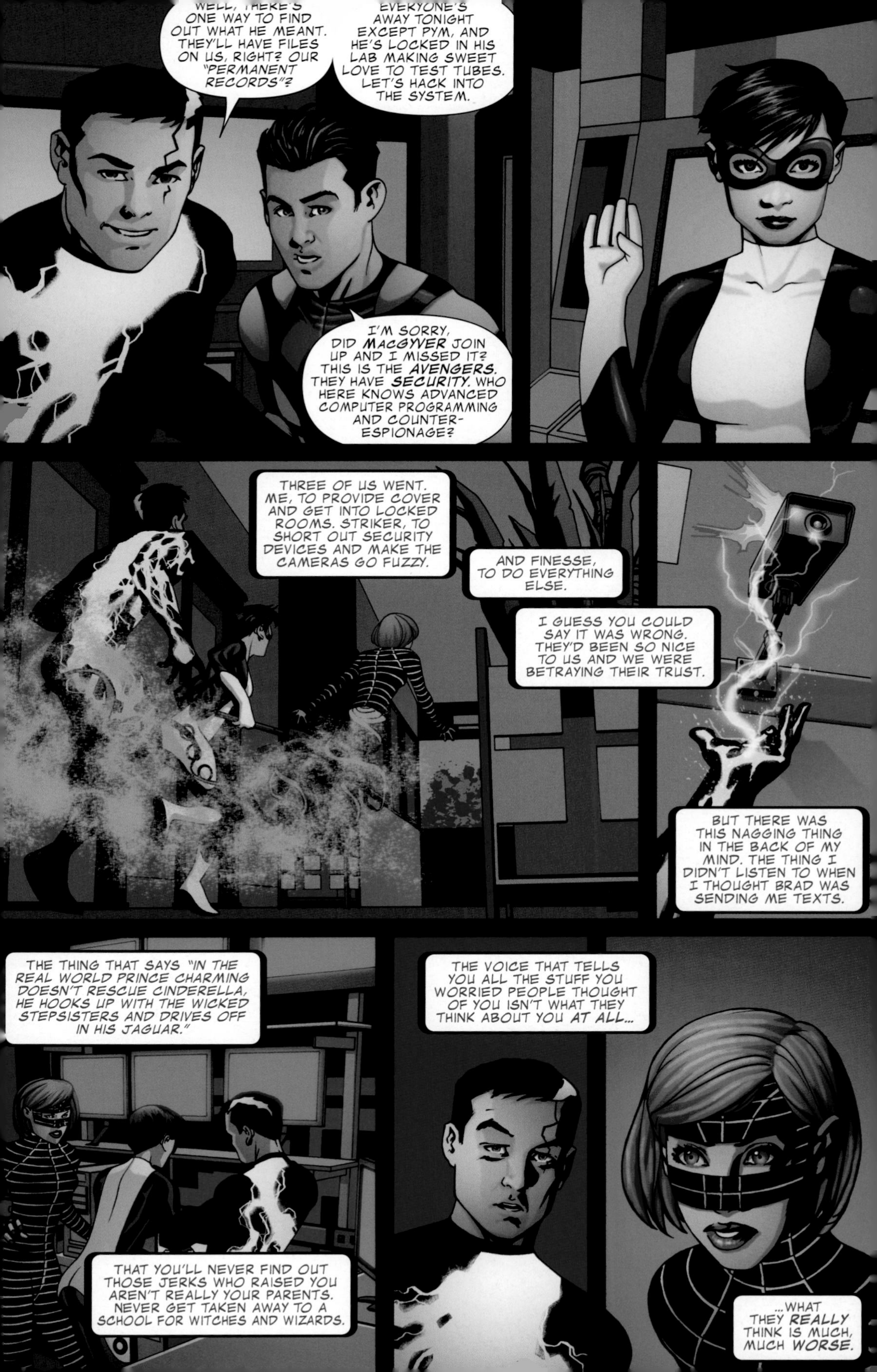
WELL, THERE'S ONE WAY TO FIND OUT WHAT HE MEANT. THEY'LL HAVE FILES ON US, RIGHT? OUR "PERMANENT RECORDS"?
EVERYONE'S AWAY TONIGHT EXCEPT PYM, AND HE'S LOCKED IN HIS LAB MAKING SWEET LOVE TO TEST TUBES. LET'S HACK INTO THE SYSTEM.
I'M SORRY, DID MACGYVER JOIN UP AND I MISSED IT? THIS IS THE AVENGERS. THEY HAVE SECURITY. WHO HERE KNOWS ADVANCED COMPUTER PROGRAMMING AND COUNTER-ESPIONAGE?
THREE OF US WENT. ME, TO PROVIDE COVER AND GET INTO LOCKED ROOMS. STRIKER, TO SHORT OUT SECURITY DEVICES AND MAKE THE CAMERAS GO FUZZY.
AND FINESSE, TO DO EVERYTHING ELSE.
I GUESS YOU COULD SAY IT WAS WRONG. THEY'D BEEN SO NICE TO US AND WE WERE BETRAYING THEIR TRUST.
BUT THERE WAS THIS NAGGING THING IN THE BACK OF MY MIND. THE THING I DIDN'T LISTEN TO WHEN I THOUGHT BRAD WAS SENDING ME TEXTS.
THE THING THAT SAYS "IN THE REAL WORLD PRINCE CHARMING DOESN'T RESCUE CINDERELLA, HE HOOKS UP WITH THE WICKED STEPSISTERS AND DRIVES OFF IN HIS JAGUAR."
THAT YOU'LL NEVER FIND OUT THOSE JERKS WHO RAISED YOU AREN'T REALLY YOUR PARENTS. NEVER GET TAKEN AWAY TO A SCHOOL FOR WITCHES AND WIZARDS.
THE VOICE THAT TELLS YOU ALL THE STUFF YOU WORRIED PEOPLE THOUGHT OF YOU ISN'T WHAT THEY THINK ABOUT YOU AT ALL...
...WHAT THEY REALLY THINK IS MUCH, MUCH WORSE.

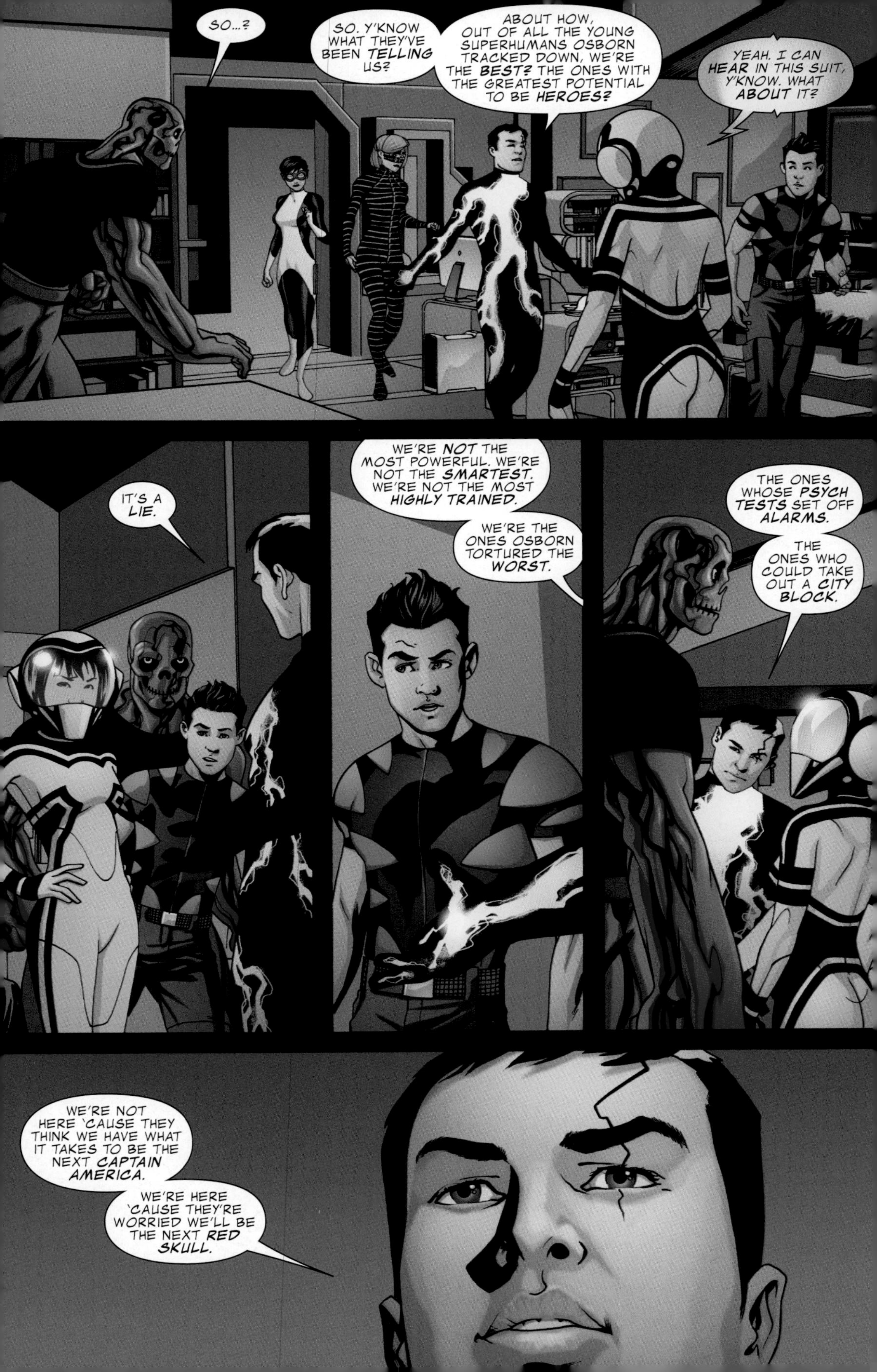
SO...?
SO. Y'KNOW WHAT THEY'VE BEEN TELLING US?
ABOUT HOW, OUT OF ALL THE YOUNG SUPERHUMANS OSBORN TRACKED DOWN, WE'RE THE BEST? THE ONES WITH THE GREATEST POTENTIAL TO BE HEROES?
YEAH. I CAN HEAR IN THIS SUIT, Y'KNOW. WHAT ABOUT IT?
IT'S A LIE.
WE'RE NOT THE MOST POWERFUL. WE'RE NOT THE SMARTEST. WE'RE NOT THE MOST HIGHLY TRAINED.
WE'RE THE ONES OSBORN TORTURED THE WORST.
THE ONES WHOSE PSYCH TESTS SET OFF ALARMS.
THE ONES WHO COULD TAKE OUT A CITY BLOCK.
WE'RE NOT HERE 'CAUSE THEY THINK WE HAVE WHAT IT TAKES TO BE THE NEXT CAPTAIN AMERICA.
WE'RE HERE 'CAUSE THEY'RE WORRIED WE'LL BE THE NEXT RED SKULL.

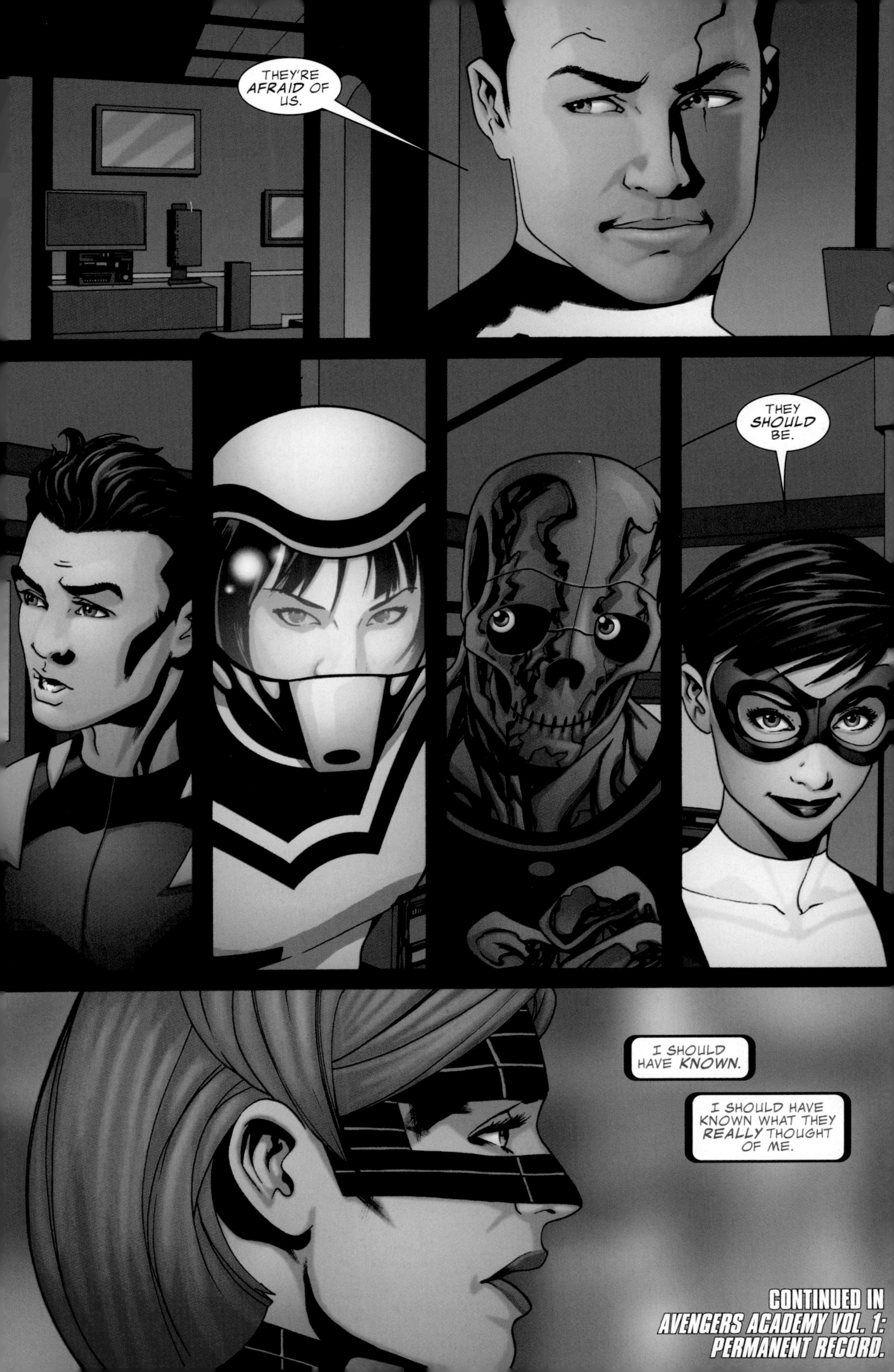
THEY'RE AFRAID OF US.
THEY SHOULD BE.
I SHOULD HAVE KNOWN.
I SHOULD HAVE KNOWN WHAT THEY REALLY THOUGHT OF ME.
CONTINUED IN AVENGERS ACADEMY VOL. 1: PERMANENT RECORD.

Tom DeFalco
Ant Man #1
Plot for 20 pages

PAGE 1

Our story opens somewhere in **Hungary** as an obviously expensive restaurant explodes in flame and fury, its concussion bursting outward to slam assorted passersby from their feet. One of these people is Hank Pym who was heading toward the restaurant.

PAGE 2

Lying on the ground, his face covered with bruises and blood, Hank reacts is horror. (We will learn that his new wife--the former **Maria Trovaya**--was in that restaurant. She was attending a dinner connected to a scientific conference sponsored by her employer, Egghead Innovations. Hank was on his way to the dinner.)

Wel move closer to a horrified Hank—

--And then we will cut to a close up of a depressed Hank whose face is healed. (He has been relating the preceding panels in **flashback**. The bombing took place six months ago.)

Pulling back the camera, we discover that Hank is relating this incident to his psychiatrist. (Hank is currently a patient in a sanatorium. He suffered a nervous breakdown after the loss of his wife.)

PAGE 3

An image of **Maria Pym** (she's a pretty brunette who looks somewhat, but not exactly like Janet Van Dyne) floats above his head as Hank explains that the authorities blamed the bombing on terrorists. He is now filled with paranoia, fearing that no one and no place is safe. No one can be trusted! (The terrorists can sneak into any place and kill any target at any time.)

As his psychiatrist assures Hank that he is safe in the sanatorium and that no one can sneak in to harm him here, we will have a three panel sequence that shows Hank noting an ant climbing up the leg of a desk or end table and walking across it.

Hank and the psychiatrist suddenly react as they hear shouting in the hallway.

PAGE 4

Warren Pym suddenly bursts into the room, demanding that Hank stop coddling himself, grow up and get back to work. The malingering has gone on too long! (Hank's father Warren appeared in **"The Man In The Ant Hill", Page 2, Panel #7**.)

The psychiatrist, of course, is outraged by Warren's appearance, but a haughty Warren reminds the good doctor that he (Warren) is paying for Hank's stay.

An angry Warren whips/turns toward a startled Hank, telling him to get ready to leave, actively pointing toward the door—

--And we have a **flashback** that shows a much younger Warren whipping/turning toward Hank's never-before-seen **mother**, telling her to get out of his house, actively pointing toward the door.

PAGE 5

Over the psychiatrist's protests, Warren hustles Hank out the door—

--And they are soon driving away from the sanatorium. (As they drive, a stern Warren and the sulking Hank will talk and we'll learn about their relationship. Warren is disappointed in his son and wants him to grow up and be man. There's a correct order to things and it's time Hank stopped being the perpetual student and committed to a career.)

Warren is particularly interested in Hank's recent theories of "Pym Particles"--

--A term that confuses Hank until Warren explains that he took the liberty of naming Hank's recent discovery.

Sulking back in his seat, Hank explains that he intended to name his discovery after Maria as the car pulls up in front of **a distinctive and modern building** that is identified as **Egghead Innovations**.

PAGE 6

Having entered the building, Warren escorts Hank past two distinctive security guards and their metal detector to introduce Hank to a serious Elihas "Egghead" Starr.

Elihas immediately expresses his sympathy for the loss of Maria, telling Hank that her death was a shock to everyone at the company.

As they walk down the hallway Elihas informs Hank that out of respect for Maria and Warren he has agreed to give Hank the use of a laboratory at Egghead Innovations.

Stating that he has heard about Hank's preliminary work on the so-called "Pym Particle", Elihas expects great things from him, but Hank tells Elihas not to expect too much because Hank only works on projects that appeal to his imagination.

In an redo of "The Man In The Ant Hill", Page 2, Panel #7, Warren will ask something like, "Ohhh...like what?" and Hank will give a serious and paranoid response.

PAGE 7

The three enter an advanced **laboratory** to discover a smiling **Bill Foster** who is turning away from an experiment to greet the newcomers. (Elihas will mention that he took the liberty of hiring Hank an assistant.)

Foster is very excited to be working with Hank and extends his hand. (Foster has read a number of Hank's published articles—especially his work on the" Pym Particle".)

Ignoring Foster's hand for a panel, Hank glances suspiciously at Elihas and Warren.

Then Hank takes Foster's hand and welcomes him aboard. (Hank's thoughts will reveal his suspicion that Foster has been hired by the company to spy on him.)

PAGE 8

Sometime later, as they leave the Egghead building, a pleased Warren claps a serious Hank on the back. (Warren is proud of Hank for getting his career back on track,)

With a serious expression on his face, Warren wonders if Hank is also interested in getting his social life back on track because his old friend Dr. Vernon Van Dyke has a beautiful single daughter—

--But Hank interrupts, saying it's only been six months since Maria's death and he isn't ready to start dating, again.

Holding his hands up in defeat, Warren heads back to the car as a suspicious Hank turns to look at the Egghead building.

This page ends with a close-up of Hank. His thoughts reveal that he is very conflicted about working for Maria's former employer.

PAGE 9

Cut to a flashback that shows a crude drawing of the **Ant Man helmet**.

Pulling back the camera, the flashback continues as a serious Maria explains the technology she is developing to communicate with insects to a curious Hank.

We have a focus shot of Maria when as she informs her husband that she intends to present this tech at the conference in Hungary.

Back in reality, Hank springs upward in bed. In his paranoia, he begins to wonder if Egghead murdered Maria for her tech.

PAGE 10

Cut to an outdoor establishing shot of the Egghead Innovations building.

Inside their laboratory, Foster apologizes for being shoved down Hank's throat and also expresses his desire to learn more about Hank's theories. (We'll also discuss the commercial possibilities for the Pym Particles.)

We will have a series of panels showing the two of them working at computers, mixing chemicals and the sequence ends as Foster watches Hank sketch a crude drawing of chamber made of glass. (While this is happening, we'll explain the basic principles of Pym Particles.

PAGE 11

Cut to days later and Hank and Foster are looking at the actual **glass enclosed chamber** which is about 6 feet high by 6 feet wide. It is also attached to a fancy gizmo so that the "shrinking gas" can be released into the confined space of the chamber.

Pleased with the day's work, Foster prepares to leave, but Hank says he's just going to check on a few things.

No sooner does Foster exit, then Hank gets down to the serious work of mixing chemicals. (Hank still doesn't trust Foster and has been doing his real work after Foster leaves at night.)

Cut to an image of Hank on a **video screen**.

Pulling back the camera, we see that a serious Elihas Starr has been secretly spying on Hank with hidden cameras because he knows these Pym Particles could be worth billions.

PAGE 12

As the weeks follow, a montage shows a few images of Hank and Foster working together.
One night after Foster has gone, Hank places a chair in the shrinking chamber,
As he releases the shirking gas, we have a three-panel sequence that shows the chair shrinking.

PAGE 13

Then an excited Hank releases a second gas as a three-panel sequence shows the chair enlarging.
An excited Hank realizes that his formula is a success.
Cut to Elihas Starr who turns from the monitor showing Hank toward the two security guards from **Page 6**. (Since it is obvious that Hank isn't going to share with Egghead, there's no need for Egghead to share this wonderful tech with him.)

PAGE 14

Moments later, Hank is startled when the two guards burst into his laboratory and demand he turn over his research and the secure passwords for his computer.
Hank is defiant—
—And receives a punch in the gut for his resistance—
—Followed by a severe beating.
Savagely beaten and bruised, Hank gives them as secure passwords.

PAGE 15

Having gotten what they want, the men decide to "disappear" him and throw Hank into the shrinking chamber.
Hank is horrified when he is exposed to the gas—
—And we have a multiple image sequence that shows Hank shrinking to the size of ant.

PAGES 16-17

It's time for a little **Hoo-Ha** action as the guards try to finish Hank off. They enter the chamber and try to squash him.
We get some wild perspective panels shown from Hank's point-of-view as he runs for his life, trying to avoid the GIANT shoes crashing around him.
Laboratory tables are bumped into, beakers crash and chemicals splash around him as Hank tries to flee the lab and escape his GIANT attackers.

PAGE 18

Reaching the outside hallway, Hank spots a **Giant janitor** in the distance.
The guards also reach the hallway.
Looking at the floor in search of Hank, they pass the janitor—
—Who pays them little mind as he continues to duties.

PAGE 19

Sometime later, the janitor heads toward the building's back door.
Outside the building, the janitor tosses his trash bag into an open **dumpster**—
—And we cut to a tiny figure jumping off his shoe.
The figure is a desperate Hank who races toward the corner of the dumpster. (Beyond the dumpster we can see a patch of grass.)
Suddenly Hank freezes. Something is wrong!

PAGE 20

Pulling back the camera, we see that Hank has gotten tangled in a **spider's web** that extends between the wall of the building to the bottom of the dumpster. A large, menacing spider is approaching Hank.

To Be Continued!

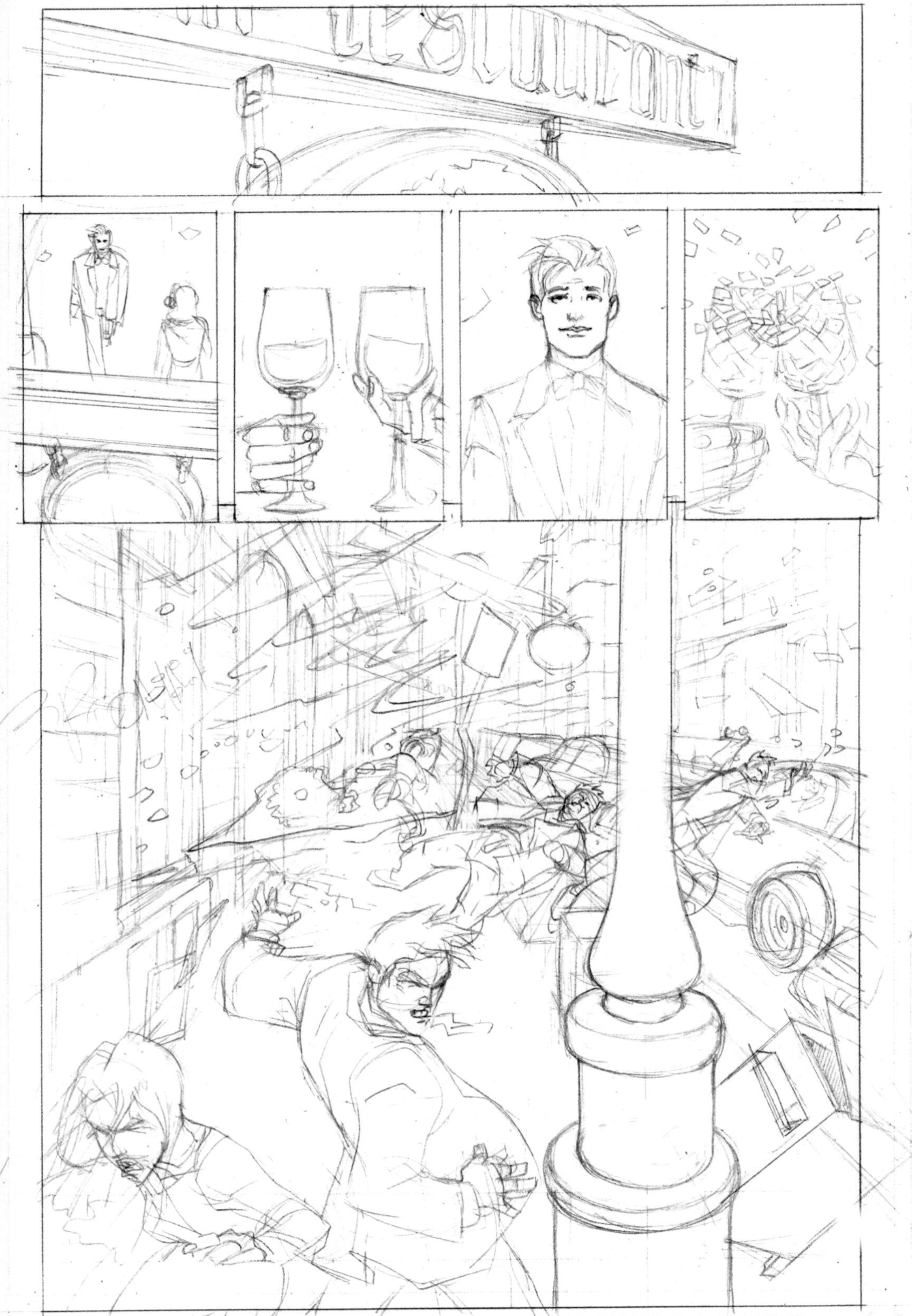
INSTRUCTIONS FOR DOUBLE PAGE SPREAD: CUT AS SHOWN, ABUT PAGE EDGES, TAPE ON BACK. DO NOT OVERLAP.
CUT RIGHT-HAND PAGE AT THIS LINE
CUT LEFT-HAND PAGE AT THIS LINE

PAGE 1 ROUGHS

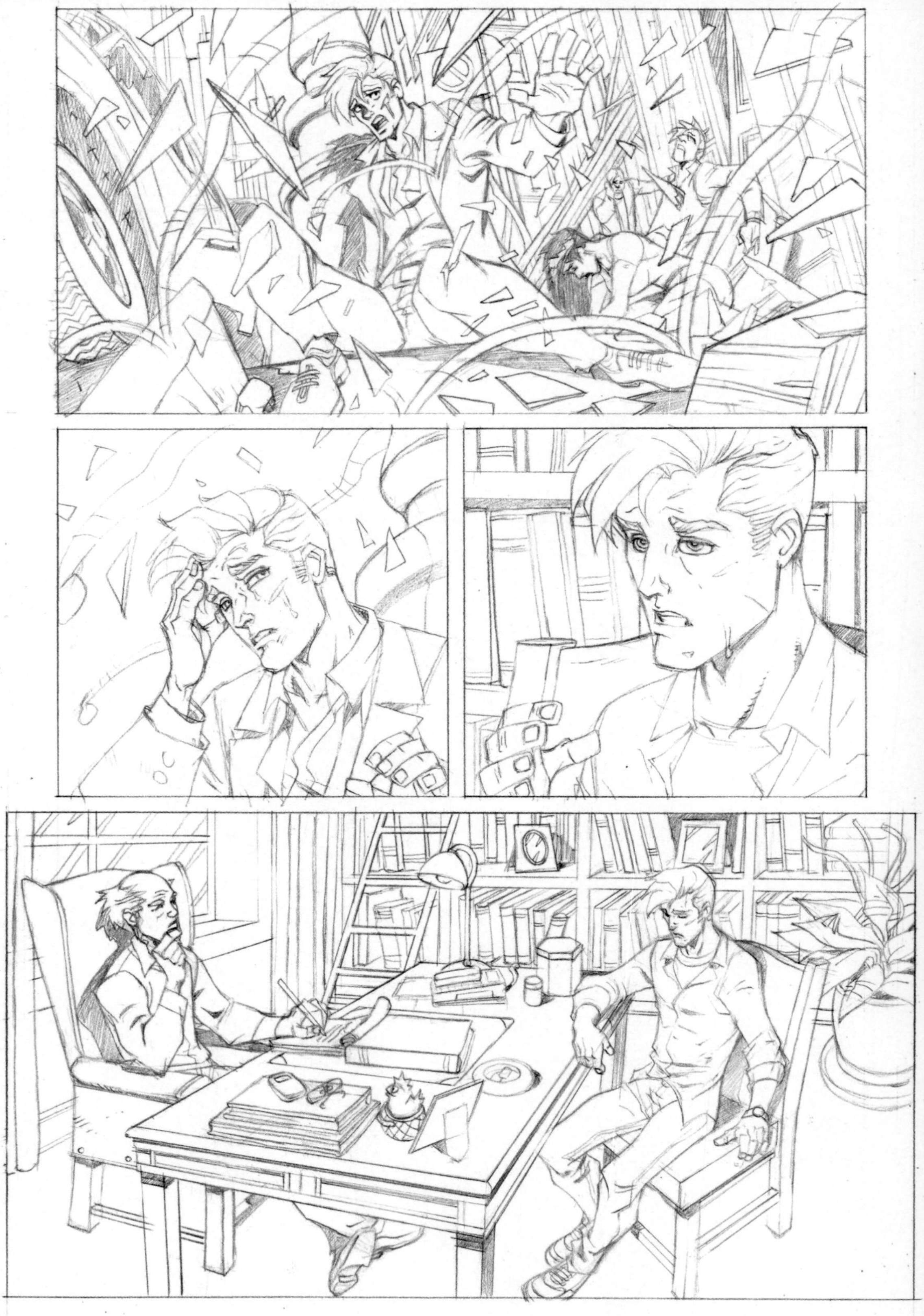

PAGE 2 PENCILS

PAGE 2 ROUGHS

PAGE 1 INKS

PAGE 1 PENCILS

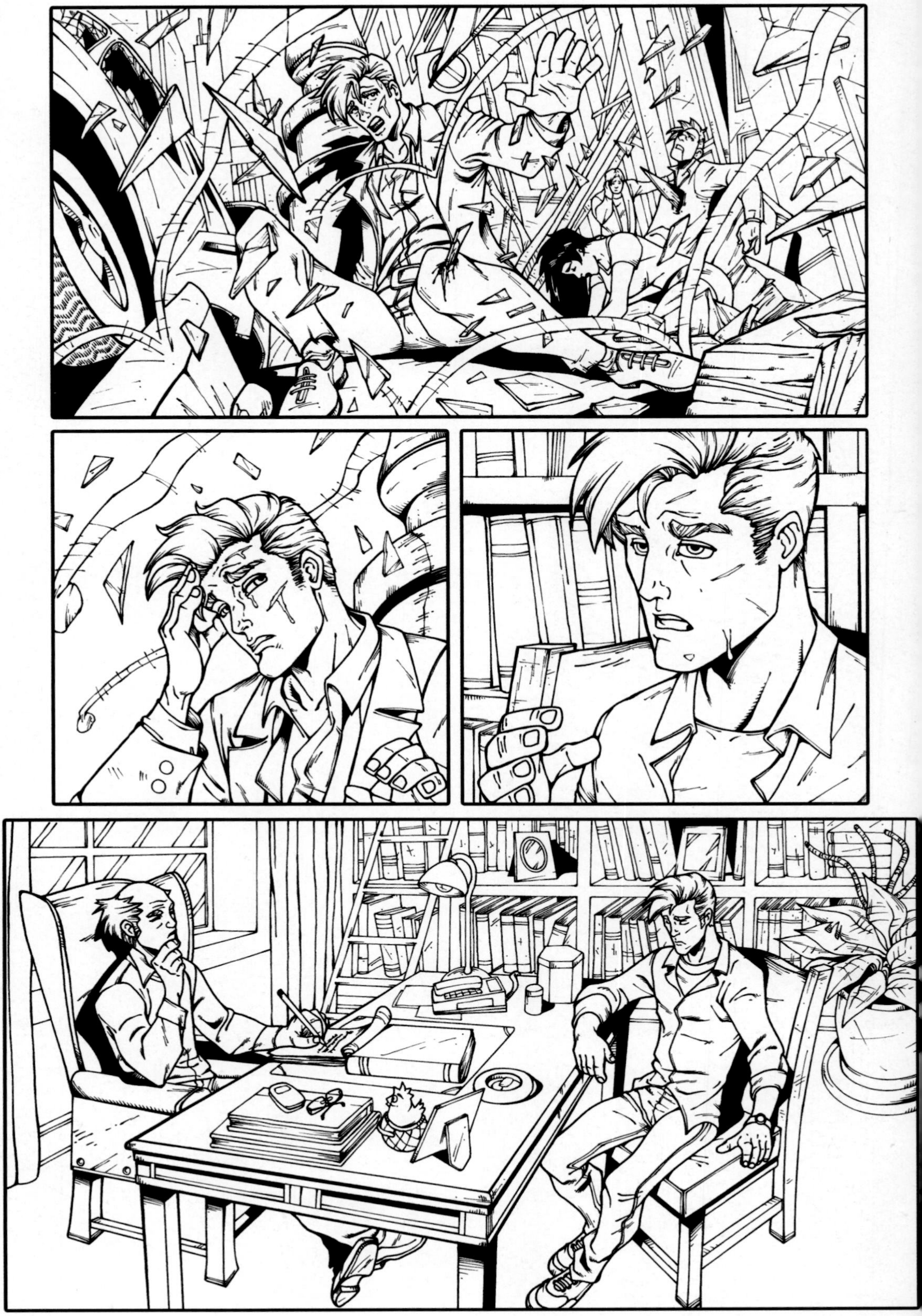

PAGE 2 INKS

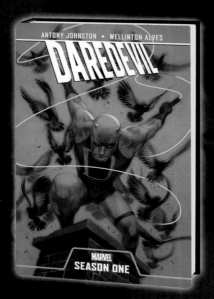

MARVEL SEASON ONE

ISBN # 978-0-7851-6386-2

ISBN # 978-0-7851-6388-6

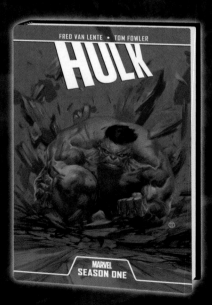

ISBN # 978-0-7851-6387-9

AVAILABLE WHEREVER BOOKS ARE SOLD.